The Idealist Guide to Nonprofit Careers

for First-time Job Seekers

by

Meg Busse

with

Steven Joiner

and contributions from

**Put Barber, David Schachter, Cathy Wasserman,
Kelley Carmichael Casey,** *and* **Valinda Lee**

Published by Hundreds of Heads Books, LLC

www.hundredsofheads.com

info@hundredsofheads.com

Book design by Eric Fichtl, with elements from Kirsten Vogdes

Library of Congress Cataloging-in-Publication Data

Busse, Meg.
 The idealist guide to nonprofit careers for first-time job seekers / by Meg Busse ; with Steven Joiner and contributions from Put Barber ... [et al.].
     p. cm.
 ISBN 978-1-933512-24-2
 1. Nonprofit organizations--Vocational guidance--United States. I. Joiner, Steven. II. Barber, Putnam. III. Title.
 HD2769.2.U6B875 2010
 331.7020973--dc22

                        2009039733

HUNDREDS OF HEADS books are available at special discounts when purchased in bulk for premiums or institutional or educational use. Excerpts and custom editions can be created for specific uses. For more information, please e-mail sales@hundredsofheads.com.

ISBN-13: 978-1-933512-24-2

Printed in Canada
10 9 8 7 6 5 4 3 2 1

The Idealist Guide to Nonprofit Careers *for* First-time Job Seekers
Table of Contents

Opening thoughts

Why do you want to work in the nonprofit sector anyway?

In this introduction you will:

- Get an overview of the purpose of The Idealist Guide.

- Learn about the thematic "threads" woven through the chapters.

- Meet the authors and learn about the organizations behind this book.

- Learn about the summary on the last page of each section.

A brave new nonprofit world

Nonprofit. Charity. Nongovernmental organization. Nonprofits have historically been defined by what they are not (profit-making) or by what they give away. These terms can conjure up images of soup kitchens run out of church basements, people collecting signatures on street corners, and organizations of "do-gooders" striving to compensate for a lack of funds by working long hours and relying on volunteers. Yet this image of the nonprofit sector is far from complete.

In the United States, today's nonprofits make up a vibrant, innovative, multi-trillion dollar sector that is continually evolving and adapting to society's needs and constraints. The list of nonprofits in the United States and in your community will probably surprise you: private universities like Harvard or public ones like Texas A&M; multi-billion dollar area hospitals; international relief organizations like Doctors Without Borders; religious organizations ranging from local congregations to national groups like Focus on the Family or the American Friends Service Committee; organizations spanning the length of the left-right, liberal-conservative political spectrum; and membership organizations like the American Bar Association, the American Civil Liberties Union, and the National Rifle Association. Additionally, the traditionally clear lines delineating nonprofit, for-profit, and government sectors are dissolving into porous borders where corporations are stepping up to be responsible social stewards, government agencies are contracting out much of their work to nonprofits, and nonprofits are becoming more lean and efficient in the face of limited funding and, yes, competition. Given these shifting borders of responsibility and focus, nonprofits are actively looking for entrepreneurial, innovative, and visionary people with the skills to take on a variety of roles.

Recent graduates who are interested in finding "work with meaning" and a way to give back to society while also earning a paycheck can find a plethora of opportunities in the nonprofit sector. This book will help you understand the vibrancy and breadth of the sector, as well as assist you in your journey along a meaningful career path to nonprofit work. Nonprofits are no longer a place where you work for a few years after college or in transition between "real jobs." Today, nonprofits are a place where you can lead a challenging and fulfilling lifelong career.

As you explore nonprofit opportunities with this book, set aside your notions of "what a nonprofit is" and prepare to discover a sector that will, we think, surprise you.

Advantages and disadvantages of working in nonprofits

There is no question that nonprofits tend to attract people with certain shared values. A typical profile of nonprofit professionals would include their desire to wed their passion for the issues that inspire them with their paid work; a focus on the bottom line of positive social change; and a real interest in making a tangible difference in the communities they serve. This merging of passion, purpose, and paycheck can be a strong pull for people seeking to find meaning in their daily lives.

This genuine appeal of meaningful work, combined with the traditional (and still often accurate) perception of nonprofits as more laid back and less formal, attracts many people to the sector. In recent interviews with nonprofit human resource professionals conducted by Idealist.org, several respondents spoke of individuals simply wanting to work in a nonprofit environment regardless of the organization's mission or structure, or the role that they would play. In other words, professionals are drawn to the nonprofit sector by a variety of perceived advantages that the work holds over careers in the private/for-profit or public/government sectors. Yet, while many of these advantages do exist, one must be careful to not blissfully overlook the challenges of nonprofit work.

The advantages

There are many reasons why nonprofit work is appealing. Some of the generalizations of nonprofits—laid back, friendly, mission-driven—are based in a reality that appeals to various types of personalities. Some advantages of nonprofit work can include:

- The ability to do **meaningful work** that focuses less on results benefiting the employer and more on creating positive change in the community at large. What that "positive change" entails is the prerogative of the nonprofit organization. A nonprofit career also allows you do to the kind of work that you might otherwise only be able to do on your own (unpaid) time.
- More **"hands-on" opportunities** that allow you to directly experience the positive outcomes of your work.

SURELY THERE ISN'T A PLACE IN NONPROFITS FOR *MY* KIND OF WORK!

The nonprofit sector has opportunities for almost every major, minor, or skill set. If you want to be an accountant, marketing specialist, actor, lawyer, baker, researcher, teacher, coach, carpenter, computer technician, or specialist in any of a myriad of other "non-traditional" professions, there is a place in the nonprofit sector for your skills and talents.

What are these text boxes all about?

For an explanation of the sidebars and "threads" that appear throughout this book, please see pages 8-9.

- A greater **flexibility** in how the work is carried out, how benchmarks are met, and which alternative strategies to employ in order to accomplish the mission of an organization.

- A more **casual work environment**. This can include a more relaxed dress code, flexible schedules, and an open physical work environment.

- The opportunity to "**wear several hats.**" Since many nonprofits are understaffed, nonprofit professionals have the chance to perform many different job functions and move outside of a strict set of job responsibilities. This allows for a greater opportunity to learn new skills and further develop pre-existing abilities on the job.

- Greater levels of **responsibility**. Professionals in nonprofits are often allowed or required to take on more responsibilities than professionals in other sectors where there may be more resources to hire additional staff. Examples include: managing staff and volunteers, working on projects outside of their expertise, and collaborating with outside individuals and organizations in a meaningful capacity.

- The potential for rapid **job advancement**. While advancement may be limited within a specific organization, it is often possible to move between organizations while also advancing up the responsibility ladder. Nonprofits see quality managers as a much sought-after commodity, allowing emerging professionals a chance to advance quickly.

- A greater organizational **culture of like-minded people**, inspiring teamwork and collaboration instead of internal competition. Often, nonprofit professionals are strongly invested in their work and this dedication can be contagious.

- More **generous benefits**. Nonprofits often offer lower wages than other sectors. However, many organizations make up for this possible salary gap by offering excellent health benefits for the employee and their family, retirement plans, more vacation time, and other "perks" that can help balance out a smaller paycheck.

- Nonprofits can sometimes **act more quickly** than government or for-profit organizations to fill a niche, meet a need, or be entrepreneurial.

Just as when you talk about working in a "business culture" or "government culture", working in a "nonprofit culture" can have many positive attributes. However, these advantages, like anything you say about the nonprofit sector, are not universal truths. They will vary depending on factors such as organizational culture, budgetary limitations, your personality and the personalities of your colleagues, and the type of work involved.

The disadvantages

A job at a nonprofit does not necessarily mean that you have found your workplace nirvana. It takes a particular set of skills and priorities to find success and happiness in the nonprofit sector. Whether or not you can deal with the following disadvantages is a crucial litmus test for your potential success in the sector.

It takes a particular set of skills and priorities to find success and happiness in the nonprofit sector."

- **Lower wages**. Nonprofits usually pay less than comparable for-profit and public positions. Usually. Mid- to upper-level nonprofit managers, especially in large organizations, often have similar salary ranges to comparable positions in other sectors. However, people fresh out of college can often adjust to this pay disparity more readily than professionals with some level of paid experience.

- **Burnout** is a common reality in the nonprofit world. Part of the personal and professional investment in a nonprofit's cause means often blurring the line that should divide your work and home life balance. Nonprofit work is commonly more than a 40-hour-a-week commitment, and this can mean anything from working long hours to attending evening and weekend obligations (fundraisers, community events, etc.). When you consistently "take your work home" or have work responsibilities seep into your personal time, you are more likely to burn out. Furthermore, many of the issues that nonprofits deal with on a daily basis have **no tangible solution**. This lack of an achievable goal (like ending poverty) coupled with an inability to objectively measure the impact of a nonprofit's efforts can also lead to frustration and potential burnout.

- **Turnover** can be high in nonprofit organizations for a variety of reasons. People move on to better paying jobs or higher level positions in other organizations, make the decision to go back to school, or decide to switch sectors. Turnover can also be more prevalent in the sector because of the large number of younger people working in nonprofits who tend to change jobs more frequently. On an organizational level, many nonprofits lack the infrastructural tools (professional development, leadership training, and so on) to retain their employees. Turnover can be especially difficult in the nonprofit sector since the nature of the work often inspires camaraderie and closeness between colleagues, and because in smaller organizations, a single person's departure can mean the loss of a good deal of institutional memory and community connections.

- Nonprofits can have **different (or fewer) structures** than other sectors. Professionals who need hierarchies with clear benchmarks, deliverables, and tasks may find nonprofit work frustrating. A nonprofit's goal is to fulfill their mission, in whatever way they see fit. In working toward meeting their mission, efficiency has not always been a priority. However, with the increasingly higher standards of accountability and the fierce competition for funding, efficiency and organization are becoming watchwords for the sector.

- Social change is slow and unpredictable. The **length of the struggle** can frustrate organizations that address social change issues. Consider how long it took for women to be allowed to vote in the United States or how long it took for the civil rights struggle or the environmental movement to start effecting real change. The unpredictability of government policy (which can change whenever new lawmakers take office); shifting priorities in social, economic, and cultural movements; and natural disasters and other crises can derail years of work invested by nonprofits.

- Nonprofits, true to their name, are often **lacking in resources**. Many nonprofits are chronically underfunded and rely largely on volunteers who, while critical to the success of the sector, may or may not be as available or reliable as paid staff. This can mean that already overworked staff members must pick up the slack.

- Many nonprofits suffer from what is called **"Founders' Syndrome"**, the propensity of an organization's founders (be it one person or a group) to have a deep sense of ownership over and responsibility for the organization. Those who have been there from the start are often reluctant to leave or to change how things have always been done. This can have several effects on subsequent staff, including limited decision-making power in matters of organizational change; a lack of succession planning within the nonprofit (few or no internal mechanisms to prepare the new generations of leaders); and a lack of clear hierarchy below the founders that makes it hard for staff to grasp the necessary steps to becoming a future manager or leader. The resulting **limited potential for advancement** within some nonprofit organizations means you may be less likely to become the supervisor of coworkers than in other sectors. This, along with the irreplaceable skill sets (at least internally) of many nonprofit leaders, often forces nonprofits to look externally when filling an upper management position.

- There is still an all-too-common misconception of nonprofits as a place for unfocused do-gooders to get together and complain about the status quo before they have to go out and "get a real job". Ironically, the nonprofit sector, despite being the backbone of much of the social change that has taken place throughout U.S. history, is **still emerging as a credible sector**. Thus, as a professional interested in nonprofit work, you will often face questions from family and friends—your support network—who may not understand why you are involved in nonprofit work, why you would "waste your talent", or why you would choose nonprofit work over a more financially rewarding career.

As with the advantages of nonprofit work, the disadvantages and drawbacks vary based on the organization. Finding organizations that are proactively looking to make these challenges a thing of the nonprofit past should be a key part of your search for meaningful work in the sector. But be aware that many of these drawbacks, to some degree, will exist. Deciding whether these kinds of disadvantages would prohibit you from finding fulfilling work is an important consideration when exploring the nonprofit sector.

The nonlinear career path

Gone are the days of 40 years of service to the company for a gold watch and a retirement dinner. The baby boomers began nonlinear career paths in earnest decades ago and subsequent generations have reinforced and built upon this current workplace reality. Members of today's workforce know that they are moving through a series of positions and responsibilities and few, if any, are settling down in one job without (at least occasionally) looking to see what else is out there.

This mobility of professionals lends itself well to building transferable skill sets. Many for-profits are looking for ways to be good stewards to all aspects of their supply chain: the employees, the customers, even the planet itself. Most for-profits are also looking to be more transparent in their dealings and to garner the trust of skeptics. At the same time, nonprofits are looking to an increasingly competitive funding market and are developing ways to both serve their mission and stay afloat. Government agencies, too, are looking to shed their image of being ineffective and unresponsive bureaucracies. As these three sectors apply techniques and best practices borrowed from other sectors, each is looking for professionals with the transferable skills that are needed to stay current, relevant, competitive, and innovative.

The nonprofit sector, being so vast in both the kinds of organizations it encompasses and the range of social missions it promotes, is an excellent place to lead a nonlinear career path. It is especially true in nonprofit work that people in leadership roles like Executive Director, Chief Program Officer, or HR Director often come to their position through a winding and indirect route. As nonprofit professionals navigate this nonlinear career path, they pick up skill sets from the various positions they fill. This accumulation of expertise—fundraising, volunteer management, community development, project management, etc.—is becoming more and more the norm for nonprofit leaders. In other words, nonprofits are both looking for *and* encouraging people who follow nonlinear careers.

Who are you? Where do you want to go? How can this book help?

Simply put, it is not enough to know that you want to work in the nonprofit sector. The *first step* you should take on your journey into the sector is to do a self-assessment of your interests. This first step can lead to a deeper **knowledge of self**. Your **second step** is to gain a thorough **knowledge of the sector**. This means making sure you have a clear understanding of the nonprofit landscape both in your geographic area and your areas of focus. This also implies understanding the opportunities for the kind of work you want to do within your community or a community where you

 It is not enough to know that you want to work in the nonprofit sector."

would like to (or have to) live. There is a clear difference between professionals who want a job in a nonprofit and professionals who are looking for a specific position or role. Nonprofit employers want professionals interested in the *job* they are trying to fill (i.e., event planner at a mental health agency), and not just interested in the kind of work environment that nonprofits offer. They want people who understand themselves and therefore understand why they will be a good fit for particular roles within an organization. The way you will truly stand out in your nonprofit career search is to make sure you have a strong sense of what you are looking for and then make sure you know how to look for it.

Chapter One offers an overview of the nonprofit sector, giving a brief discussion of the diverse historical and legal space occupied by nonprofits as well as the societal benefits that accrue from these organizations. Chapter Two discusses the psychological swings of the job search and ways to stay motivated during your transition. Chapter Three takes you through the process of assessing your needs and understanding the current nonprofit environment.

From here, the ***third step*** is to ***find the synergy*** between what you want and what is available. Chapters Four, Five, Six, and Seven are all about getting out and involved in your career search. Covering activities like networking, volunteering, furthering your education, and conducting research, these chapters can guide you as you move along the career continuum in search of new opportunities.

Chapters Eight and Nine focus on how you present yourself to potential employers—from resume and cover letter basics to interview preparation and advice on making the right first impression. Chapter Ten will help you understand compensation packages and whether to accept a job offer, while Chapter Eleven provides reasons for and tips on continuing your job search even after getting an offer.

In the Reality Check section, Chapter Twelve outlines pros and cons of nonprofit hiring practices and Chapter Thirteen tackles some of the misconceptions and somber realities of the nonprofit sector as a whole. The intent of these chapters is not to discourage you from considering nonprofit work. Rather, they are meant to ensure that you have all the information you need, both positive and negative, to make the best decisions during your career exploration. And if you are considering starting your own nonprofit organization, Chapter Fourteen is essential reading.

It is our pleasure to support you as you begin this exciting journey of discovery. We hope that you will find the information, activities, and advice in the book helpful as you explore both where you are in your career right now and where you want to go within the wonderfully vibrant slice of society known as the nonprofit sector.

An explanation of this book's "threads"

This book contains text boxes with information that falls under common themes. The themed text boxes, or "threads," are explained on this page and the next. Some "threads" don't appear in every section of the book, but every section features some.

IMAGINE, CONNECT, ACT

Self-assessment is an essential component to finding a fulfilling career path. Therefore, it is best if you can regularly block out short periods of time in your schedule for self-assessment. This three-pronged thread helps you break this task into manageable parts.

- First, the **Imagine** boxes ask you basic questions about yourself, where you're starting, and what you want. These activities will help you answer the question, "What is my ideal?"

- Next, the **Connect** boxes will help you frame your research and set goals to fill in any gaps you discovered in the Imagine stage. At this point, you should start connecting your ideal with real opportunities in your community. These activities will help you answer the question, "Where does my ideal meet reality?"

- Finally, the **Act** boxes will give suggestions and opportunities for you to take action in the community and connect with other people. These activities will help you answer the question, "How can I take action?"

These three stages should be completed in conjunction with each other; however, if you're short on time or if a particular section doesn't fit your stage in the job search, feel free to take these components à la carte.

THE GREAT DEBATE

Finding total consensus on aspects of the job search process is like getting a unanimous vote on the greatest movie ever made. Is a one-page resume always best? Should you ever ask about salary during the interview process? How do you best research an organization before an interview? What is the best way to get a job in the nonprofit sector? Since there are no universal answers to these questions (and many others), you'll see **The Great Debate** text boxes whenever an issue arises for which there are multiple perspectives. Sometimes there will be anecdotal evidence, sometimes data will be available, but for the most part, it will be up to you to make a choice based on your personality, your search, your potential employer, and your unique situation.

COMMON MISTAKES

Ask any hiring manager what common mistakes they see in job applications, and you're likely to get much more than a quick, one sentence answer. The **Common Mistakes** text boxes cover many of the widespread errors that are found in all stages of the job search process.

These issues range from basics like not proofreading or following directions, to more subtle but similarly off-putting mistakes like not turning off "Track Changes" before emailing a cover letter or resume. Hiring professionals have very little time to select candidates from a pile of resumes and, when you factor in the intense competition for many positions, you can see why even the slightest mistake can cause your application to be placed in the recycling bin without a second thought.

This symbol indicates a spot where it can be helpful for you to record some of your own thoughts on a given section of the text.

Gray sidebars

Gray sidebars appear throughout the book. Technically, these aren't thematic threads. Instead, these sidebars provide useful clarifications, insightful anecdotes, and other supplementary materials in order to offer you more perspective on the topic of a particular section of the main text.

Gray text boxes

Similar to gray sidebars, these gray text boxes appear throughout the book, interspersed in the main text column. They serve to highlight particularly important or exemplary cases and points, or to list useful resources.

Learn more

The chapters in this book cover many aspects of the job search, but depending on your interests, focus, or experience, you may need more in depth information on particular topics. The **Learn More** threads will point you in the direction of resources that deal with many of the topics discussed in the book in much more detail. Resources listed in the Learn More thread may be a page on Idealist.org or another website, a PDF you can download, or books and other materials that you can find at a library or book shop. All the resources were carefully selected to broaden your understanding of points discussed in this book.

JOB SEARCH 2.0

Technology is essential in almost all aspects of our lives, and the job search is no exception. Especially in today's wired workplace, in order to stay competitive, you need to take advantage of tech tools to network, research, and find opportunities ranging from volunteer projects to graduate education programs. The **Job Search 2.0** threads are not about highlighting the newest technology gadgets and gizmos; we'll leave that to the tech experts. Instead, they point out useful, reliable, and proven tools as well as the multitude of ways you can utilize them to make your job search more effective and efficient.

ROADMAP

A job search is one place where it's not only okay to ask for directions, it's probably the best way to get where you want to go. The **Roadmap** text boxes offer useful checklists and a series of guided conversations that can help you communicate your questions, concerns, or requests along the way. While some of the roadmaps are written in dialogue format, these should not be scripts; you'll need to rework them to ensure that they reflect you and your unique situation. Hopefully, though, these roadmaps will give you a sense of the direction to take, while allowing you to map your own route to get there.

The organizations behind this book

Action Without Borders is a nonprofit organization founded in 1995 with offices in the United States and Argentina. **Idealist.org**, a project of Action Without Borders, is an interactive site where people and organizations can exchange resources and ideas, find opportunities and supporters, and turn their good intentions into action.

The Idealist Guide to Nonprofit Careers for First-time Job Seekers is a product of Action Without Borders' Nonprofit Careers Program based in Portland, OR. This team works to support individuals and organizations with graduate education options; HR and volunteer management resources; and job, internship, and volunteer opportunities.

This book was made possible by a grant from the **Lumina Foundation**, a private, independent foundation that strives to help people achieve their potential by expanding access and success in education beyond high school. In particular, we'd like to thank **Gloria Ackerson**, Grants Manager, and **Caroline Altman Smith**, Program Officer, for their incredible support.

About the authors

Meg Busse

Meg is a native (and ardent fan) of New Jersey. However, she's also enjoyed living in Philly, Boston, Washington DC, San Francisco, NW Connecticut, and Seattle. Currently, Meg resides in Portland, OR with her best friend, Ian, Rufus the puppy, and Boris the grumpy cat. In just the few years she's been in Portland, Meg's fallen in love with its outdoor adventures, incredible bridges, amazing wine, and food carts. In her pre-Idealist years, Meg was a middle school reading and writing teacher, a coach, and a writer and editor. In her free time, she has been a white water rafting guide, pet pig owner, competitive board game player, dark chocoholic, and long distance runner. Some of these labels still apply. She has one of the best interview stories ever, dreams of being Ira Glass someday, and is continually floored by Tom Waits, Edward Abbey, Bill Moyers, and Calvin & Hobbes. As for her work at Idealist, the best thing about her job is her colleagues—a continually surprising, engaging, awe-inspiring, passionate bunch of folks.

Steven Joiner

Steven joined the Action Without Borders/Idealist Nonprofit Careers and Partnerships Team in February 2007 after his second stint in Japan. He was born on the U.S. East Coast and spent the first 12 years of his life in seven different cities before stopping for a while in North Carolina. After finishing a B.A. in Secondary English Education at North Carolina State University, he left for three years of life in Japan. Upon returning to the United States, he drove across the country three times during his "Reorientation Tour of America," fell in love with San Francisco, and went on to finish an M.A. in International Adult Educational Development at San Francisco State University. After two more years in Japan, he returned to wonderful Portland, OR to settle down... for now at least. Steve loves learning, cooking, reading sci-fi, watching movies, writing, and his super-cool black cat Fortuna. He is an avid fan of sumo wrestling and baseball, though he completely understands—yet also completely disagrees—when people think either or both are boring.

Featured contributors

Put Barber

Put Barber joined Idealist.org in October of 2004 when the Nonprofit FAQ was added to the website. He has been the editor of the FAQ since its earliest years and worked with Cliff Landesmann (founder of the Internet Nonprofit Center) and Michael Gilbert (of The Gilbert Center) to design the user interface and add content. He founded The Evergreen State Society in Seattle to build strong nonprofits and strong communities in his home state of Washington and continues that work as a Senior Consultant to Executive Alliance. He serves on the editorial board for *Non-*

profit and Voluntary Sector Quarterly and on the board of directors of the Thomas C. Wales Foundation, and is a frequent author and speaker on issues affecting nonprofit organizations in the United States. He's an avid amateur photographer; you can see some of his photos at http://putnam.smugmug.com.

David Schachter

David Schachter is the Assistant Dean for Career Services and Experiential Learning at the NYU Robert F. Wagner Graduate School of Public Service, where he oversees all career-related services and programs to Wagner's students and alumni. David has more than 20 years of hands-on experience in nonprofit staff and volunteer management. He has offered training, consulting, and facilitation nationally in the areas of leadership, staff development, supervision, team building, training of the trainer, and career planning. David received the 2006 NACE/Chevron Outstanding Achievement Award for Innovative Programs in Career Services for his partnership with Action Without Borders/Idealist.org on the creation of the Institute on Public Service Careers, a series of conferences designed to educate college career services professionals from across the country on how to increase the visibility and accessibility of public service careers to their students. David received his Master's Degree in Public Administration from NYU's Wagner School and a Bachelor of Fine Arts from NYU's Tisch School of the Arts. He is a member of the Idealist Mid-Career Transitions Advisory Board. http://wagner.nyu.edu

Cathy Wasserman

Cathy Wasserman provides career, executive, and depth coaching to a wide range of individuals seeking to increase their personal and professional success, actively direct their life, and realize their one-of-a-kind core strengths and goals through her business, Self-Leadership Strategies. She has 16 years of experience in the nonprofit sector and beyond including work as a training director, a recruiter, and an organization development consultant. Additionally, she has served as career coaching expert with her column, *Ask Cathy*, on Idealist.org. *Working Mother* magazine also featured her as expert of the month on switching from corporate to nonprofit work. She began her career as an advocate for youth and women and she is published in the book *Front-line Feminism*. Cathy holds an MSW in Clinical Social Work from Smith College and a B.A. in Psychology from Wesleyan University. You can contact Cathy at cathy@self-leadershipstrategies.com or visit her website www.self-leadershipstrategies.com.

Kelley Carmichael Casey

Kelley Carmichael Casey is the Education and Community Engagement Director for Life by Design NW in Portland, OR. In her private practice, she provides personal career counseling to mid-career transitioners seeking their passion and purpose in work and community engagement. Kelley has more than 20 years of experience in counseling and nonprofit work. Kelley has researched, written, and presented in numerous venues on midlife women and mentoring, baby boomers and volunteerism, and work with meaning over 50. She is a member of the Idealist.org Volunteer Management Advisory Board and serves as Vice Chair of the Board of Directors of the School & Community Reuse Action Project. Kelley has a Doctor of Psychology from George Fox University and an M.S. in Counseling from University of Portland.

Valinda Lee

Valinda Lee is a Career Counselor at Scripps College, the women's college of The Claremont Colleges. After changing her major three times during her first year at La Sierra University in Riverside, CA, she earned a B.A. in Psychology and decided to make a career of helping other people navigate their own career decision making. Her graduate training at California State University, Northridge in Career Counseling has given her the opportunity to work in community colleges, graduate schools, and liberal arts colleges counseling students who want to change the world. At Scripps, Valinda works individually with students to help them pursue internship or post-college plans, organizes events to bring alumnae to campus to share their experiences, and is currently working on creating a podcast series to provide students with more ways to interact with her office. You may contact Valinda through her LinkedIn profile at www.linkedin.com/in/valindalee.

Acknowledgments

We thank the **entire staff at Action Without Borders** for their contributions, ideas, and continuous support during the creation of this book. Special thanks go to the people in and outside our organization who provided useful suggestions and insightful comments that have improved the book in so many ways—**Bill Alberta, Linda Arra, Put Barber, Erin Barnhart, Jay Bloom, Jake Brewer, Amelia Byers, Kelley Carmichael Casey, Ami Dar, Joe DuPont, Jung Fitzpatrick, Jillian Glazer, Lauren Gordon, Rose Grech, Cary Hixon, Valinda Lee, Chris Machuca, Chelsea Maricle, Alicia Ng, Nancy Paul, Amy Potthast, Anna Pozolova, Gary Prehn, Stephen Ristau, David Schachter, Mike Sciola, Lorene Straka, Julia Sylla, Dee Thompson, Mary Vance, Cathy Wasserman, Linda Weiner,** and **Gail Wootan.**

Thanks go to **Dave Amos**, who created the webspace for this book (www.idealist.org/careerguide); to **Eric Fichtl**, who guided the book's editing, production, and formatting for publication; and to **Russ Finkelstein**, who provided constant support and leadership to the entire team behind the book.

Grateful acknowledgment is made to **New York University** for permission to reprint excerpts and adaptations of the work of **David Schachter**, Assistant Dean of Career Services and Experiential Learning at NYU's Robert F. Wagner Graduate School of Public Service © 2008. These specific sections are reprinted with permission of New York University and David Schachter.

We also thank and acknowledge the members of the Idealist High School and College Nonprofit Career Transitions Advisory Board who have reviewed this book and enhanced it through their tireless feedback and valuable insights: **Bill Alberta** (Associate Director, Cornell Career Services), **Cathy Wasserman** (Founder, Self-Leadership Strategies), **Joe DuPont** (Director, Hiatt Career Center, Brandeis University), **Linda Arra** (Director, Career Services Center, Lafayette College), **Mike Sciola** (Director, Career Resource Center, Wesleyan University), and **Nancy Paul** (Director, Career Development Center, Binghamton University).

Our thanks go to the following career services professionals from Portland, OR area colleges and universities, each of whom gave insightful feedback on early versions of many of the book's texts: **Bonnie J. Jerke** (Director of Career Services, George Fox University), **Amy Cavanaugh** (Director, Office of Career Services, University of Portland), **Jill Cain** (Co-Coordinator of the Career Resource Center, Portland Community College), **Louise Paradis** and **Mary C. Vance** (Career Counselors, Portland State University), **Julie Maxfield** (Administrative Assistant, Career Services, Reed College), and **Heather Dittmore** (Administrative and Recruitment Coordinator, Lewis & Clark College).

We gratefully acknowledge **Kerstin Vogdes** of kvdesign (www.kvdesign.net), who created the original graphic design elements and page templates for this book.

We also wish to say thank you to all of those individuals who, in so many ways, express their desire to spend their lives doing good work. It is their passion to make an impact that has motivated us to create this book.

ABOUT THE SUMMARY BOX AND LAST PAGE OF EACH CHAPTER

These blue boxes on the last page of each chapter provide a **short summary** of the main points made in that text. You'll also find handy **page number cues** that point you to the precise pages in the text where you can read more about a particular topic.

CHAPTER ONE

What exactly is a nonprofit?

(The answer will surprise you)

In this chapter you will:

- Learn why nonprofit organizations exist.

- Explore the variety of services, causes and missions, and types of organizations.

- Examine the difference between the nonprofit, for-profit (business), and public (government) sectors.

- Consider statistics about the benefits of working in the nonprofit sector.

As discussed in the **Introduction**, the nonprofit sector offers a diverse range of exciting career opportunities. In this chapter, we'll explore some of the ways to understand the sector (e.g. mission, tax status, role in community) and more clearly define why you are considering a nonprofit career. While there are an infinite number of reasons why people consider nonprofit work, one that resonates with most people is the desire to create positive change. Whatever your reason, having a clear understanding of the sector will help you assess and explain how you fit into the nonprofit landscape and, more importantly, into the organizations where you apply.

Understanding nonprofits

What is a nonprofit? There is no definitive answer to this question. Nonprofits can be defined by tax status, what they do with surplus revenue, the existence of a volunteer board of directors, or the fact that their work is directed by a mission statement. The nonprofit sector is also referred to as the not-for-profit, tax-exempt, civil, independent, third, social, charitable, or voluntary sector. Internationally, nonprofits are typically called nongovernmental organizations (NGOs), charities, or foundations.

The nonprofit sector is comprised of organizations that are trying to create a better world, as defined by their missions. These organizations have varying levels of government oversight depending on the state in which they are located and the percentage of their funding that comes from the government. Within the nonprofit sector, organizations with opposing missions co-exist; there are many other organizations whose work is guided by similar values, goals, and visions, but which take different approaches to achieve success.

> **What do nonprofits mean by "mission"?**
>
> When people at a nonprofit organization say the word "mission", they're referring both to the general goals of the organization and the specific role the organization seeks to play in the community it serves.
>
> For a useful glossary of nonprofit terms, see **Appendix One**.

While youth centers and soup kitchens are often the first type of nonprofits that come to mind, the sector also includes religious institutions, universities, hospitals, trade associations, unions, and museums. The sector includes organizations with values all along the liberal to conservative political spectrum; it's a misconception that nonprofits are all left-wing. Organizations with traditionally right-leaning constituents—like the National Rifle Association, the Heritage Foundation, the Republican National Committee, and the Moral Majority—are nonprofits, while organizations with stated neutral agendas, such as the Red Cross or Doctors Without Borders, are also nonprofits.

What type of work do nonprofits do?

Think about the nonprofits that you know. What kind of work do they do? What other groups do similar work? What would it be like if nonprofits didn't exist? If you think about what our society would be like without groups such as the Sierra Club, YMCA, American Cancer Society, Boy Scouts of America, local food banks, Habitat for Humanity, local private schools, many hospitals, most museums and private universities, and the Red Cross, you'll have a good idea of the incredible contribution that nonprofits make to society. Many nonprofits exist to provide services that business enterprises and government do not or cannot address. However, succinctly stating *why* nonprofits exist is difficult because the scope of their work is so vast.

While the scope, structure, and size of the nonprofit sector changes constantly, the reason that nonprofits exist is the same today as it was when they first emerged. As U.S. society evolved, it needed to address common concerns such as education, adoption, fire prevention, and health care. Since a gap has always existed between what the private sector can profit from and what the public (government) sector can afford, citizens joined together voluntarily and created early versions of nonprofit organizations. Citizen action is at the root of the nonprofit sector, and it is what continues to drive most nonprofits today.[1]

The societal benefits of nonprofits

The societal benefits of nonprofit organizations are vast and varied. Nonprofit services and their constituents are equally diverse. This incredible range of work, missions, and benefits is what makes the nonprofit sector such a vibrant and effective force in our society. Below are a just a few of the causes and issues the nonprofit sector addresses.

Low-income housing	Education
Environmental preservation	Conflict resolution
Activism	Research
Grassroots organizing	Community development
Lobbying	Urban planning
Public radio	Civil rights advocacy
Health care	Social services
Legal services	International aid

---

[1] For a deeper discussion of these themes, see: Salamon, Lester M. *America's Nonprofit Sector: A Primer, Second Edition.* (Foundation Center, 1999).

A tale of two youth outreach programs

The **Virginia Woof®️ Dog Daycare** in Portland, OR works with youth who want to improve their lives through employment training programs. These youth can use their training at Virginia Woof to pursue permanent employment or further training and schooling in animal care.

The **All-Star Project, Inc.** is a national nonprofit that uses theater and performance-based activities to teach young people leadership skills, performance skills, and technical theater skills. The opportunities provided by the All-Star Project give their participants the groundwork to pursue professional paths that may not otherwise be open to them.

Thus, while both programs aim to teach youth useful professional and life skills that they can use to be productive members of society, the approaches these two nonprofits take are quite different.

Nonprofit organizations not only provide the societal benefits of direct services, they also provide a tangible, monetary contribution to the overall U.S. economy through jobs and products. Over 12 million people are employed in nonprofit organizations, representing roughly 9 percent of the entire U.S. workforce. The annual assets of the nonprofit sector total $2.9 trillion, a sizable contribution to the overall economy.

Due to the unique nature of nonprofits, they also create less quantifiable, more intangible societal benefits. Nonprofits provide opportunities for people to invest in and give back to their communities, raise awareness of issues, and help foster a sense of community and trust.

Finally, the line between strict "nonprofit" work and "business" priorities is becoming blurred. The incredible societal benefits of the for-profit sector's increased attention to what have traditionally been nonprofit concerns are becoming more widespread. This is evident in the business world with the development of Corporate Social Responsibility (CSR) departments, the increase in cause marketing (emphasizing fair trade practices, fair labor policies, etc.), and the emphasis on the triple bottom line (a type of accounting that takes into consideration economic, societal, and environmental performance). In these ways, the nonprofit sector has profoundly influenced the practices, perspectives, and priorities of the for-profit sector.

Common characteristics

Despite all of the ambiguity about the definition, size, and scope of the nonprofit sector, there are several distinguishing characteristics:

- **A focus on mission or purpose**: Central to every nonprofit's work is a vision of why the organization exists, how it serves its constituents, and the goals it aims to achieve.
- **A standard form of organization**: Nearly every nonprofit has a volunteer board of community leaders who oversee the organization, a corps of volunteers who help the organization do its work, donors who contribute financially, and staff members who share a commitment to the mission.
- **Independence**: Businesses answer to their owners—whether proprietors or shareholders. Government agencies implement programs and follow rules that legislatures create and, ultimately, the public demands. Within the boundaries set by law, nonprofits answer only to themselves and to their circles of supporters. These supporters can include funders, volunteers, and constituents. Such independence allows for creativity and innovation, and encourages the development of new approaches to meet community goals and expectations.
- **Public benefit**: Both by law and by custom, nonprofits are focused on providing benefit to the community at large and to serving public—not private—ends.
- **Voluntary board leadership**: The direction, innovation, and "feel" of an organization is often created by its board of directors. Ideally, the board has

HOW DO YOU MEASURE SUCCESS?

the GREAT DEBATE

Measuring success in the nonprofit world is as tricky as defining the sector. Just as it is difficult to quantify the success of a school (do you use attendance rates, graduation rates, grade point averages, or test results?), measuring the impact of nonprofits in numbers is a real challenge.

Is a nonprofit successful if it builds a certain number of affordable homes or delivers a certain number of warm meals? Do you measure the success of an advocacy organization based on the legislation it gets passed? Do you measure the success of a support organization like Idealist.org by the number of partnerships it forms? Is the success of a museum only measured in ticket sales or should you factor in estate bequests and the expertise of the staff?

Also keep in mind that there are some nonprofits that deal with causes for which there is no "solution." Groups involved in women's advocacy, the environment, and poverty alleviation, among other issues, will be fighting for their causes as long as their causes exist.

the interests of the organization at heart, leads with the mission statement foremost in their minds, and makes decisions on the organization's structure and activities as they relate to achieving the mission.

A snapshot of the nonprofit sector

The box below gives an indication of the scale and scope of the U.S. nonprofit sector. But despite these significant numbers, most recognized nonprofits are small; roughly 70 percent of organizations that report to the Internal Revenue Service (IRS) have annual revenues of less than $500,000. Not surprisingly, the largest nonprofits tend to be hospitals and universities, which generally have the biggest budgets, the most assets, and the largest staffs. Meanwhile, there are many small organizations that focus on the arts, human services, and environmental causes.

"PUBLIC" DOESN'T MEAN EVERYONE

While most nonprofits work toward "public good," the demographics they serve may be more focused. Organizations like March of Dimes, Girls Incorporated, and Food for the Poor have missions that are directed at helping specific segments of the population. While the benefits of their work are undoubtedly felt far beyond the clientele they serve, it is important to note that the "public" in phrases like "public good" and "public benefit" may be more focused in order to create lasting improvement in society at large.

- The Internal Revenue Service (IRS) recognizes **over one million non-profits** in the United States (see sidebar page 22 for more detail).
- The nonprofit sector's assets are estimated at **$2.9 trillion**. This is the same amount as the **2008 federal budget blueprint** proposed by Congressional Democrats. This figure is also roughly equivalent to **one third of the U.S. Gross Domestic Product**.
- Some **70 percent** of nonprofit organizations operate on annual budgets under $500,000.
- About **4 percent** of nonprofits have budgets over $10 million.
- **Thirty-one percent** of the sector's funding comes from government grants and contracts.
- Over **50 percent** of funding for **health and human services** comes from the government.
- More than **100 new nonprofit organizations** file with the IRS **each day**.
- In the United States, **12 million individuals** (about **9 percent** of the U.S. workforce) work with nonprofit organizations. That means that one of every ten workers in the United States is employed by a nonprofit.
- An example of nonprofit scale and reach: America's Second Harvest, the largest charitable food distribution network in the United States, now **helps more than 25 million people** (more than the population of Texas).

Nonprofits work in communities throughout the country. In rural areas and small towns, a single organization (such as a church or community center) may provide a wide range of services and host many groups of community volunteers. In larger urban areas, there are a multitude of organizations that undertake more focused missions and serve more specific demographic groups. Nonprofits serve communities, address community problems, and build community assets in such diverse ways that there is no simple categorization for the work that they do.

Various types of nonprofit organizations

Nonprofits can also be understood by sorting them into three broad groups based on:

- Who they serve: their **member base** or the **general public**
- The **role** that they play in the sector
- The **cause(s)** on which they focus

These groupings are not strict or mutually exclusive. Rather, this is a framework with which to think about the variety of organizations, the populations served, and the services provided. This will help you to better understand how organizations view their roles within the sector. This framework can also show the multitude of ways in which you can get involved in the nonprofit sector.

Member-serving and public-serving organizations

Member-serving organizations target specific segments of the population such as political parties, professional associations, and labor unions. *Public-serving organizations* are what most people think of as nonprofits; these are charitable organizations, social welfare institutions, and religious organizations. The distinction between member-serving and public-serving organizations has to do with the tax status of the organization and the effect this has on the taxation of individual donations—a complicated issue beyond the scope of this introductory discussion.

Roles of the organizations

Nonprofits essentially play four roles in the community: service providers, support providers, funders, and advocacy organizations.

- *Service providers* offer direct services to their constituents. Direct service can take many forms such as education, counseling, medical care, and outreach. These organizations represent the bulk of nonprofits and include schools, homeless shelters, and hospitals.
- *Support providers* offer assistance to other nonprofit organizations. For example, Idealist.org helps organizations find qualified candidates for job openings, and offers resources to support internal nonprofit functions like Human Resources (www.idealist.org/nonprofithr) and Volunteer Management (www.idealist.org/vmrc).
- *Funders* provide financial resources for nonprofits. These generally fall under two categories: foundations and funding intermediaries. Foundations can be family (The Bill and Melinda Gates Foundation), community (Oregon Community Foundation), or corporate (Nike Foundation). Funding intermediaries are organizations that "collect private donations on behalf of a number of service organizations."[2] The United Way, American Cancer Society, and

Nonprofits essentially play four roles in the community: service providers, support providers, funders, and advocacy organizations."

> **What's tax got to do with it?**
> Tax policy provides another way to understand the nonprofit sector. Because nonprofits focus on providing public benefit (rather than receiving private reward), nonprofits and their supporters are eligible for certain tax-related benefits. For an explanation of tax-exempt status as it relates to nonprofits, see page 21.

---

[2] Salamon, Lester M. *America's Nonprofit Sector: A Primer, Second Edition.* (Foundation Center, 1999) p. 29

American Heart Association are all examples of organizations "that raise funds from individuals and corporations on behalf of a number of local social service agencies."[3]

- *Advocacy organizations* shape public policy around specific causes. These organizations represent views or interests and then, through issue advocacy, lobbying, or political activity, work to change public opinion or policy. Examples of advocacy organizations are the American Society for the Prevention of Cruelty to Animals (ASPCA), Sierra Club, the NAACP, Republican National Committee, National Organization for Women (NOW), and AARP. Organizations that engage in advocacy need to follow strict guidelines regarding how much time and money they devote to lobbying and how they engage in political advocacy—activities which can affect whether or not donations to their organization are tax-deductible.

These categorizations are not strict. Nonprofit organizations can perform several or all of these roles simultaneously.

Cause focus

Organizations can also be grouped based on their mission. Since organizations work on so many missions and causes, and because a single organization may focus on several causes, creating a comprehensive list that encompasses the range of nonprofit services and constituents is difficult. The following list gives some idea of the range of causes on which nonprofits focus.

• **Advocacy and community development**	• **Environment and conservation**
• **Animal welfare**	• **Foundations, grantmaking organizations, and philanthropy**
• **Arts, culture, and humanities**	
• **Business, professional, and trade associations**	• **Health and science**
• **Education**	• **Human/social services**
	• **Religious organizations**

One of the most exciting aspects of nonprofits is their ability to work on multiple causes to find innovative solutions. For example, an award-winning nonprofit magazine based in Portland, OR, *The Bear Deluxe*, explores environmental issues through the arts. Not only does it focus on how the arts can be used to view and discuss environmental causes, it engages in education and advocacy work as well. This multi-issue approach is part of what makes nonprofit organizations so effective in the community. It is also what makes nonprofit work such an enriching career.

Nonprofits can multitask

The Leukemia and Lymphoma Society is an example of a nonprofit organization performing all four roles. The Society **provides services** to individuals with blood cancers, **supports** blood cancer awareness and advocacy, **funds** cancer research, and helps **raise awareness** of leukemia and lymphoma.

---

[3] Salamon, Lester M. *America's Nonprofit Sector: A Primer, Second Edition.* (Foundation Center, 1999) p. 29

Nonprofits and tax-exempt status

A common attribute shared by most U.S. nonprofits is that they are recognized by the IRS as tax-exempt. This status is granted if an organization's work serves one or more of the "exempt purposes" defined by section 501(c)(3) of the Internal Revenue Code. This large group—nearly one million organizations across the United States—includes both the "public charities" that provide a broad spectrum of community and public services, as well as the grantmaking "private foundations" that focus primarily on supporting other nonprofits.

Being tax-exempt means that an organization does not have to pay corporate income taxes to the U.S. government on revenues it receives from mission-related activities; other taxes can still apply to nonprofit organizations, and their employees still pay personal income taxes on wages. IRS tax-exempt recognition also means that contributions to an organization may be deducted from donors' income when they calculate their personal income tax. It is also the case that most foundations will not make grants to organizations that are not recognized as 501(c)(3)s by the IRS. Securing and maintaining tax-exempt status can be very important to a nonprofit in gathering the resources it needs to do its work.

Along with these advantages, tax exemption also carries some obligations and restrictions. Nonprofits must demonstrate their continued qualification for exempt status via a yearly report to the IRS. Exempt organizations cannot distribute "profits" to anyone, and they must avoid providing "undue compensation" to anyone who performs work for them. There are limits on the ways exempt organizations can work to influence legislation by "lobbying" and 501(c)(3) nonprofits are prohibited from doing anything that directly affects the outcome of an election for public office. Keeping the records and filing the reports necessary to maintain tax-exempt status requires specialized knowledge and a significant amount of effort.

While 501(c)(3) status is the most common one for U.S. nonprofits, there are many other classifications of tax-exempt organizations in the Internal Revenue Code, each bestowing particular advantages to support or encourage a type of nonprofit work. These classifications cover a diverse range of organizations including labor unions, credit unions, membership groups, political action committees (PACs), advocacy groups (the NRA, MoveOn.org), retirement funds, and chambers of commerce.

The differences among the nonprofit, for-profit, and public sectors

As opposed to the public (government) sector and the for-profit (business) sector, the nonprofit sector (also referred to as nongovernmental, independent, philanthropic,

ADVOCACY AND LOBBYING IN 501(C)(3) NONPROFITS

There is confusion even within nonprofit organizations as to exactly how much advocacy and lobbying a 501(c)(3) nonprofit is legally allowed to do. The rules affecting advocacy and political work in 501(c)(3) nonprofits are different from the other types of tax-exempt organizations mentioned here.

Here are three basic rules governing 501(c)(3) nonprofit advocacy and lobbying:

1. There are no restrictions on 501(c)(3) nonprofits with regard to advocacy.

2. 501(c)(3) nonprofit lobbying, while restricted, is not illegal. Congress has a formula based on revenues that outlines how much of a 501(c)(3) nonprofit's budget can go toward lobbying.

3. 501(c)(3)s cannot engage in any activities that directly influence the election of an individual to public office. This process, called electioneering, is flatly illegal.

In addition to these considerations, nonprofits are also covered by local rules in the states and cities where they operate, so it is a good idea to carefully consult those before starting an advocacy campaign or a lobbying effort.

or third sector) is often defined by what it is not (i.e., profit-making). The easiest way to understand the difference between the public, for-profit, and nonprofit sectors is to understand the constituents that each serves.

Public sector

The public sector—federal, state, county, and city government agencies—by definition serves the public good. Through taxation (a form of wealth redistribution), public money (taxes) goes toward making sure that everyone in society has a minimum set of rights and services. These funds help to ensure that programs and laws are put into place for all citizens to enjoy their rights without impinging on or impairing the rights of others.

Public programs include public transportation; roads, sewers, and water systems; public universities and community colleges; and a myriad of other services that most of us simply take for granted. Public money goes toward projects that benefit the public good, but it is impossible for the government to meet all of society's needs. The public sector relies on nonprofits and businesses to provide the services and programs that it doesn't have the capacity or capability to do itself.

For-profit sector

The for-profit sector—giant corporations, local businesses, mom-and-pop stores—serves a very select constituency: their owners, shareholders, and consumers. As the name implies, for-profits operate to make a profit. Employees and owners work to make money and shareholders invest money in order to make returns. Projects and decisions in the for-profit world all have the same bottom line: profit. The recent explosion of socially responsible business practices has raised awareness of the impact that business decisions can have on society and the environment, creating what is commonly called "multiple bottom lines". The increased visibility of for-profit companies (such as Nike) and businesspeople (such as Bill Gates) creating foundations that fund the work of nonprofits further demonstrates the growing connections between the for-profit and nonprofit sectors. However, even as companies gain greater social awareness and increase their support of nonprofits, profit is still the major driving force behind their business.

Nonprofit sector

If you consider the public sector and the for-profit sector, you'll notice a gap between the services provided by the government and the activities from which for-profit businesses make money (even with multiple bottom lines); this is where the nonprofit sector exists. Take, for example, issues such as clean air or homeless youth. The government enacts legislation that provides some regulation and oversight. For-profit industry can legitimately say they are "doing something about the environment" or "helping the community." But most of the actual work and direct service is done by nonprofit organizations. It is within these problem-solving gaps that nonprofit organizations thrive.

Think of this gap that nonprofits fill as a space where people can come together to provide a service to either a specific group of people, like homeless teens in downtown Baltimore, or a far-reaching issue of public concern, such as the AIDS epidemic. Nonprofits have the freedom to address causes that range from very narrow to very broad without having to worry about appeasing all members of the public *or* making a profit. However, they still must often cater to public and for-profit sector funders.

The "gap position" and the freedom to approach causes creatively are two distinct qualities of nonprofits that allow them to provide services that are essential to society. Because of these services, nonprofits receive both a tax exemption from the IRS and varying financial support from the for-profit and public sectors. For example, your local city opera is most likely a nonprofit. If this is the case, it has tax-exempt status. The public sector might provide a subsidy in the form of public funding, but in order to bring in enough revenue to support its goals, the opera house will also woo corporate sponsors, apply for grants from foundations, and generate revenue through ticket sales. In this example, funding is generated in four ways with benefits for all involved: the government supports a socially valuable institution, corporate partnerships increase their community visibility, foundations provide grants that support their mission and goals, and opera enthusiasts get a chance to support an art form about which they are passionate through ticket purchases, donations, "Friends of the Opera" groups, and bequests.

In practice, the nonprofit sector's means of reaching its goals are as varied as the tens of thousands of mission statements that drive organizations' work. This also means that a nonprofit can serve a niche group without worrying about addressing all of the public's needs. Yet just as there are expectations in government work to provide services that benefit the general public, and in for-profit businesses to constantly increase revenue, nonprofit organizations also have expectations. Nonprofits are mission-driven and, as such, the mission often dictates the action and management of a nonprofit. For example, if a nonprofit's mission centers on "creating a voice for children," it might do advocacy work and would most likely try to do a significant amount of outreach and public engagement work. However, if a nonprofit's mission is focused on "providing resources for local individuals and groups," it would make sense to expect that organization to provide direct services. Or, if a nonprofit exists to support other nonprofits, expect a priority to be placed on collaboration and partnership at the organizational level.

These are only a few examples of how the mission drives both the actions and the management of a nonprofit. The commonality comes from the fact that the desired outcome or mission of any organization is intimately connected to the structure and work of that organization.

the GREAT DEBATE

SO MANY NAMES FOR THE SECTOR

Civil society, nonprofit, nongovernmental, charitable, third, social, voluntary... These terms reflect distinct perspectives on the sector's place and purpose. "Nonprofit" draws a distinction with the activities of profit-seeking entities while "nongovernmental" implies a separation from the state. "Third" and "social" similarly distinguish the sector from the "public" and "private" sectors. "Charitable" not only has associations with religious concepts of charity, but also with 17th century British laws that defined certain charitable actions (education, poverty reduction, religious mission) as being beneficial to society.

"Civil society" is a concept used differently by various people. It is common to hear of the "flourishing of civil society" in the globalization era, which partly refers to the explosive growth of citizens' groups (often nonprofits) in the wake of the collapse of authoritarian regimes, the spread of elections, and the liberalization of economies around the world from the late 1980s onward. Similarly, "voluntary" doesn't just mean that work is done by volunteers, but also denotes that people voluntarily associate to perform certain activities rather than being obliged to act by government regulations. In this perspective, the sector is composed of "voluntary" agents working to achieve their goals, rather than people required to do so by law. This also applies to funding, since these groups do not have the power of government to raise taxes and instead tend to rely on voluntary contributions.

Some view this citizen capacity positively, and others argue that this rise in voluntary activity derives from reforms which have "shrunk the state" by reducing governments' regulatory reach and service provision. In this view, the nonprofit sector has grown in a void left by the retreating state, leaving citizens' groups to organize services that were (or could be) mandated by law and funded by taxes, or to monitor harmful practices previously (or possibly) regulated by governments. This is just one of many interesting debates you may encounter in the sector–whatever you call it.

Conclusion

There is an incredible range of organizations, missions, tax statuses, and job opportunities within the nonprofit sector. One of the misconceptions about working in the nonprofit sector is that it is all direct service work such as grassroots organizing, social work, teaching, or serving food. Nonprofit organizations also need people to take care of finances, human resources, website management, maintenance, outreach, and leadership. In addition, organizations often have indirect service roles like volunteer managers, fundraisers, and grantwriters. Because of this diversity of jobs, responsibilities, organizations, and missions, there is a vast number of ways to have a career doing meaningful work in the nonprofit sector. This combination of attributes also creates a work environment that many people (even outside the sector) see as stimulating and rewarding, as the survey data in the table on the next page details.

 One of the misconceptions about working in the nonprofit sector is that it is all direct service work like grassroots organizing and serving food."

 **Jot your thoughts** Use the space below to identify connections you have with organizations from each sector.

Benefits of working in nonprofits

In 2002, the Brookings Institute[4] surveyed workers to gauge their perceptions of the nonprofit, for-profit, and government sectors. While it is interesting to see how each sector perceives itself, the results also showed some surprising contrasts with commonly held stereotypes, particularly about nonprofits. For instance, the nonprofit sector ranked highly in terms of innovation, trustworthiness, and efficiency, as the statistics below indicate. While every nonprofit is different, the overall perceptions of the nonprofit sector—from those who work in it, as well as those who don't—suggest a vibrant, stimulating work environment with plenty of benefits for individuals who choose to make it their career.

Benefits of Working in Different Sectors: Nonprofit, For-profit (Business), and Federal (Public)	Nonprofit employees	For-profit employees	Federal employees
Regarding their jobs, in general, respondents state that:			
They strongly disagree that their work is boring (Q10a)	75%	58%	57%
They are very satisfied with their opportunity to accomplish something worthwhile (Q14d)	66%	41%	47%
They strongly agree that they are given the chance to do the things that they do best (Q10b)	68%	52%	46%
They are very satisfied with their jobs overall (Q11a)	58%	44%	49%
They are very satisfied with their opportunity to develop new skills (Q14b)	48%	43%	36%
In terms of their organizations, respondents state that:			
Their organization does a very good job at helping people (Q36b)	73%	51%	51%
They feel very proud of the organization they work for (Q38)	67%	54%	51%
Their organization does a very good job of running its programs and services (Q36a)	56%	44%	41%
They feel that the word "innovative" describes their organization very well (Q9a)	38%	40%	29%
They feel that the word "trusted" describes their organization very well (Q9d)	67%	56%	45%
They feel that their organization does a very good job at spending its money wisely (Q36d)	44%	36%	22%
In regard to colleagues, respondents state that:			
Their coworkers are willing to help other employees learn new skills to a great extent (Q6c)	67%	51%	52%
The people they work with are open to new ideas to a great extent (Q6b)	46%	36%	33%

Extrapolating from the Brookings data (Q41), an interesting **portrait of the perceptions of workers in each sector** emerges. By excluding the views of workers about their own sector, and focusing on just the views of workers in the remaining two sectors, it becomes clear that nonprofits are highly regarded by peers in the for-profit and public sectors. In one result, nonprofits were seen as spending money the most wisely. In another question, nonprofits were overwhelmingly viewed as the sector that does the best job of helping people. While these findings are not conclusive evidence, they suggest that the nonprofit sector is both financially responsible and beneficial to the community–a combination increasingly sought by both potential employees and the community at large.

36 percent of for-profit and federal government workers think that **nonprofits spend money the most wisely**.

30 percent of nonprofit and federal government workers think that **for-profits spend money the most wisely**.

4 percent of nonprofit and for-profit workers think that the **federal government spends money the most wisely**.

49 percent of for-profit and federal government workers think that **nonprofits do the best job of helping people**.

5 percent of nonprofit and federal government workers think that **for-profits do the best job of helping people**.

9 percent of nonprofit and for-profit workers think that the **federal government does the best job of helping people**.

---

[4] Brookings Institute. *Final Topline Report: Health of the Nonprofit, For-profit, and Public Service Sectors.* February 2002. Available at www.brookings.edu/views/papers/light/NonprofitTopline.PDF

SUMMARY

Learning about the nonprofit sector is essential to being informed and successful in your nonprofit career search. This information can help you prioritize elements of your resume, craft a persuasive cover letter, and answer interview questions with depth and focus.

Why do nonprofit organizations exist? Organizations today serve much the same purpose for which they were originally created (pages 15-18).

However, the **variety of services, causes and missions, and sizes of organizations** has expanded to serve a much broader range of constituents (pages 19-20).

Many nonprofit organizations have a type of **tax-exempt status** in common (page 21).

The distinctions between the nonprofit, for-profit (business), and public (government) sectors are growing increasingly unclear. While the three sectors all serve distinct purposes, they often complement one another's services, as well as collaborate to utilize the best aspects of each (pages 21-23).

Read **what nonprofit workers have to say about their work,** based on a Brookings Institute survey. When surveyed, nonprofit, for-profit, and public sector employees rated the nonprofit sector as trustworthy, thrifty, and efficient—quite the opposite of the outmoded stereotypes (page 25).

CHAPTER TWO

Balancing act

The psychology of the job search

by **Kelley Carmichael Casey**, PsyD, Career Counselor *and*

Cathy Wasserman, LMSW, Career, Executive, and Depth Coach

In this chapter you will:

- Understand that although there are inevitable highs and lows in a job search, there are aspects of the search that you can control.
- Identify how your personality affects your job search and how a strong self-perception can help your search.
- Be aware of several key factors that can help you make your job search a more positive and effective process.

Keeping confident in the search

by Kelley Carmichael Casey, PsyD, Career Counselor*

The story goes: an eccentric billionaire offered one million dollars to the first team of scientists to successfully teach a gorilla to write poetry. Many techniques were employed by ambitious teams of researchers around the globe, all vying for the million dollar prize. One prestigious group of top government scientists built an elaborate multimedia feedback laboratory and employed graduate students to read poetry to the gorilla around the clock and give measured banana-flavored incentives when the gorilla appeared to have an inclination to put pen to paper. All to no avail. Another team hired a poet laureate to give the gorilla hours of exceptional, expert instruction—with no success. At a small, Midwestern university, a set of hardworking researchers in a lab equipped with an old wooden desk and undersized chair simply offered the gorilla a pen and paper. Patiently waiting for the gorilla to make a move, one scientist remarked to the other, "You know, he looks like a genius sitting there." Apparently overhearing the researcher's comment, the gorilla looked up thoughtfully, picked up the pen, and wrote a sonnet…

What other people tell us—and what we tell ourselves—greatly impacts what we believe we are capable of accomplishing in life. And while we are not our job titles, our careers significantly influence our self identities. When in a job search, you are

LEARN MORE

Know where you are

This book is designed to help you structure your job search toward a meaningful career. Evaluating your personal strengths and exploring the opportunities that match your abilities is the subject of **Chapter Three**. There you'll find a number of tips, exercises, and exploratory frameworks that can help you connect your self-knowledge to career options in the nonprofit sector.

* This section is by Kelley Carmichael Casey. Kelley is the Education and Community Engagement Director for Life by Design NW in Portland, OR. In her private practice, she provides personal career counseling to mid-career transitioners seeking their passion and purpose in work and community engagement. Kelley has more than 20 years of experience in counseling and nonprofit work. Kelley has researched, written, and presented in numerous venues on midlife women and mentoring, Baby Boomers and volunteerism, and work with meaning over 50. She is a member of the Idealist.org Volunteer Management Advisory Board and serves as Vice Chair of the Board of Directors of the School & Community Reuse Action Project. Kelley has a Doctor of Psychology from George Fox University and an M.S. in Counseling from University of Portland.

more vulnerable than ever to your perceived shortcomings and failures. You need someone to notice that you "look like a genius sitting there." During this process, it's important to seek out those people who will remind you of your strengths and help you stay confident during a time when it might be easier to identify with the gorilla than the researchers.

An emotional rollercoaster

You probably already know this, but the job search is one of the hardest processes you'll go through. Through it all, you must appear confident, eloquent, well groomed, and informed. You need to present meticulously crafted and proofread documents and offer up well researched answers. While obviously looking for a job, you must never seem desperate for one. And you need to do all of this while facing more rejection than you were ever subjected to during your middle school foray into the dating scene.

There are several points to remember as you weather the ups and downs of the job search:

1. Your personality matters
2. Self-perception is essential
3. A support network can make the difference

1. Your personality matters

There are certain personality traits that are helpful in a job search. For example, the most successful job searchers tend to be people who are outgoing or well organized. And those who look harder are likely to be more optimistic. People who are extroverted may actually enjoy the process of interviewing and meeting new and potentially exciting people and workplaces. Highly organized people tend to be very conscientious about networking and following up on job leads.

"That doesn't mean that introverts or less conscientious individuals have poor re-employment prospects," says Ruth Kanfer, a professor in the School of Psychology at the Georgia Institute of Technology.[1] "But those personality traits are less conducive to the path that they're up against. In contrast, some people are naturally outgoing or predisposed to set goals and follow through. In a job search, it's often the little extras that can make a difference in impressing employers."

If you are not very outgoing, you will need to put forth more effort in your job search to achieve the same edge that extroverts have from the start. Being aware of your own personality strengths and their relation to the challenges of the job search is invaluable. It will help you to determine when you need to focus more energy on get-

I HAVE TO SPEND ALL MY TIME ON MY JOB SEARCH

common **MISTAKES**

A job search is a time-consuming process. However, for a multitude of reasons, it's important to spend time doing other activities that don't involve resumes, cover letters, or trolling through Idealist.org job listings just in case something new was posted in the last eight minutes. By making time to do the things that refuel you like volunteering, going to shows, or playing a game of pick-up basketball, you will be able to not only return to your job search refreshed, but you will have interesting things to talk about in your cover letters and interviews, you will meet people and expand your network, and you'll be able to remind yourself that there is more to who you are than just your job search.

---

[1] Ruth Kanfer quoted in Becker, T. J. "Shopping the job market: Persistence and a positive mindset pay off in a job search" *Research Horizons*, Fall 2002. Available at http://gtresearchnews.gatech.edu/reshor/rh-f02/jobs.html

ting out there to network, interview, and make valuable contacts, or when you need to slow down, pause to reflect, and take care of other aspects of your life.

2. Self-perception is essential

Why is self-esteem so vulnerable during a job search? Career identification is a big piece of how we perceive our worth and value to others. Self-image can determine job search success because it informs our job search behavior. Like the poetry-writing gorilla, how we see ourselves shapes our hopes, actions, and—ultimately—our successes.

Those who are successful in their pursuits often have secure and realistic self-perceptions. They are open to information and feedback, even if it is discouraging or critical. They learn from their mistakes and make course corrections along the way. People who lack strong self-esteem may ignore, forget, or misinterpret information that is threatening to their self-image (which is already in a fragile state during a job search!). These job searchers may be unable to accept and correct their shortcomings and are vulnerable to making the same mistakes over and over again.

It's important to acknowledge disappointments and corrective feedback on the way to achieving goals, and to concentrate on the next opportunity by moving ahead with confidence. This can help you welcome challenges and transitions, get excited about overcoming obstacles, and take pride in transforming problems into opportunities. In other words, you can embrace change with a sense of adventure and assurance.

What does confidence look like?

- Good posture
- Sense of humor
- Strong handshake
- Relaxed and comfortable small talk
- Thoughtful and interesting questions for the interviewer
- Genuinely interested in the interviewer's responses
- Eye contact (see **Chapter Nine** for advice on the right and wrong ways to maintain eye contact)
- Appearance that you have other employment options (without saying things that aren't true. Statements like "I'm exploring a variety of opportunities at this point" show that you are out there and engaged, but be ready to back up your talk!)
- Well prepared (have a pen, some paper, a copy of your resume)

Another critical component in successful job searches is how much of your career destiny you perceive to be within your control. In the inevitable discouragement of a job search process, it's easy to fail to recognize the myriad elements of success that you can influence. However, if you frame the job search as an activity you can steer and influence, you will increasingly do just that—it can become a self-fulfilling prophecy.

How we see ourselves shapes our hopes, actions, and–ultimately–our successes."

the GREAT DEBATE

CONFIDENCE LOOKS DIFFERENT TO DIFFERENT PEOPLE

As you look over these ways to convey confidence, you may disagree with or find elements missing from the list. It is not meant to be exhaustive nor does it touch on all of the ways different people, cultures, and generations view confidence. The best way to identify what confidence looks like is to find your own examples. Become an avid people watcher and try to identify what makes confident people seem this way. Is it what they're wearing or how they're wearing it? How they're walking or sitting? What they're doing with their hands or mouth while listening? What they're saying or how they're saying it? Try to identify an element or two that makes certain people exude confidence. Try these out the next time you are with people you don't know and see how it works.

Also be aware of the fine line between being confident and appearing arrogant. If you are sincere about your abilities and personality, you can display confidence without giving off an air of self-importance.

When your self-esteem takes a beating from the job search, it's difficult to do your best in an interview. Your success in vying for a competitive nonprofit position often lies in demonstrating personal confidence and efficacy. This is an essential quality to convey to employers, as it's the confident job seekers who leave the right kind of impression. This confidence does two things: it makes employers think you have other options (which is useful in both interviews and negotiations) and shows you can keep your cool in a stressful situation. Although it's frequently overlooked, maintaining strong and resilient self-esteem is as important a priority as managing the job search itself.

3. A support network can make the difference

Having people you can share the trials and tribulations as well as the triumphs of your search with can make a huge difference, especially if you're currently unemployed. Spending all day home alone firing off applications or doing hours of research can drive anyone crazy! So, let the people you trust know how things are going and, whenever possible, give them specific ways they can be helpful, even if that occasionally means listening to you have a brief job search whining session. And don't worry, you'll have the opportunity to return the favor later on; nowadays, the average person searches for jobs many times during their lifetime. It also can be helpful to find other job seekers because you'll likely understand one another's challenges and frustrations. Networking organizations that provide discussion forums, online groups, or events are a particularly good way to connect with other job seekers. You might want to set up a regular meeting time with old or new friends, in person, online, or on the phone to check in and cheer each other on. At the same time, be careful not to join any pity parties where you repeatedly bemoan your jobless status. Those can be major downers and don't move you any closer to finding great work.

It may be the first, but it won't be the last...

by Cathy Wasserman, LMSW, Career, Executive, and Depth Coach*

Initially, you may experience your first job search process as frustrating and even daunting because there are a plethora of skills, emotions, and nuances to figure out, balance, and put into perspective. The good news is that it gets easier and you don't have to get it all right the first time; you'll have plenty of time to practice!

"So, what do you do?"

How many times has this happened to you: you meet someone new or run into an old friend and the discussion turns to work. You're asked the innocent, conversational, and ubiquitous question, "So what do you do?" Regardless of how much (or little) your self-image is tied to your career, this question can be dreaded if you don't have a job. It can also be harmful to answer bluntly, "Well, actually I'm unemployed..." By not providing any specifics about your situation and goals, you've missed an opportunity to possibly expand your network. The person to whom you're speaking may well have a contact or friend who'd be perfect for you to talk to.

A better way to answer this question is to address what you're doing now and what you plan to be doing in the future. For example, you could say, "Lately, I've been volunteering with Friends of the River in order to gain an awareness of the state's water issues so that I can find a job doing marketing and development for an environmental organization here in California." With this kind of response, you will provide enough information so that people can find specific ways to connect you to their networks. Additionally, you will sound active and engaged, which is always much better than unemployed, unconfident, and desperate.

---

* This section is by Cathy Wasserman. Cathy provides career, executive, and depth coaching to a wide range of individuals seeking to increase their personal and professional success, actively direct their life, and realize their one-of-a-kind core strengths and goals through her business, Self-Leadership Strategies. She has 16 years of experience in the nonprofit sector and beyond including work as a training director, a recruiter, and an organization development consultant. Additionally, she has served as career coaching expert with her column, *Ask Cathy*, on Idealist.org. *Working Mother* magazine also featured her as expert of the month on switching from corporate to nonprofit work. She began her career as an advocate for youth and women and she is published in the book *Front-line Feminism*. Cathy holds an MSW in Clinical Social Work from Smith College and a B.A. in Psychology from Wesleyan University. You can contact Cathy at cathy@self-leadershipstrategies.com or visit her website, www.self-leadershipstrategies.com.

According to the National Association for Counseling and Development, the average person goes through five to seven careers and 10 to 12 job changes during their lifetime. The U.S. Department of Labor's Bureau of Labor Statistics estimates that the baby boomer generation held nearly ten jobs before they turned 36. Because of the frequency with which people change careers these days, it's become commonplace for people to be upwardly, horizontally, and even downwardly mobile as it suits their individual desires and life circumstances.

Here are four critical points to keep in mind during your job search, whether you are looking for your first, second, or 32nd new career opportunity.

Know your strengths (and limits)

Self-assessment is essential in the job search because it can help you zero in on a job or field in which you are interested or skilled. It can also help remind you of your strengths and the many areas in which you excel. Set aside time to review all of your best qualities: personal, professional, social, etc. As weeks go by where you don't hear anything about the gazillion resumes you've sent out, reminding yourself that your combination of writing, interpersonal, and IT skills are unique and eminently hireable can help motivate you to schedule just one more informational interview before the week is over. Scheduling time for this kind of positive reinforcement will not only help you stay focused during your job search, it can also help you stay confident and positive in your daily life.

A realistic sense of your self and of your situation is also important in your job search. For many people, being out of work for three months is economically impossible. For others, staying at a job that's driving them bonkers is mentally impossible. So before you begin your search, try to give yourself some kind of timeline and map out a rough outline of your steps, including how and when you get support during the process. It could be beneficial to break your search into a couple of phases. Phase one might consist of securing what is sometimes called a "B" or "hold it together" job—one that brings home some bacon but doesn't take as much energy as a job where you're head-over-heels for the position. After you get a "B" job, then you can begin phase two: the more in-depth process of looking for "right" work without having to worry as much about survival issues. The downside of this strategy is that a "B" job is still a job and since the job search is a second job in and of itself, it can take a lot of energy to do both at the same time. Whatever strategy you settle on, the key is to know what is most sustainable for you, even if that means making choices that are less than ideal.

Continually reassess your search process and your goals

Because a job search incorporates so many factors, you need to regularly refine your search process to make sure your efforts are well spent. It's important to remain open

Put yourself out there effectively

There's something to the old cliché that a job won't come and find you–you have to go and find it. And yet there are so many ways to put yourself out "on the job scene" that it can be difficult to choose how to begin. Chapters Four, Five, and Six highlight a range of ways to get out there and get involved, from networking and informational interviews (**Chapter Four**), to volunteering, interning, and other opportunities to gain experience (**Chapter Five**), to researching *all* the opportunities in your desired location (**Chapter Six**).

In a similar vein, **Chapter Seven** gives you practical tips on how to research and evaluate whether a specific organization would be a good fit for you. Don't underestimate the importance of reading up on a potential employer!

Control your job search

How you get out and stay active in your job search is important (see sidebar above), but other key ways you can control your search lay in how you represent yourself on paper and in person. **Chapter Eight** is all about how to build effective resumes and cover letters that speak to your strengths, while **Chapter Nine** discusses strategies you can use to make a good impression at interviews. These job search elements are among those over which you have the most control–be sure to put your best foot forward.

to changing directions if something isn't working. Strategies that might have been helpful at the very beginning of your search might not be as helpful by month five. For example, at the beginning of your search, it can be extremely beneficial to go on lots of informational interviews, but after you've gained clarity on the parameters of the field, position, or organizations you're interested in, your time might be better spent volunteering at a few key nonprofits to get some hands-on experience.

Additionally, make sure your search "portfolio" is diversified; you want to be careful not to focus too much of your energy on sending out applications, for example, and too little on networking. Having a concrete document like a "Search Diary" or "Job Log" (see page 34) can make it much easier to see exactly where you've been spending your time and help you to plan the most effective next steps. Checking in with people who are currently working in the kind of jobs or field you're interested in or speaking with a career coach or even a friend can be helpful. Let them know what you're spending your time on and listen to their feedback; this outside perspective can help keep your career compass on target.

Remind yourself that finding the right work can take time

This may seem obvious, but often people put inordinate pressure on themselves to find a great job very quickly. The pressure is understandable because it can be unnerving to your pocketbook, not to mention your peace of mind, to be without work—especially in a society where so much value is placed on what you do. While it depends on what you're looking for, the truth is that most job searches take at least three months, and many take longer—particularly if you're changing fields or positions.

Reminding yourself that there are some very real and concrete reasons that your search is taking some time may help put things into perspective.

- Relationship building is at the heart of finding new work and is definitely not a process you can rush.
- The local or state economy may have an impact on your search: Is there a slow economy? How about high unemployment?
- What does the nonprofit community look like: Is there a high demand for nonprofit jobs? Are there fewer nonprofits in your community?
- Be sure to take these and other concrete reasons into account as you ask yourself, again, why your search is taking so long.

For those days when you feel you've really "had it," keep a running list of every single thing you do for your search, dating each task and noting any outcomes. At the end of another hard week at the job search "office", go through your "Search Diary" to take stock of all of your efforts and remind yourself that you're doing everything you can to find meaningful work.

Giving away your time while unemployed?

When you are immersed in the job search process, it can seem counterintuitive to volunteer or intern. You should spend your time looking and applying for jobs, right? Not necessarily.

Donating your time to a nonprofit may be one of the smartest job search steps you can take. Volunteering raises your visibility within an organization and many nonprofits look to their network of volunteers and interns when they need to hire. Additionally, volunteering and interning keep you active, out of the house meeting people, and contributing to the community. Instead of sitting in front of your computer launching resumes off into cyberspace, your time could be much better spent out in public making connections with people and organizations that resonate with you.

For more on why volunteering and interning are essential in the job search process, see the section on nonprofit hiring practices in **Chapter Twelve**.

A few hours a day...

If you're not spending all day on your job search, you're not doing it right, right? Wrong. A job search is most effective when it's highly focused for a few hours a day rather than being an all-consuming activity. Schedule three to four hours a day to research new job opportunities, craft individualized resumes and cover letters, and keep up with and develop your network. What should you do with all of this free time? Volunteer, go out for coffee with new or existing contacts, explore a new park or trail, read a book, take a class, pet dogs... Use this time to do activities that you enjoy so that by the time you return to your job search the next day, you'll be refreshed and will feel better about yourself and your search.

Structure your day (but keep things in perspective)

Finding a job is real work. Just as with any job, setting up task lists, daily schedules, and weekly goals will help you be as efficient as possible during a time when the details really do matter. As you consider what kind of structure to create for yourself, think about how and where you do your best work. Is it in the same carrel in the library? Do you get into your zone at a local coffee shop with the buzz of others around? How about your dining room table or desk at home? Your routine shouldn't be arbitrary or based on how others do their best work; by this point in your life, you should have a good idea of what works best for you. Once you've established location, consider how your time should be spent. Will you spend an hour trolling through Craig's List, an hour reviewing new Idealist job posts, and an hour preparing resumes for the two or three jobs that caught your eye? Be sure to set aside at least an hour for networking, whether it is maintaining your profile on LinkedIn, going out for coffee with a friend or contact, or researching for an informational interview—this is one of the most valuable parts of your job search and should be scheduled as such.

While you're scheduling, be sure to set aside enough time for exercise, being with friends, and relaxing. Collectively, these three pieces are essential in your job search as they can help remind you that you are so much more than your job search. They will also provide a break from your search and allow you to return refreshed and ready (more or less) to begin again. Individually, there are benefits to each one. So many studies show that people are significantly more productive after exercising; unfortunately, this is often one of the first things to go when schedules get tight or self-esteem drops. Setting aside time for friends is not only therapeutic, it can be counted as networking (see the sidebars on pages 28 and 32)! Finally, reserving time for yourself to do whatever else fills your tank is imperative. Whether this is cooking, crafting, or reading a (non–career-related!) book, give yourself permission to be human and happy during your job search.

The best part of all of these non–job-search-related activities is that they'll allow you to keep the job search—a process that can become all-consuming—in perspective.

Roadmap

DO YOU NEED TO MEASURE SUCCESS TO FEEL SUCCESSFUL?

Some people need measurable goals and tangibles to feel like they are successfully moving forward in their job search. If you are the kind of person that likes crossing to-dos off a daily list or tracking accomplishments, set up a metric for success: Contact two different members of your network every day; send in three resumes and conduct an informational interview every week; and research five new organizations every month. The keys to creating metrics for success, however, is to keep it realistic and grounded in journaling, daily routines, managing stress, and perseverance.

common MISTAKES

DOUBTING YOUR JOB SEARCH SKILLS

With people changing jobs an average of once every three years, chances are very good that one of your friends has been through a job search recently. Think of a few people you know who have recently taken a new job and plan to chat with them about their experiences. Even if they seemed to navigate the job search process with ease and confidence, ask your friends if they ever felt unsure of themselves during the process. You will probably hear some very familiar stories about insecurities, concerns, and moments of self-doubt.

Hearing these experiences will help you recognize that a job search is hard on everyone, but that with lots of preparation, a healthy appearance of (sometimes faked!) confidence, and a little luck, it won't be long until the offers start rolling in.

Date of contact: 5/12/08

Name of organization: School & Community Reuse Action Project

Contact name and title: Sam Exampleson, Media Director

Contact email address: examples@scrapaction.org   Phone number: (503) 555-1212

Referral source: Karen at the Nonprofit Roundtable

Action(s) taken: 5/12/08 emailed Sam using Karen as reference and requested an informational interview.

Information about the organization: SCRAP's mission is to promote creative reuse and environmentally sustainable behavior by providing educational programs and affordable materials to the community. They have a really cool storefront in the industrial area and creative reuse workshops. They're featured on the Master Recycler tour.

Questions to ask: How did you get started on this career path?

Which skills and abilities are most valued in your field?

What do you wish you had known about this field when you were starting your career?

Is there someone at one of your community affiliates that you would recommend me meeting with?

Funding: want to ask, but I have to think of a good way to do that.

Summary of thoughts and feelings: Sam responded the next day and proposed times to meet over coffee. I was heartened and impressed that she responded so quickly. I've heard good things about the organization. I realize that I can get overly enthusiastic about potential opportunities. It will be important for me to remind myself throughout the interview that I'm gathering information about the organization and her job specifically.

Next Steps: I will gather information that will help me assess my interest and skills in relation to a small, grassroots organization with big potential.

I will draft some questions that inquire about funding issues in an appropriate way.

Date of contact: _____

Name of organization: _____

Contact name and title: _____

Contact email address: _____

Phone number: _____

Referral source: _____

Action(s) taken: _____

Information about the organization: _____

_____

_____

Questions to ask: _____

_____

_____

Summary of thoughts and feelings: _____

_____

_____

Next Steps: _____

_____

_____

SUMMARY

People's careers play a significant role in **how they define and perceive themselves**. During a career search, people may experience a **range of emotions** (pages 27-28).

During a career search, it's important to take into account how **your personality will affect how you search**. In particular, it may influence which aspects come naturally and which components of your search you will have to put more effort into (pages 28-30).

Your success during a job search is often based on a secure and realistic **self-perception**. Being open to feedback, learning from mistakes, and acknowledging your shortcomings will allow you to grow and evolve during your job search (pages 29-30).

While much of your job search is a solitary effort, establishing and **maintaining a strong support network** of family, old friends, and new acquaintances will help you find a commiserating ear, words of encouragement and wisdom, and plenty of people to celebrate with once you've found a great job (page 30).

In order to keep your search focused and your outlook positive, be sure to **assess your strengths and your limits**, continually **reassess your search process** and goals, **create a structure** for your day, and recognize that **finding a great job can take time** (pages 30-33, Job Search Log page 34).

CHAPTER THREE

Self and career assessment

The foundation of a successful job search and career

by **Cathy Wasserman**, LMSW, Career, Executive, and Depth Coach *and* **David Schachter**, Assistant Dean for Career Services and Experiential Learning at NYU's Robert F. Wagner Graduate School of Public Service

In this chapter you will:

- Understand the vital role that self-knowledge plays in both your job search and your career.

- Grasp the kind of work that will appeal to you and communicate that connection during your career search.

- Clarify your mission, values, priorities, and greatest skills.

- Create a realistic picture of where your passion fits into the nonprofit sector through the "Career Tracks Exercise."

- Use the "Four Lens Framework" to better understand what draws you to the nonprofit sector.

- Learn a short exercise to help you rate your interest in applying for a position.

- Begin researching your potential salary range–and learn why research is critical to a successful career search.

Why is self-knowledge so critical?

by Cathy Wasserman, LMSW, Career, Executive, and Depth Coach*

The big question on most job seekers' minds is: What can I do to make myself stand out to employers? While there are a myriad of ways to increase your "wow" factor, all of them essentially involve "knowing thyself," not "selling thyself." While selling yourself can come across as pushy and insincere, knowing yourself inside and out— your core strengths, experience, passions, and goals—greatly increases the likelihood that you will stand out and land a fulfilling job where you can contribute, be supported, and continue to develop and grow professionally. The benefits of professional self-knowledge can be broken down into:

1. **Strategically directing your career**
2. **Identifying jobs and organizations that fit**
3. **Authentically and specifically communicating your fit to employers**

The rewards of self-knowledge

As you read through the resources in this book and think about taking the next steps on your career path, put some time and energy into deepening your professional self-knowledge. While this takes effort, the information you uncover will undoubtedly save you time in the long run and serve you in all areas of your life–in fact, it might be one of the best time investments you make, both personally and professionally!

---

* This section is by Cathy Wasserman. Cathy provides career, executive, and depth coaching to a wide range of individuals seeking to increase their personal and professional success, actively direct their life, and realize their one-of-a-kind core strengths and goals through her business, Self-Leadership Strategies. She has 16 years of experience in the nonprofit sector and beyond including work as a training director, a recruiter, and an organization development consultant. Additionally, she has served as career coaching expert with her column, *Ask Cathy*, on Idealist.org. *Working Mother* magazine also featured her as expert of the month on switching from corporate to nonprofit work. She began her career as an advocate for youth and women and she is published in the book *Front-line Feminism*. Cathy holds an MSW in Clinical Social Work from Smith College and a B.A. in Psychology from Wesleyan University. You can contact Cathy at cathy@self-leadershipstrategies.com or visit her website, www.self-leadershipstrategies.com.

1. Strategically directing your career

Most fundamentally, self-knowledge can serve as a kind of North Star, helping you to determine where to invest your time, energy, and focus. It is difficult to make good decisions about your career without knowing your likes and dislikes, experience and skills, strengths and weaknesses, and the environments in which you do your best work. Lack of self-knowledge makes it more likely that you will end up treading professional water or embarking upon a career path that does not maximize your abilities.

In contrast, knowing yourself provides you with lots of detailed information from which to make informed and powerful choices about everything from developing a networking strategy to creating a professional development plan that will maximize your impact and satisfaction over the long term.

2. Identifying jobs and organizations that fit

Similarly, without having a good sense of yourself, it is challenging to know the specific positions and organizations that are likely to be the best match for you and therefore a good use of your job search time. Having clarity around your strengths, background, and goals will allow you to discern whether, for example, you are more suited to the day-to-day work of grantwriting or donor relations or, perhaps, both.

It is equally important to know the kinds of organizational cultures that help you to flourish. Seemingly small cultural details such as dress code can have a big impact, not to mention more subtle elements such as how decisions get made. So, for example, knowing whether you prefer working within a more or less formal environment, whether in terms of dress code or decision making, is key.

If you have a clear sense of the elements that accentuate your effectiveness, you will be in a good position to gather mission and culture-related information through networking and organizational research to assess your fit. Because it is impossible to get a complete picture of an organization's culture and the day-to-day responsibilities of a position before you actually begin, it is all the more vital to know beforehand the basics of what works for you.

3. Authentically and specifically communicating your fit to employers

Finally, taking an ongoing inventory of yourself provides you with the details you will need to create outstanding application materials, as well as to position yourself for a promotion and raise.

Let's say, for example, that you would like to write a "wow" cover letter for a job that you really want. If you have not identified what specifically attracts you to

Lack of self-knowledge makes it more likely that you will end up treading professional water."

> **Your unique self (knowledge)**
> You will naturally stand out if you know how to briefly and vividly articulate the key pieces of your self-knowledge, because no one else in the world has the exact combination of skills, experience, interests, and approach to work that you have.

the position and organization, and how your skills and experience will help you succeed, it is unlikely that you will be able to convey your true connection to the work and the added value that you would bring to the organization.

If you have a clear sense of how the position fits with your interests and expertise, along with what you are excited to contribute, it is much easier to communicate why you are applying. In the end, there is no need to sell yourself when you can simply and straightforwardly describe the nuances of your enthusiasm and fit with a particular position and organization.

Key elements of professional self-knowledge

True professional self-knowledge requires knowing not just the specifics of your skills and experience, but also your values and goals. Indeed, without having insight into both, it is difficult to land the right job.

Below is a list of some key questions that will assist you in building self-awareness. These questions will take time to answer thoroughly so if you have an hour or less, you may want to break them up into a few sittings.

Big picture insights

1. What are your professional mission, values, and priorities? Do the jobs and organizations that you are interested in fit with your mission? (On page 40 you will find an exercise to start writing your mission.)

2. What are your short- and long-term professional goals? Do the jobs and organizations that interest you make sense as a next step, given your goals?

3. What is and is not included in your ideal job description? Be sure to address not just what you enjoy doing most in a given day, but also the kinds of cultures and organizations that are the best fit for you. Do the jobs and organizations you are interested in make sense as a next step, given your ideal job description?

Skill and experience insights

1. What are your greatest skills and strengths? What skills do you need to work on? (On page 43, you will find an exercise to start clarifying your skill set.)

2. What are your greatest knowledge areas? What areas can you build?

3. What are your greatest professional accomplishments?

4. What are your greatest professional curiosities?

5. What are your greatest professional passions?

6. What are the key positive elements of your working style? For example, how do you do your best work? What aspects of your work style could benefit from some tweaking?

> **Finding time to know yourself**
> It takes a lifetime to fully know yourself, and that is if you're moving quickly! So how do you take an express bus to self-knowledge? Well, there are a lot of steps you can take to jump-start or deepen this journey. Setting aside even 10-20 minutes each week to complete any of these activities or answer these questions can go a long way toward helping you to understand yourself and plotting your professional development in just a couple of months.

Steps to continually deepen your self-knowledge

- **Make the commitment** to "just do it": In this case, Nike has it right. Just making a formal commitment to periodically check in on everything from your skills to your ideal job is a great way to grow your self-knowledge. Before you know it, it is likely that you will have accumulated lots of useful information to effectively direct your search or on-the-job focus.

- **Try to stay open**: Consciously making the effort to keep your mind open to new professional roles, goals, and skills can greatly open up your professional possibilities. While "job hopping" could be detrimental, trying out new experiences—whether through volunteer work or expanding your responsibilities in a current job (within reason, watch out for burnout)—is a great way to test-drive emerging skills and passions.

- **Assess your past experiences**: Formally assessing every volunteer and professional experience you have had in order to see what you learned and what you would do differently next time can build your self-awareness and help you to refine and clarify where you want to go.

- **Ask for ongoing feedback**: You usually gain valuable information when you ask for feedback from colleagues, supervisors, professors, mentors, friends, or others. Asking people to think about both your strengths and areas you can work on will help you further assess how to build your skills and experience and see what kinds of roles and organizations might be the best fit.

- **Work with a coach**: It can be very beneficial to formally work with a coach at some point as you move through the self-clarification process. It is useful for many people to have a sounding board as well as someone to ask thought provoking questions of you as you stretch not just your knowledge of yourself but also your possibilities. Sometimes we underestimate ourselves, and a coach's job is to remind you of your highest vision and goals, especially when you are feeling uncertain or stuck.

- **Strategically build your skills, experience, and knowledge**: Take note of where you would benefit from skill or experience building and keep in mind your long-term goals as you plan your professional development. For example, you may want to periodically enroll in a certificate program, take a workshop on an area of interest and/or of importance, or seek out a mentor. At a minimum, it is a good idea to focus on developing or deepening *at least one skill a year*.

- **Periodically refuel your "inspiration tank"**: It is important to make time to do things that inspire you, whether going to your favorite museum or setting aside a few minutes each day to consciously daydream. In order to know yourself, you need to take good care of yourself and give yourself the inspiration and downtime that allow creativity, self-knowledge, and new directions to emerge.

 **Jot your thoughts** Use the space below to jot down some ideas on how you can develop your self-knowledge.

 It is a good idea to focus on developing or deepening at least one skill a year."

Activity 1: Clarifying Your Mission, Values, and Priorities

A great way to further clarify where you want to head professionally is to write a mission statement. Mission statements help to prevent "mission drift"–taking on jobs and responsibilities not consistent with your true purpose and values, making it difficult to actively and intentionally direct your life and career. While your mission, values, and priorities will change throughout your life, having something to start with gives you important information for making informed choices and increases the likelihood of living a meaningful life, both personally and professionally.

Writing a personal and professional mission statement can take time. Indeed, meaningful mission statements are the product of deep reflection and thinking. However, even if you do not currently have a lot of time to invest in the process, it is incredibly helpful to create a brief statement that you can add to or edit later.

1. Define Your Values

Start writing your mission statement by reflecting on your values: these are the principles that guide your decisions, form the bedrock of your worldview, and make you passionate. Clarifying your values helps you develop a potent mission statement since values motivate us to take action and actively live our purpose. Below are some examples of values:

- Creativity
- Perseverance
- Compassion for all people, including myself
- Friendliness
- Family orientation

List five to ten of your most important values:

1. _____
2. _____
3. _____
4. _____
5. _____

6. _____
7. _____
8. _____
9. _____
10. _____

Now order these values from most important to least:

1. _____
2. _____
3. _____
4. _____
5. _____

6. _____
7. _____
8. _____
9. _____
10. _____

2. Define Your Priorities

Next, clarify where your personal and professional priorities lie. Where do you truly want to direct your personal energy, time, and resources? The priorities that form the backbone of a mission statement should be broad and overarching. Below are examples of priorities:

*   To provide my daughter with emotional and financial support.
*   To make sure I get adequate exercise and rest each week.
*   To provide my staff with the support that they need to be the best leaders and managers of themselves and others.
*   To continually educate myself in my field of "_____."

List five to ten of your most important priorities:

1. _____   6. _____
2. _____   7. _____
3. _____   8. _____
4. _____   9. _____
5. _____   10. _____

Now order these priorities from most important to least:

1. _____   6. _____
2. _____   7. _____
3. _____   8. _____
4. _____   9. _____
5. _____   10. _____

3. Craft Your Mission Statement

Your mission statement should incorporate your values and priorities, as well as the personal and professional impacts that you would like to make. You should feel strongly, if not passionately, about everything that you include in your statement so that you are motivated to live it on a daily basis. Your mission should include the personal qualities that you want to exhibit and/or develop, and the kind of person that you want to be rather than just what you want to do. Your statement may be short or long. Typically they run from a couple of sentences to one page in length. Whatever the statement's length, if it does not move you to read it, then it is a good idea to continue the reflection process and tap into more of your core purpose.

A very short mission statement might say:

> I am committed to living my life with compassion and caring for all people, including myself and with a strong emphasis on and attention to my family. Professionally, I am passionate about helping to elect progressive candidates through highly innovative fundraising, event planning, and the development of persuasive campaign material. I am also committed to devoting the time necessary to develop my staff's skills and to assist them in meeting their own mission statements as best as I can. Personally, I am passionate about raising a self-aware, engaged, and happy daughter, and ensuring my physical, spiritual, and mental health by exercising, meditating, and taking time to refuel with friends every week.

Begin your mission statement below, considering the values and priorities you listed above, along with your reflections on who you want to be and the impacts you want to make personally and professionally:

Activity 2: Clarifying Your Greatest Skills

Being explicitly clear with yourself about your skill set allows you to enthusiastically communicate what you have to offer both during a job search and on the job. It is a good idea to periodically check in with yourself and reflect on your greatest strengths.

This does not just mean knowing that you are, for example, a good communicator. Instead, focus in on the precise ways in which you are a good communicator. For example, if you are a great listener, how do you listen to people? What are some specific examples of how your listening skills have made particular impacts? As you work through the exercise below, it also can be very informative to ask a supervisor, mentor, or colleague to assess your skills. Noting any differences between your respective assessments serves as a great starting point for further reflection and clarification.

When breaking down each skill, be as specific as possible.

Sample

Summary of the skill	Why do you feel passionately about this skill? Rate your passion from 1-10 (10 being most passionate)	Detailed breakdown of this skill (What is your knowledge base? What are your connections? What is your experience? What are your sub-skills?)	What have been the specific impacts of this skill in your previous positions? (Focus on measurable and quantifiable results.)
Example: Community Outreach: I am skilled at community outreach in urban youth organizing, which works to increase youth involvement in middle school leadership.	I love helping young people identify their leadership spark and then put it into action by planning and making concrete contributions to their middle school community. It really makes me feel like I am giving back because I had some amazing mentors when I was that age. I rate my passion for this skill as a 9.	I am well versed in the personal, family, and educational issues facing young people in New York City. I have dozens of personal connections to youth empowerment groups across the city representing a wide range of ages, races, and socioeconomic backgrounds. I know how to engage large groups of young people (200+) in working to spread the word about campaigns to increase their voice in their schools and to build their leadership skills, utilizing face-to-face contact and outreach. I know how to build broad support within the schools for increased youth voice in school governance by meeting individually with each stakeholder group (parents, teachers, administration, and students) and organizing meetings in which young people play leadership roles.	I have a track record of assisting young people in playing substantive roles in their middle schools. For example, when I worked for Vocalize Youth last year, I guided 50 seventh graders in developing a group art exhibit and fundraiser where they raised $5,000 for a sister youth development program in Ghana and I also helped to facilitate a discussion with teachers and administration on expanding the international sister school program.

Your Greatest Skills

Summary of the skill	Why do you feel passionately about this skill? Rate your passion from 1-10 (10 being most passionate)	Detailed breakdown of this skill (What is your knowledge base? What are your connections? What is your experience? What are your sub-skills?)	What have been the specific impacts of this skill in your previous positions? (Focus on measurable and quantifiable results.)

Career tracks exercise

by **David Schachter**, Assistant Dean for Career Services and Experiential Learning at NYU's Robert F. Wagner Graduate School of Public Service*

Whether or not you are sure what you want to do, the following activity is a great way to fully understand your interests and desires while also developing a thorough understanding of the existing opportunities in the nonprofit sector. This activity creates a clear picture of where your passion fits into the nonprofit sector. It stresses both idealism and realism and is a perfect place to get started.

Data collection

Look at online or newspaper job postings, and copy or cut out any posting (a "clip") that appeals to you either by (A) the type of organization or by (B) the job description.

> **A.** You are drawn to this **kind of an organization**. You like its mission. You would like your work to have an impact on this issue, population, or area. You like the agency's approach to the work and you could see yourself, someday, working for an organization like this. Do not worry about where it's located or whether you like the job description that's attached to the organization. Just focus on the agency's overall purpose. Circle the part you like and put it in a folder.

> **B.** You are drawn to this **kind of job description**. You like the way the responsibilities are bundled. You like the skills needed to perform the function of the position, and you could see yourself, someday, doing work like this in your day-to-day activities. Do not worry about the agency the description is associated with or whether you have the skills to perform the job. Just focus on the actual job description. Circle the part you like and put it in your folder.

Remember, the only criteria you are using to select clips are either organization or job description. *The location of the organization or job should not be an issue for now.* By broadening your search outside of the area where you live (or plan to live), you get a much fuller sense of the opportunities that are out there. For now, you are not concerned with finding a job with a ten minute commute.

Repeat this activity until you have at least 50 clips. The more you collect, the better.

Remember, when collecting, you do not evaluate along the way, you just collect ideas. Once you have a minimum of 50 clips, continue to the **analysis** phase.

> ### Your job does not choose you
> If you are new to thinking about self-knowledge and how it relates to your career, know that you are not alone. There's an old stereotype that a job is what you get when you graduate from high school or college and is contingent on either your degree or the first offer you receive. The simple act of reflecting on what inspires and motivates you and then connecting that knowledge to the search for your next opportunity has profound implications. Get rid of the notion you may have that you should simply take the first job that becomes available to you. Your job should not choose you, you should choose your job... and know exactly why!

* Grateful acknowledgment is made to New York University for permission to reprint excerpts from and adapt the "Career Tracks Exercise" by David Schachter, Assistant Dean of Career Services and Experiential Learning at NYU's Robert F. Wagner Graduate School of Public Service © 2008 Reprinted with permission of New York University and David Schachter. http://wagner.nyu.edu. Modifications to the original text have been made by the staff at Idealist.org.

Analysis

Take the clips out of your folder and see if you can find any patterns or common themes. Points to look for might include: issue, population to be served, approach to the work, geography, kind of organization, unit or department within an agency, and role and responsibilities.

For example, you might notice that a large number of your clips focus on direct service with homeless teens and adults, and most of the organizations you are drawn to are large organizations located in urban areas.

Synthesis

Using the data gathered from your collection and analysis phases, create at least one and no more than five potential career tracks for yourself. A *career track* is a way to put parameters around and frame your potential career interests, and can include any of the following attributes that have meaning for you:

- Issue or field of interest (homelessness)
- Subcomponents of the issue that are of interest (workforce development that gets people off the street and into paying work)
- Approach to the work (individual training/mentorships, training classes, outsourced trainings)
- Kinds of organizations that do this work (religious groups, nonprofits with heavy federal funding, local groups that focus on specific neighborhoods)
- Where these organizations are located (urban, rural)
- Size of the organizations (three paid staff, 50 paid staff operating within a larger community organization)
- Potential departments within organizations (Fundraising department, Event Planning department)
- Roles that you aspire to play (curriculum developer, community liaison)
- Requirement of skills, education, experience, and knowledge to fulfill those roles (background in education, mental health, rehabilitation, Master of Social Work)

Take stock of your qualifications and experiences as they relate to your potential career tracks. Your track should inform which groups you join, the people you seek out, the internship/job experiences you look for, and how you present yourself in a resume, cover letter, and interview. (See **Chapter Eight** for more advice on cover letters and resumes, and **Chapter Nine** for a discussion of interview techniques.)

Remember to reflect along the way to determine if this track feels like a good fit for you. If it does, continue on this path. If not, seek out additional tracks.

Jot your thoughts

Use the space below to jot down one to five potential career tracks that you can explore.

Application

After you identify your possible career tracks, draft a different resume for each position you identify that fits into each of the tracks. This can be an entry-level position or a "dream job"; the point of drafting a mock resume is to get a clear view of the skills, experiences, and qualifications (which can include certifications or licenses) you will need in that particular job.

Now, fill in the resume with the skills, experiences, and qualifications that you already have for the position. Look at any areas that are blank.

Your task now is to fill in those blanks.

- If you need more **management experience**, try to lead a project team in school or take on a leadership role in a campus or community group.

- If you need more **direct service experience**, volunteer to tutor adults, mentor children, or reach out to families in need.

- If you need more **fundraising experience**, organize a campaign through your network of friends, your church, or your workplace to raise money for a cause that is important to you. You can even participate in an endurance event (walks, half-marathons, triathlons) and raise money through your training.

- If you need to demonstrate more **commitment to an issue area**, find organizations in your area that work in the area you care about. Do an internship with them. Participate in a year of service. Volunteer and strive to become a volunteer leader that takes initiative and gains the trust of the staff working in the organization.

- If you need more **professional experience,** find out what national professional associations exist in your area of interest and become a member. Attend the annual conference. Membership organizations are great for networking and they look good on your resume. They show commitment to an issue area and demonstrate to employers that you are up-to-date on the trends and issues affecting their profession.

- Take courses at the local college in **finance** or **administration**. Get a certification online through a reputable organization. Attend workshops held by local nonprofits and businesses.

Whatever the blanks are on your resume, you can find a time and place to fill them. While it is unrealistic to fill all the blanks in all of your resumes in a relatively short amount of time, many of the skills you wish to have should be transferable between resumes.

START ASKING

After the "Synthesis" phase of the Career Tracks exercise, you will have a much clearer sense of the kind of work you wish to do. Although you are planning to make your "dream resume" into reality, don't be afraid to reach out to professionals already doing this work.

Consider setting up a few informational interviews with these professionals in order to get a sense of the steps you should be taking to achieve your goals (see **Chapter Four** to learn how).

Ask for recommendations of organizations to join, publications to read, courses or certifications to complete, volunteer and intern positions to apply for, or even intentional opportunities to create, and any other avenues you can think of to help you on your way (see **Chapter Five** for more ideas on how to get out and involved).

There is no better place to seek guidance in finding your ideal job than from the people who are doing the job right now.

Ideally, you will have **_at least 12 months_** for the Career Tracks process. Realistically, you will only have three to six months. Here is how to schedule your tracking for each of the given time constraints:

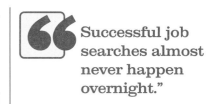

	12 month timeline	6 month timeline	3 month timeline
Part One: Data collection	First to third months	First month	First two weeks
Part Two: Analysis & **Part Three:** Synthesis	Fourth month	Second month	Second two weeks
Part Four: Application	Fifth to twelfth months	Third to sixth months	Second and third months

What if I need a job right NOW?!?

If you really need a job as soon as possible, you should take a "hold it together" job for now. Instead of trying to find your ideal work *today* (and frustrating yourself in the process), your focus should be on finding interim work: a job that meets your basic needs and allows you to cover the monthly bills. This "hold it together" position should last no more than 18 months. While doing your interim job, start the Career Tracks exercise and stick with it. If you do it right and stay committed, your next job shift will be a lot more meaningful.

If you are looking to find a new job immediately, don't expect to step into your ideal job at this point. You may need more time to research available positions, develop transferable skills, network through professional associations, and gain experience you will need to make your materials stand out in a pool of applications for your ideal work.

Successful job searches—especially job searches that cross sectors—almost never happen overnight. The more you put into the search, including *time* and *energy*, the more you stand to gain.

In the margin:
> " Successful job searches almost never happen overnight."

The four lens framework

by David Schachter, Assistant Dean for Career Services and Experiential Learning at NYU's Robert F. Wagner Graduate School of Public Service[*]

Simply saying "I want to work in nonprofits" is not enough. People don't enter the for-profit or public sectors without a specific job, organization, or specialization in mind. An education major knows they want to teach tenth grade math, a business major knows they want to work in print advertising, and a political science major knows they want to work as a policy analyst in the State Department. Approaching the wonderfully diverse nonprofit sector means understanding what draws you to the work.

With the Four Lens Framework you can start from where you are right now and figure out where you want to go next. People typically enter the nonprofit career conversation from one of four lenses:

1. An **issue** (and/or **value**): a matter of public or personal concern
2. An **organization**: a structure through which individuals cooperate systematically to conduct business
3. A **role**: a function or part performed
4. A **system**: a group of interacting, interrelated, or interdependent elements forming a complex whole

If you enter the nonprofit sector through the lens of an **issue** or **value**, you may be passionate about and want a career concerning a specific cause; for example, education, the environment, public health, or anti-racism.

If you enter the nonprofit sector through the lens of an **organization**, you might really want to work for a specific organization like Doctors Without Borders, the United Nations, or Habitat for Humanity.

If you enter through the lens of a **role**, you may have decided that you would like to have a specific position like a grantwriter, a program manager, or a volunteer coordinator.

If you enter through the **system** lens, you might be interested in the interplay, patterns, and connections between and among the other three lenses, looking at how they work together, influence each other, and shift based on the movement of external dynamics.

Activity

How are you thinking about your professional next steps? On the next page you'll find some questions to ask yourself:

Reflecting on past work experiences

As you begin to direct your career, identify jobs and organizations that could be a good fit, and understand how to communicate your fit with the organization, take time to reflect on the aspects of past jobs or experiences that you've really enjoyed.

- Was there a particular manager or professor you loved working with?

- Is there a certain work environment that you know you prefer? Why?

- Was there a specific aspect of a job or project that you enjoyed doing?

People often reflect on a past job or experience as a "whole". Dig a bit deeper and look at various aspects of each role you've had and ask yourself: "What part of this did I like and why?" Keep track of your answers to refer to as you begin to assess whether an organization will be a good fit for you.

Consider organizations in the orbit of your target employer

If you are interested in working with a larger, well-known organization—like the Gates Foundation—research small organizations that they fund, contract out to, or collaborate with, and explore working with those smaller organizations first.

---

[*] Grateful acknowledgment is made to New York University for permission to reprint excerpts from and adapt the "Four Lens Framework" by David Schachter, Assistant Dean of Career Services and Experiential Learning at NYU's Robert F. Wagner Graduate School of Public Service © 2008. Reprinted with permission of New York University and David Schachter. http://wagner.nyu.edu. Modifications to the original text have been made by the staff at Idealist.org.

Issue/value

1. Why is this issue a matter of public concern? Why should anyone care about this issue? How can this issue be broken down?

2. Which of these issue areas am I interested in? Which do I want to find out more about?

Organization

1. Which organizations am I particularly drawn to?

2. What is it about these organizations that appeals to me?

3. What other organizations exist that share these qualities? (You can search www.idealist.org to explore other organizations.)

Role

1. Do I have a role in mind that I'd like to take on?

2. What are some common roles with organizations that work on issues I care about?

3. How are the responsibilities within job descriptions bundled, and do I have the requisite skills, education, and experience to fulfill them?

System

1. Do I want to be in a very established organization or a start-up? Do I want to be in an agency that already has a lot of influence in the field, or with an agency that can afford to push an agenda firmly? Which well-funded organizations are very established and in the mainstream? Which radical grassroots organizations are on the fringe? Where do I want to have influence?

2. Do I want the scope of my work to be local, national, or international?

3. What are some approaches to doing this work? (For example: direct service, philanthropy, capacity building, policy, research/analysis, marketing, advocacy.)

After contemplating the four lenses and their related questions, you should be able to formulate a statement reflecting your specific aims and approaches in your nonprofit career search. This will be a lot more focused than simply saying, "I want to work in nonprofits." For example:

*I am passionate about learning and education (**issue/value**). Since my issue area is broad, I need to look at organizations that are doing educational outreach that interests me. I want to work with an **organization** that embraces the train-the-trainer model since I want to help teachers and trainers become better at their work, thus impacting a larger number of students than I could impact in a single classroom. Therefore, my **role** would be that of a trainer, curriculum developer, or education program manager. I've worked in several types of nonprofits from well-established and financially secure to new, unknown, and unfunded, and I like the stature afforded to well-established agencies within the **system**.*

Rate your interest in applying for a position

Use the space below to assess your interest in a job opening using this activity.

by **Cathy Wasserman**, LMSW, Career, Executive, and Depth Coach*

Job applications take a lot of time and effort so it is crucial to assess whether each job of interest is worth the effort of actually applying. If you find yourself really struggling to explain why you want the job when crafting a resume and cover letter for that position, you may want to reconsider applying. Moreover, it is helpful to formally rate your level of interest in the job, the organization, and its fit with your skills and experience. This exercise will help you do that.

Step one

First, rate your level of interest and **passion for the position** on a scale of 1-10, with 10 being most passionate. Then, make a note about why you gave it the rating that you did. If you rate a job as less than a 7, then it might not be the right position for you.

Step two

Next, rate your level of interest and **passion for the organization** itself on a scale of 1-10. Again, if your rating is less than a 7 (even if the position itself looks really great), and if you do not see a fit between yourself and the organization's mission and culture, it may not be the right fit for you.

Step three

Now go through the job announcement and note whether you meet the **job requirements**. If you meet at least 80 percent of the requirements, then it is probably a good fit (assuming the last 20 percent is not a major component of the position).

Step four

Lastly, go back through all of your ratings and take a "**big picture view**" in making your final assessment. For example, you might have rated the position a 7, but the organization as 8, and your skill match at 85 percent. Taken together, this is a pretty strong fit and probably worth the effort of applying.

* This activity was developed by Cathy Wasserman. Cathy provides career, executive, and depth coaching to a wide range of individuals seeking to increase their personal and professional success, actively direct their life, and realize their one-of-a-kind core strengths and goals through her business, Self-Leadership Strategies. She has 16 years of experience in the nonprofit sector and beyond including work as a training director, a recruiter, and an organization development consultant. Additionally, she has served as career coaching expert with her column, *Ask Cathy*, on Idealist.org. *Working Mother* magazine also featured her as expert of the month on switching from corporate to nonprofit work. She began her career as an advocate for youth and women and she is published in the book *Front-line Feminism*. Cathy holds an MSW in Clinical Social Work from Smith College and a B.A. in Psychology from Wesleyan University. You can contact Cathy at cathy@self-leadershipstrategies.com or visit her website, www.self-leadershipstrategies.com.

Research your salary range

The final piece of the self-assessment process is understanding your market value. While it can be frustrating to try to reduce your worth to a dollar figure, this is powerful—and essential—knowledge to have in mind both when deciding to apply for a job and when deciding to negotiate. So while negotiation may seem a long way off in this process, investing time to figure out your worth in terms of salary will help you further refine how you choose to engage with the sector, which positions you want to apply for, and whether a particular job is right for you. And while this process focuses on salary assessment, remember that a job offer comes with a complete compensation package. Other components of this are harder to put a price tag on, but are no less important to consider as you weigh an offer and decide if it will meet your needs. **Chapter Ten** has more information on the multitude of options that you may find (or ask for) in an offer that reflects your true market value.

Salary surveys and anecdotal research

Nonprofit salary information is particularly hard to find. There are a number of salary calculators and surveys that you can begin with. Take what information you can from these online tools and then begin your "on the ground" research. As you are conducting informational interviews, ask questions like: "For someone [with my skill set/seeking a specific position/coming in at entry-level], what kind of salary could I anticipate in the nonprofit sector?" Do *not* ask the person what they earn! However, if you phrase the question so that it relates to your experience and skills, you will often get a useful answer without having to ask a personal question.

Factors that affect salary

There are several factors to take into account as you figure out what salary range you should expect in a job offer: experience, education, geography, and both the issue area and size of the organizations you're targeting.

Experience

Your experience level generally refers to the full-time years you've worked. However, part-time jobs, internships, volunteer work, and course projects can also count as experience depending on their scope and duration. As a first-time job seeker, your coursework may be all of the experience you have; be sure to highlight it on your resume.

Education

Studies show that your salary correlates with the highest level of education you've achieved (see the table on the next page). As you assess your earning potential, take into consideration not only the degree(s) that you have earned, but also the relevance of the degree(s) to the positions you're pursuing. Another factor that may

> "While it can be frustrating to reduce your worth to a dollar figure, this is essential knowledge when deciding to apply for a job."

Salary surveys

For a list of free salary calculators and surveys, see the online resource page for Chapter Ten (which covers compensation packages) at: www.idealist.org/en/career/guide/ch10resources.html

Financial self assessment

Idealist.org partnered with the National Endowment for Financial Education (NEFE) to create a free guide to financial self assessment called "Making a Difference: A Guide to Personal Profit in a Nonprofit World."

Find it here: www.idealist.org/en/career/financialadvice.html

get taken into account is the institution where you received your degree. Right or wrong, a degree from a prestigious institution may increase your perceived worth.

Unemployment rate in 2006 (%)	Education attained	Median weekly earnings in 2006 ($)
1.4	Doctoral degree	1,441
1.1	Professional degree	1,474
1.7	Masters degree	1,140
2.3	Bachelors degree	962
3.0	Associate degree	721
3.9	Some college, no degree	674
4.3	High school graduate	595
6.8	Less than high school diploma	419

Data are 2006 annual averages for persons aged 25 and over; earnings are for full-time wage and salary workers. Source: U.S. Bureau of Labor Statistics, Current Population Survey.

Geography

You will generally find higher salaries in big cities as compared to more rural areas. Even among big cities, salaries in cities like New York, San Francisco, or Washington, DC will be higher (on average) than those in Kansas City or Atlanta. However, don't make a beeline for a big city just because your salary will be higher; the cost of living in big cities is also significantly higher than in rural areas. If you're curious how salaries translate from one town or city to another, try several combinations of salaries and cities in CNN's cost of living calculator (http://cgi.money.cnn.com/tools/costofliving/costofliving.html). This tool will also help you compare housing, utilities, transportation, and health care costs.

Size of organization

Bigger organizations tend to have larger budgets to put toward compensation packages as compared to smaller organizations. However, the nonprofit sector in general, and small nonprofits, in particular, are often very creative in their compensation package offerings. So even if the salary isn't as high at a small organization, you may be able to negotiate benefits like more vacation time, a flexible schedule, or tuition reimbursement to make the offer work for your needs.

The value of research

Investigating your potential salary range is only part of the research you'll need to do during your career search. As the exercises in this chapter have shown, and as the sidebars on this page note, research comes up at every stage of the job search. Rather than viewing research as one more time-consuming task that keeps you from finding that perfect job, take it for what it really is: intelligence gathering that will help you find an opportunity that meets—and hopefully exceeds—your needs and aspirations. If you value your long-term fulfillment and sustainability, you should recognize the value of research in your career search.

I DON'T HAVE TIME TO RESEARCH

In your job search, the more you know, the better you will fare. This is true for all aspects of the job search, from having a clear awareness of your worth in terms of salary to being well versed in the work and plans of organizations you're interviewing with. This kind of in-depth understanding will allow you to craft specific and tailored cover letters, ask thoughtful questions during your interview, and negotiate a fair compensation package.

At every stage of the job search, you should make thorough research a priority. It will pay off.

Further ideas on research

Research is a critical part of the nonprofit career search. You can find more research tactics in several chapters of this book:

Chapter Six has ideas for researching work opportunities near and far.

Chapter Seven explains how to research and evaluate organizational culture, while **Chapter Nine** has tips on researching an organization before your job interview.

Chapter Ten includes useful advice on researching an organization's compensation package so you can negotiate more effectively.

SUMMARY

Self-knowledge greatly increases the likelihood that you will stand out in your career search and obtain a fulfilling job where you can contribute and grow professionally. Self-knowledge also helps you to strategically direct your career and authentically communicate your fit to employers (pages 36-38).

The two key elements of professional self-knowledge are big picture insight, and skill and experience insight (page 38). Take steps to **continually deepen your self-knowledge** on a regular basis (page 39).

Your mission statement is a great way to further clarify where you want to head professionally and helps to prevent **"mission drift"**–taking on jobs and responsibilities not consistent with your true purpose and values (Activity 1, pages 40-42).

Clarifying your greatest skills means being explicitly clear with yourself about your skill set, so you can communicate what you have to offer both during a job search and on the job (Activity 2, pages 43-44).

After developing your self-knowledge, **finding a nonprofit career path that is right for you** is the next step in the process of locating work in the nonprofit sector (pages 45-50).

Career Tracks Exercise. Collect, analyze, and synthesize nonprofit job postings (regardless of geographic location) to better apply your energies toward seeking fulfilling nonprofit career paths (page 45-48).

The Four Lens Framework. People tend to view possible nonprofit careers through the lens of **issue**, **organization**, **role**, or **system**. Answering some questions for each lens can help you formulate a strong and clear statement about your ideal position in the nonprofit sector (page 49-50).

Rating your interest in a position is a simple analytical method that can help you decide whether applying for a specific job is worth the effort (page 51).

Start researching your salary range as a natural part of your career search. The more you know, the better you can advocate for yourself! (pages 52-53)

CHAPTER FOUR

Networking

Is it really all about who you know? Yes.

In this chapter you will:

- Examine the role of community in networking and think about ways to strengthen involvement in your preexisting groups.

- Consider both strong and weak links in your life and how they can help you network.

- Explore informal and formal networking and how to better engage in each.

- Develop your "elevator pitch" in order to quickly and concisely convey your networking needs.

- Discover how to request and conduct an informational interview.

- Learn how to follow up with your networking leads.

Building relationships

While the word "networking" might conjure images of people in suits making agonizing, self-promoting small talk, it is something that you have done countless times (even if you've never owned a suit). Instead of a forced conversation or the exchange of business cards, think of networking as building relationships. Does this sound more like something you've done before?

The value of a strong social and professional network is impossible to overestimate. Nurturing new contacts, making your professional and social needs known, and connecting colleagues with the people who can help them (networking is about reciprocity)—all of these can lead to a positive career transition for you. Your preparations for starting work in a new sector should be about leveraging relationships to make your transition successful.

A strong network helps you to:
- Gain access to information and job leads
- Find and pass along opportunities
- Connect your work and ideas with other people and organizations

What network? The one you already have.

A mid-career professional often enters the nonprofit world with a strong network in place, while younger people may feel at a loss to locate their networks. Even if you think you do not know anyone in the nonprofit world, chances are that you do simply because of your daily activities. Involvement in religious groups, social clubs, professional organizations, libraries, hospitals, Boy or Girl Scouts, Big Brothers/Big Sisters, Campfire USA, local soup kitchens, and schools or colleges, to name just a few, will have already put you in touch with people in the nonprofit world.

Relying on weak links

In 1973, sociologist Mark Granovetter developed a theory called "The Strength of Weak Ties"[1] that has important implications for job searching and networking. The idea behind the strength of weak ties (which are different from strong ties like family and close friends) is that you have plenty of tangential friends, acquaintances, and other people who pass through your world more than once. These are the people you see a few times a year at friends' parties, the barista at your favorite cafe, old friends from high school and college that you stay in touch with, or the professor you interviewed for a research paper on urban planning.

The two key advantages that these weak ties have for building relationships and networking are size and awareness. Your weak ties far outnumber your close friends and family. Also, your close social circle will know that you are starting or switching careers, so they will already be on the lookout to help you. If they had job leads, they'd have already given them to you. Your weak ties, once made aware of your situation, can help make connections and open doors that you didn't even know existed.

Although networking is often viewed as a "business" skill, it is vital to the nonprofit world because of how much weight a personal reference holds. While networking is how many people find their jobs in the for-profit sector, it is even more instrumental in nonprofit job searches. Since much of the work that nonprofits do is driven by a combination of skills and passion, many nonprofit employers prefer to hire a candidate who comes with a personal recommendation. Networking is also a crucial conduit to locating nonprofit positions because of the lack of centralized promotional channels for nonprofit job announcements (see **Chapter Twelve** for more on nonprofit hiring practices and the challenges of the job market). And once you've been hired, your network will help you to be more effective at doing your job, since much of the work done in nonprofits often involves collaboration and relationship building.

Your communities, your network

Start with what and who you know

You can define your communities as any group of people with whom you share common interests, passions, or skills—people with whom you take classes, spend time, or have discussions. Some of these people may be in several of your circles, while you may know others through only one activity or event. The people who populate these groups can be connected to you through both weak and strong ties.

Many nonprofit employers prefer to hire a candidate who comes with a personal recommendation."

---

[1] Granovetter, Mark. "The Strength of Weak Ties" *American Journal of Sociology*, Vol. 78, Issue 6, May 1973, pp. 1360-1380.

Below are examples of different communities of both weak and strong ties. Be aware that you may belong to several communities of one type. For example if you volunteer at an animal shelter and in a kindergarten classroom, you may have two volunteer group communities. This list is by no means exhaustive—you can probably think of several more communities in which you are active.

- Volunteer groups
- Colleagues
- Family and relatives
- Faith community
- Sports teams
- Friends from work, your neighborhood, childhood, or school
- Professional associations
- Blogger groups
- Classmates from crafts, language, or cooking classes
- Neighborhood groups
- Alumni networks
- Fitness class acquaintances
- Online chatrooms
- Musical ensembles
- Parenting (or other) support groups

Being aware of the communities to which you are connected is essential in recognizing the expanse of your network of strong and weak ties. It is also essential in understanding the commonalities of the participants in these groups. Are there certain interest areas that are common to many of the groups? For example, do you have a large number of friends involved in music? Are most of the people you spend time with passionate about volunteering? Did you meet a large number of people through online groups? Are most of the people in your network your age?

While it is important to know the strengths of your network, it is also important to recognize the gaps. The strengths represent your interests, connections to exciting opportunities and contacts, and invaluable information in those areas. The gaps are important to understand because once you've identified areas in which you don't know as many (or perhaps any) people, you can also begin to identify ways to expand your network.

Keep expanding your community network

In order to continue expanding your network, it is best to again start with your preexisting communities. This may seem counterintuitive: if you are trying to branch out from your immediate network, why would you want to begin with them?

This goes back to the idea that most people value the opinions of people in their network more than an anonymous suggestion. If you show up at an event, club, or group meeting by yourself, you will undoubtedly meet people and probably make some connections, but you will, in essence, be a "face in the crowd." You seem nice but no one knows you. You have no one to introduce you and, by doing so, suggest: "This person is okay. You should get to know them." However, if you attend an event

TAKING AN ACTIVE ROLE IN YOUR COMMUNITY

What kind of active role can you see yourself taking in your community? Would you like to expand your involvement in an organization that you already work with? Would you like to get involved with a new group in your community and see what active role you can play there? Take a moment to imagine two ways in which you can become more active in your preexisting community groups as well as two interest areas in your life that you would like to further cultivate, rekindle, or explore. This can be anything from playing intramural sports to taking on a leadership role in a faith organization, from starting to paint again to making a point to get out into the wilderness more often.

DO YOU HAVE TIME FOR ALL OF THIS?

Now that you have thought about your preexisting groups and some new areas that you would like to explore, sit down with a calendar and figure out what kind of realistic time commitments you can make. Your goal here is to find a happy medium between taking a more active role in your community groups (reconnecting with a group that you have lost touch with or taking a leadership role in a familiar group) and finding new community groups to connect with (arts organizations, job seeker support networks, trail maintenance groups at a state park), as well as seeing how much time you really have to pursue these endeavors. Does your work schedule make weekend activities easier to attend than weeknight meetings? Can you volunteer for a new organization once a month? Can you commit to coaching an entire basketball season? Does the meeting time for the watercolor group conflict with another engagement?

with a friend (or a friend-of-a-friend), you will also meet people, but with an added bonus—you'll now have an informal endorsement as the person you accompanied to the event introduces you.

Take on a leadership role

Step back and examine the distinct groups in your network. For each group, do you see any missed connections, unrealized potential, or areas for improvement? For example, is there a natural connection between your local neighborhood group and the urban renewal nonprofit where you volunteer? Would members of your Spanish language class enjoy the opportunity to volunteer with a local school to tutor English as a Second Language students? Does your college alumni network need a local chapter?

A leadership role is not necessarily synonymous with being the president. There are plenty of opportunities for leadership where you can achieve significant results without taking on the responsibility of being elected or given a title. In these instances, the results can often be quantified and included in your resume, and can also prepare you to be a serious candidate for an "official" leadership position in the future (if you so choose). As with all networking, remember to "build it before you need it." If you are considering being elected to a position, take on a leadership role well before an election; it will allow your leadership and relationships to evolve naturally.

Make connections and ask questions

While it is important to clearly and concisely talk about yourself (see "The elevator pitch" discussion below), it is equally important to find out as much as you can about the people in your community. At events, practice asking questions that allow people to talk about themselves, their career paths, and their interests and passions. Consider these situations to be mini-informational interviews (see page 66 for more on informational interviewing). They are not formal or scheduled, but you can still get an incredible amount of information, advice, and potential referrals from more casual conversations that are framed by the right questions. Find a friend or contact you have heard ask good questions; see if they would be willing to let you shadow them at a party or event. This is one area where a script is a particularly bad idea, as it usually sounds canned—the opposite of your goal. The best way to learn effective questioning skills is to watch others do it and then get out there and practice.

The only question you **SHOULD NOT ASK** is if someone can give you a job. This question puts people on the spot and there are much more effective ways to convey your interest in a position without creating an awkward and potentially negative situation.

Informal and formal networking

Informal networking

This is the kind of networking you've already done quite a bit. You may not have called it "networking," but it's what you were doing when you struck up a conversation with a new person, when you volunteered for an organization, or when you reconnected with an old friend. Some people are more comfortable with this than others, but just by doing what you do every day, you have already accumulated quite a significant network of contacts. Many of the contacts that you have made through informal networking constitute your "weak ties."

Informal networking is a beneficial, long-term form of networking because you aren't looking for anything specific yet. Instead, you're building relationships and letting people get to know you. With this kind of networking, opportunities naturally arise as many people enjoy recommending strong (and close) candidates for professional and personal opportunities.

Say you want to talk with someone who is in the environmental field. Who would you call? Is there someone who could put you in touch with another person who might know more? How about a request for general advice on your resume? Or an opinion on recent political events? Chances are good that you have at least one person you would call for each of those scenarios. And chances are that one of those people would in turn call you for information on a topic about which you have some expertise. This conversational give-and-take is much of what informal networking is about.

> Some examples of **informal networking**:
> - Volunteering
> - Participating in your faith community
> - Posting messages on mailing lists, chat rooms, listservs
> - Emailing an old friend (or two) to get back in touch
> - Setting up an action group with people in your community
> - Inviting friends to join a new book club
> - Talking with the person behind you in the grocery store line, on the bus, etc.

Formal networking

Compared with informal networking, formal networking focuses on professionally beneficial partnerships, ideas, and job leads. Formal, targeted networking is the type that gives networking its bad reputation because of the misconception that it is all

IT TAKES TIME TO LEAD

If you volunteer to organize an event, lead a group, or present a workshop, be forewarned that these activities will require significant time and energy. It is not something you should do if you may not have enough time to do it well.

However, if you can prepare for and successfully conduct a workshop or organize an event, this will allow you to have a much more visible presence in your community. It may also allow you to meet people you might not have otherwise met. Look into opportunities to present workshops for clubs, organizations, or even online communities to which you belong. Similarly, there are many opportunities for hosting an event (end of season party, post-yoga class breakfast, or faith group social) for a community in which you're involved. This is an incredibly valuable experience in terms of meeting people and taking on a higher profile in your community. Plus, it looks good on your nonprofit resume.

about schmoozing and fishing for important contacts. Instead, think of formal networking as strategic relationship building. Along with more targeted relationships, formal networking also involves an awareness of, and intentionality about, the process. The people you meet at networking events know that conversations, contacts, and connections are good for relationship building in general, but they are also aware that such networking is very helpful for professional purposes.

Formal networking is also about creating a connection that allows you to pass on resources to those in your network. Everyone has the potential to be a valuable connection because of the relationships, resources, and perspectives they can provide.

Just like informal networking, formal networking can take a wide variety of forms. The main characteristic of formal networking is that it can help you be more strategic about whatever it is you're currently looking for (a job, information, a good pair of shoes, etc.).

Examples of **formal networking**:
- Participate in conferences, workshops, presentations for your current job
- Participate in networking events (professional association events, local business publication events, Young NonProfit Professionals, Net Impact, Green Drinks, etc.)
- Email/phone friends, family, and staff at your alma mater regarding their contacts
- Conduct informational interviews
- Join professional associations
- Apply for internships (advertised opportunities as well as internships you've solicited)
- Join online social networking sites (LinkedIn, MySpace, Facebook, etc.)
- Become involved in your alumni networks

Your formal networking roadmap

Your formal networking efforts will be more effective if you take a strategic, intentional approach. There are three tasks to do before you jump headfirst into a nonprofit networking event (like an informational interview, a meeting with an alum, or an online forum):

1. **Research**
2. **Prepare an elevator pitch**
3. **Develop a system**

Research

In order to get the most out of your networking, make sure to research:
- Basic information about the relevant field, organization, and position
- What you hope to gain from this specific meeting or event

Natural networkers

Do you know people who seem to know everyone? Think about what they do at parties, sporting events, lunchtime, or even while walking around town. These people probably always have a story about "a new person I met" or "a great conversation I just had." The next time you're with a natural networker, watch how they interact with everyone: their colleagues, their best friends, and acquaintances, strangers, and colleagues. By watching a few of these networkers in action, you'll see that there isn't one particular way to network, but rather a variety of effective styles.

Formal networking and informational interviews

Informational interviews are a great example of strategic relationship building. The key point of an informational interview is to glean useful knowledge from a professional in the field. One byproduct of an informational interview, therefore, should be adding one more person to your professional network. When done correctly, an informational interview creates a type of mentorship in which you can keep your contact abreast of your successes as you explore your new field. Most people who agree to informational interviews are eager to be "kept in the loop" and will usually enjoy an email or quick phone call letting them know how you are getting along. This follow-up effort is good for keeping you on that person's professional radar. See page 66 for more on informational interviews.

You do not want to ask questions that make it evident you didn't prepare. Be familiar with information about the constituency that an organization serves, the main responsibilities of people in their position, and some of the general concerns that the specific industry faces. If you know some basic information before your conversation, you will make the most of your meeting time by asking thoughtful questions that will help you get what you need out of the meeting. You will also leave an impression of yourself as a knowledgeable, insightful, and prepared person whom your contact will remember and be comfortable recommending when that perfect job opportunity arises. Not adequately preparing yourself may leave a poor impression and undermine your chances of future connections, references, or job leads.

Here are some ideas for research:

An organization's website: This is your best source of information for an organization's mission, constituents, recent grants, annual report, new initiatives, advisory board, and influential people in the organization. Site maps, when available, are a great way to get a sense of what information is available.

The Nonprofit Times and *The Chronicle of Philanthropy*: Use these publications to search for articles about a particular field, organization, or person as well as getting good, general sector information.

Career Opportunities in the Nonprofit Sector by Jennifer Bobrow Burns (New York: Checkmark, 2006): This book is available in libraries and bookstores and provides a great overview of major nonprofit positions, education requirements, and career trajectories.

GuideStar: GuideStar (www.guidestar.org) provides a comprehensive listing of nonprofit organizations. You can search for an organization's old 990s (the annual tax report that nonprofits need to file with the IRS) in order to get a sense of their financial status from a few years back.

General Google search: This should be a last stop to catch any information that your more focused searches didn't uncover.

Finally, as much as you should know about the basics of a person's job or their specific organization, you will also need to know what you want to get out of this meeting. This knowledge will help you frame, shape, and articulate your research to make sure your networking endeavors are productive and strategic.

YOUR PUBLIC PROFILE IS PUBLIC

common MISTAKES

A word of warning about online networking programs: be aware potential employers may view anything that you post. While you may not recognize MySpace, Friendster, or Facebook as a business tool, many potential employers do. A good rule to keep in mind is that you should only post information, photos, or opinions that you would like your parents, children, or a current or potential employer to see.

Another tip: Employers often Google applicants, so you should be aware of the links that pop up when your name is "Googled." Do a search for yourself and see what comes up.

LEARN MORE

Researching organizations

Further advice on researching organizations is available in the following chapters of this book:

Chapter Six has ideas for researching work opportunities near and far.

Chapter Seven explains how to research and evaluate organizational culture, while **Chapter Nine** has tips on researching an organization before your job interview.

Chapter Ten includes useful advice on researching an organization's compensation package so you can negotiate more effectively.

The elevator pitch

If you were in an elevator actually talking with a potential employer, your normally quick elevator ride would seem even shorter as you tried to convey why you are the perfect candidate for a job. However, if you have prepared and practiced a concise, persuasive statement conveying your best attributes in approximately 30 seconds, then that short ride would be more than enough time to articulate your value.

You will use your elevator pitch for informational interviews, networking events, or chance meetings. No matter where you are, you will want to be able to succinctly state who you are, what you are looking for, and how the person you're speaking with could help you. If done well, 30-45 seconds is plenty of time to convey your need without losing your audience's attention. Always try to be brief. This will leave more time for a conversation with your new contact around ways that you can help one another out.

Here's what you should include in your elevator pitch:

1. **Who are you?**
2. **What you're looking for and why**
3. **A specific outcome**

1. Who are you?

"Hi, my name is Edgar."

While it may seem obvious, be sure to state your name! State it clearly, slowly, and with confidence. Practice this beforehand several times. This is how the person you're talking with will remember it. If you have business cards, handing one to the person will provide a visual reminder of your name, as well as a means to contact you in the future.

"I majored in finance at SUNY Binghamton and served as the president of our campus accounting club. Before graduating this past spring, I spent much of my time off campus helping a local organization get their financial records in order."

After stating your name, mention something else specific that defines you at this point in your life. Are you still in school or have you recently graduated? If so, what was your major and minor? What extracurricular activities did you excel in? What school did you attend? The trick here is to be as specific as you can without boring the listener with unnecessary details.

2. What you're looking for and why

Be specific! The bulk of your elevator pitch should explain exactly what you are looking for and why. Have at least a general idea of what you're looking for, whether it is a job, advice, or a referral for someone to contact in a particular organization.

TWO NETWORKING ACTIVITIES A DAY...

Commit to following up with two networking activities every day. This could mean making a phone call, sending an email, attending an event, researching an organization, conducting an informational interview, writing a thank you note, or closing out a dead end lead. By making a conscious decision to pursue two networking activities a day, you will help ensure that you do not become passive in locating work; a job search should be active.

"I am interested in applying both my education and my community service experiences to the nonprofit sector. I would ideally like to work in development and fundraising for a larger, local organization that focuses on environmental advocacy."

Clearly explaining what you are looking for can be tricky if you have not prepared. Spend the most time practicing this part of your pitch to make sure it is direct, concise, and polished.

3. A specific outcome

Do you want an informational interview, online or published resources, or advice? If you know what you want to get out of the conversation, you can find a way to subtly work it in to the end of your elevator pitch and allow the person to offer it. Of course, be aware that a specific request can put the person you're speaking with on the spot, and if they can't help you with your exact request, the conversation may end there. Open-ended requests will likely lead to a fruitful conversation.

"I would love to know if you have any contacts in larger nonprofits who I could speak to regarding my interests. As I continue to explore my career opportunities in the nonprofit sector, I am always looking out for interesting people doing interesting work, as well as any good advice on publications or other resources that I should be familiar with."

Open the door for conversation without demanding anything. Often, you will get a response such as, "Oh, I know exactly the person you should talk with. Let me get you their contact information." This way, you get what you're looking for while allowing the people you're speaking with to determine how they can help you.

Here's how to develop and practice your elevator pitch:
- **Write it out**
- **Practice it out loud**

Write it out: You should write your pitch out first and then practice saying it until it feels natural. You can also begin by speaking what you think you want to say and writing it down as you go; once your words are down on paper, you can polish them. Either way, be sure to work on both the spoken and written versions of your pitch. The written version is to make sure that you're saying exactly what you want to say as you want it to be heard, and can also be useful for email introductions and written requests for informational interviews. The spoken version is what your audience will hear and it is essential that you are able to say a close approximation of the essential details you have on paper (without sounding like you are reciting a list from memory).

Business cards for beginners

You don't need to have a job to have a business card! In fact, since they're basically a pocket-sized marketing tool, they're great to have during your job search. While you may have a resume that you can hand out, resumes are not easily portable for casual networking events. Another point to consider is that handing out a resume can create an interesting power dynamic. Handing out a resume conveys "I need a job." Exchanging business cards with someone instead establishes more of a peer relationship and a sense of collaboration.

Your personal business cards should have a simple, clean layout that includes your name, phone number, email address, and possibly your permanent address or website if either are relevant to your search. The address will show you're local (a plus for many nonprofits) and the website could have your resume and work samples, or serve as an online portfolio. With the huge number of online and inexpensive printing options, it may be worth it to spend the money to print quality business cards (often they are $20 for 250 cards).

Remember that one of the most valuable reasons to hand out your business cards is that you will get someone else's in return. Since most folks will not contact you from a first meeting—it's up to you to use their business card as a way to follow up and contact them!

Practice it out loud: Once you've practiced it in front of the mirror and you feel like the wording sounds natural and concise, find some friends or family members who will give you honest feedback on all aspects of the pitch. Ask everyone who listens to provide you with at least one aspect to improve, as well as one aspect that works well. Have your practice audience pay attention to your content, clarity, tone, and pace, as well as to your body language and poise.

Develop a system

In order to better manage your network, you will need a system to keep track of all of the details that are essential in developing relationships. The process of gathering contacts needs to be supported by some mechanism for organizing this information. If you do not have a detailed and organized system for your contacts, you risk losing track of potential leads, wasting time pursuing information that you should already have, or even worse, confusing contact details and consequently coming across as very unprofessional.

Think about your personal relationships. Do you send family members and friends cards or presents on their birthdays? Perhaps you keep track of the dates on a calendar and store current addresses on your computer. A professional networking system is very similar in that it allows you to store essential information about people you meet so that you can cultivate relationships by keeping track of details. People appreciate the fact that you take the time to learn details about their work, organization, and accomplishments. Tracking details makes sure they know you are paying attention.

There are plenty of networking system styles, but the best ones are easy to use, detail-oriented, and allow you to keep track of ongoing aspects of the relationship. A system can be as simple as a Rolodex, as portable as an address book on your PDA, as connected as an online networking website (for example, www.linkedin.com), or as customized as an Excel spreadsheet tailored to your needs. The most important part is that you are diligent about using your system, so pick one that will work for you. Ask friends, family, colleagues, instructors, "natural networkers," and career service professionals to describe what systems they use.

Page 65 is a sample sheet that can be printed, copied, and attached to each individual's business card and kept in a three-ring binder or some other alphabetized filing system. You can create a similar document in Word and use a file naming system that helps you keep track of the information. It's not fancy but, if used consistently, it can be an effective way to keep track of your contacts. If you choose to use another format, consider using the prompts from this system to ensure that you include all necessary details.

"I DON'T KNOW WHAT I WANT TO DO."

Don't start any networking situation by saying, "I don't know what I want to do."

If you are open to a variety of opportunities, you can still tailor your pitch to each situation. Perhaps you are considering careers in either grantwriting or teaching. You don't have to confess your conflicted thoughts on whether grantwriting or teaching is the ideal career for you; you don't even have to mention it in your pitch. For the purpose of any conversation, your "What are you looking for and why?" component should be tailored to that conversation. Be prepared to answer questions like, "Why are you interested in this career?" or "What relevant work have you done so far?"

You can answer these questions honestly and thoughtfully based on your passion and experience. Your desired outcomes will be clearer and the person you're speaking with will be able to be more specific in their referrals and advice.

Also, bear in mind that if you seem unsure about what you want to do, or likely to make a poor impression, people in your network will be less willing to hand out contact information because you could reflect poorly on them. Nobody wants to gain a reputation for wasting their peers' time.

Network Management System

Contact name: _____
(including Dr., The Honorable, III, etc.)

Basic information

Title/Position: _____

Org/Company: _____

Org URL: _____

Contact information

Email addresses

Work: _____

Personal: _____

Phone numbers

Cell: _____

Work: _____

Other: _____

Physical address: _____

_____

_____

_____

FILE UNDER	DATE OF 1ST MEETING

MEETING DETAILS

Where did we meet? Include event, place, date. _____

_____

_____

Who introduced us? _____

_____

Details from our conversation:

_____

_____

_____

_____

This person has knowledge about/experience with/contacts in the following areas:

He/she is okay to approach (circle one in each pair): casually/often or formally/rarely

Date of last meeting	Venue (phone, event, etc.)	Specific details of last interaction	Referred me to these resources (people, sites, articles, etc.)	Any specific outcomes?	Did I follow up? (card/email/call)	Resources/ contacts that I've given to them	Down the road: when to contact again, next steps, etc.

Informational interviews

Relax. People love to talk about themselves...

One way to learn about your career options is to interview the people who are already following a similar path. An informational interview is usually a very brief (about a half hour) exploratory chat with a person who has insights into a position, educational field, career path, organization, field of expertise, or issue area. It is *not* a job interview, nor is it ever an appropriate time to ask for a job.

In an informational interview, your objective is to gather as much information and advice as possible, and to make contacts in the occupational areas and/or organizations that most interest you.

Informational interviews can serve a variety of functions:

- Provide background on a field of work
- Offer specific information about a type of organization
- Find out about hiring trends (but don't ask for a job)
- Explore a particular organization
- Connect with local decision makers in the nonprofit sector

> An informational interview is *not* a job interview, nor is it ever an appropriate time to ask for a job."

Think back to the Four Lens Framework (see **Chapter Three**) as you begin to map out your informational interview schedule. Try to locate people who:
- Work in the **roles** or **organizations** that interest you.
- Work within a **system** that interests you.
- Work on the **issues** that interest you.

Tap into your network of contacts to help you identify people with whom you should chat. Be sure to get permission from your contacts to use their names in requesting interviews; perhaps ask them send an introductory email before you contact the person in order to "e-introduce" you. Using your network should help make cold-calling or "cold-emailing" potential informational interviewees unnecessary. If your network does not turn up any leads, it's preferable to cold-email someone rather than cold-call them.

Before you talk with your potential informational interviewee, be prepared and practice what you are going to say. This is your first chance to sound competent, polished, and professional. Remember, and practice again, your elevator pitch. Whether you are emailing or calling to ask for an interview, here are some things you can mention:

- Who referred you to the potential interviewee
- Why you are asking them for an interview (be sure to include any specific, positive aspects about them or their work)

- What kind of information you are seeking (information about the organization, issue area, job function, etc.)
- A request for a roughly half-hour chat, at a time and place of their choosing or by phone if they are not in your area

Here's an example of what this might sound like:

Hello. I'm Edgar Hernandez. Kathy Liu suggested I get in touch with you to request an informational interview. I've majored in finance at SUNY Binghamton, where I served as president of the campus accounting club and helped a local charity improve their bookkeeping practices. I've been considering a career in nonprofit finance. Kathy said that you have 15 years of experience in fundraising and development and that you are highly respected among your peers. I am sure you are busy, but I was wondering if you would have time for a short conversation over coffee, or at your office; my schedule is flexible. I'd love to ask you some questions about how you got started and the trajectory of your career so far.

What if they say no?

It is possible, though usually unlikely, that the person will turn you down for an interview. They may not have the time right now or may not feel that they can actually help you. If they have said that they are too busy right now, follow up by asking if you can contact them again in the future and, if so, when would be a good time. If they say they cannot help you, thank them for their time and ask if they can refer you to another person in a similar role, field, or organization.

If they say yes...

More than likely, people will be happy to give you a bit of their time. Once you've scheduled the informational interview, prepare yourself well. Your to-do list should include:

- Researching their accomplishments (try Googling them) and their organization online. Working their accomplishments into your conversation ("I saw that you spoke at the Gates Foundation. What was that like?") is a great way to learn information while letting them know you have taken the time to prepare.
- Finding something that the person has written, a speech they've given, or research they've published, and then developing a few questions about it. The more you show you are aware of their work, the more impressed they will be.
- Preparing thoughtful questions ahead of time (see below).
- Dressing professionally (or at least appropriately for the situation).
- Being on time. Be sure to call if you think you are running late.
- Bringing a pad of paper and a pen to take notes, and a watch to keep track of the time.
- Planning to pay for their order if you are meeting for a beverage or a meal.

USE SOCIAL NETWORK SITES

Are you on Facebook or MySpace every day? Why not use them to help you network for your job search? Use keywords relating to your interests (like AIDS, environment, or nonprofit) to find others in your extended network who have similar interests, or who are working in related fields. Try a search using the names of organizations you're interested in. In Facebook, once you've searched a keyword, click on "People" to make sure you're searching individual profiles. If you go to a traditional college-age school, set the age limit in the advanced settings to people who are over 22–this should get you alumni. You might start a message to these people by saying something like, "Hi–I know this is a little strange, but I see on your profile that you're working at...". After you acknowledge the awkwardness, most people will be happy to tell you about their experiences. Just be sure to follow up with a prompt and appreciative "thank you."

–Valinda Lee

Below are some questions to consider asking. Choose the most relevant ones for your situation in advance, and remember that your interviewee may be pressed for time. It's unlikely you'll be able to ask all of these questions.

 **Jot your thoughts**

Use the space below to jot down a few other questions you would like to ask in an informational interview.

- How did you get started on this career path?
- Why did you choose this type of work—what drew you to it?
- What do you do in a typical day?
- What are the most and least rewarding aspects of this type of work?
- If I were to look for a job in this field (or career path), what are the best known organizations or types of employers I should be aware of?
- How would you recommend I start the job search?
- What other local (regional, national, international) employers have positions in this field?
- What do you wish you had known about this field when you were starting your career? What would you do differently?
- Which skills and abilities are most valued in your field? Which ones are currently in demand?
- How would you recommend someone with my background demonstrate these skills through my resume? (This is a great question to ask if you want them to offer to look over your resume. Don't directly ask them to do this.)
- What is the salary range for this position in this area based on my level of experience?
- Are there peak hiring seasons in this field?
- What is the turnover/burnout rate? Why is it that way?
- What degree(s) do you have? Where did you earn it/them?
- What degree(s) would you recommend someone in this field getting?
- What do you consider the best schools for that kind of degree?
- Are there any books or publications I can read to learn more about this work?
- Who else would you recommend I chat with for more information?
- May I use your name when I contact them?
- What haven't I asked you that I should have?
- May I contact you if necessary, in the future?
- Again, **DO NOT ASK** for a job!

If you are performing a long-distance job search (see **Chapter Six**), make sure to ask these questions:
- What are some local nonprofit resources that I should be aware of?
- Is this the kind of career field for which a national search might be conducted?
- Who else would you recommend I chat with for more information?

Before you leave, politely ask for a business card, brochure, and if available, a copy of their organization's latest annual report (make sure the annual report isn't already online). If possible, give them your business card, too.

After the interview

After you leave, it is essential to send a thank you note. You can have the thank you note stamped, addressed, and ready to go (except for writing the note itself) when you go to the interview. After you leave the interview, take a few minutes to write the note and pop it in the nearest mailbox. Make the note meaningful, and mention something specific that you learned.

When you get home, jot down some impressions and notes in your networking management system (see pages 64-65). Ask yourself:

- What did I learn?
- How interested am I in exploring this field further?
- What values, skills, and interests of mine fit—or don't fit—with this type of work?
- What are my next steps from here? (Websites/articles to read, people to contact, events to attend, etc.)

If your informational interview leads to any positive professional steps, make sure to contact the person again to thank them. Everyone appreciates follow-up and it makes people much more likely to help you again in the future. It also shows your attention to detail and can be a reminder that you are still searching for work (or a signal that you have found a position).

If the person you interviewed gave you the name of a new person to contact, begin the process again. Over time, you will have created an expanded network of people well-positioned to help you in your career.

Follow up

Whatever type of networking you do, following up is essential. After any networking event or informational interview, as you are recording details in your networking system, review past contacts and determine if there is anyone with whom you need to follow up. This could mean emailing a new contact that someone gave you or sending a thank you note to someone who provided you with valuable information. Informational interviews are particularly important to follow up with a thank you note.

Contact the contact

This is extremely important, particularly if you were given a name and contact information. Following up with referrals is vital because the person may have been told to expect your call. Furthermore, if you fail to follow up with a suggested contact, the referrer will be far less likely to give you other leads that could be helpful to you in the future. It is also too good of an opportunity to pass up; if you've got

---

Following up on new leads

Remember, if the person you are interviewing has any other contacts that they think can help you, they will probably mention them without you asking. That said, it may be useful to double-check toward the end of the interview if the person has not mentioned anyone to follow up with for future informational interviews.

Ask how to spell the name of any new contacts, and request a phone number and email address. If you feel the conversation is going well and the interviewee is eager to help you out, consider asking if they would be willing to "e-introduce" you to the new contact.

HAND-WRITTEN NOTES AND CARDS Should you avoid handwritten notes and cards when sending a thank you message to your informational interviewees? While thank you notes are meant to be a form of professional correspondence, it is possible to add a personal touch. If you left an informational interview feeling like you made a personal connection with the interviewee, a handwritten note may be in order. If the entire informational interview process felt very formal and professional, however, then a handwritten note may not be appropriate.

If you choose to send a typed note, use business letter formatting and keep it to the three-paragraph structure detailed in the interview follow-up discussion of **Chapter Nine**.

an introduction to talk with someone, take advantage of the opportunity. Even if the person may not seem to be able to offer anything that is directly relevant to what you're looking for at the moment, a key aspect of networking is its cyclical nature. A relationship you develop and cultivate now may be the connection that helps you land a great job several years or decades later. Similarly, a contact that you think may not have any relevant leads for you may surprise you with some great information or resources. You never know when a contact may prove useful or when you, in turn, may be able to help that person out.

Thank you notes

As you follow up with connections, referrals, or resources, be sure to also follow up with your original contact. Thank you notes are always a good idea. Mention a specific detail from your interaction in your note to remind your contact about your conversation. This type of note will likely leave an impression of you as a thoughtful, detail-oriented person who appreciates and acknowledges people's time and insights. There are few people who wouldn't want to refer such a person to others in their network.

REMEMBER, NETWORKING IS A TWO-WAY CONNECTION

Networking should be a mutual give-and-take relationship. Neglecting to give back to those who help you can lead to shut doors in the future.

A reciprocal networking arrangement allows you to not only receive advice, references, and opportunities from your contacts, but also to pass on opportunities, articles, or events to your network of contacts. During all of your informal networking, be sure to keep track of your contacts, conversations, and information with a structured system.

SUMMARY

Networking, the building of relationships, is essential to any successful job search in the nonprofit sector. In this section, we explored several key themes that will help you in your networking efforts (page 55).

Your **weak ties** (page 56) are those acquaintances and tangential friends or former coworkers who can help you expand your networking opportunities exponentially. **Strong ties** (page 56) are your close friends and family who have the time and energy to help you network.

Using your preexisting community groups to create new connections and contacts is a key way to network. This kind of **community involvement** means joining groups or exploring new opportunities that can expand your network (pages 56-58).

Informal networking is the day-to-day interactions with friends, family, and colleagues that lay the groundwork for future opportunities and reciprocal relationships (page 59).

Targeted, intentional **formal networking** can include assessing your community/informal networking community to find job leads, attending professional networking events, and conducting informational interviews with professionals in your field of interest (pages 59-61).

Your elevator pitch should clearly and concisely convey who you are, what you are looking for and why, and a specific desired outcome from your conversation with a potential networking lead (pages 62-63).

To be an effective networker, you need to have a very organized **network management system**. This will ensure that you do not let any opportunities slip through the cracks and that you are making the most efficient use of both your own and your contacts' time (pages 64-65).

Informational interviews can reap many rewards, from new contacts to useful knowledge. Prepare a thoughtful range of questions in advance, but **never** ask for a job at an informational interview (pages 66-67)!

Following up with network contacts keeps the door open for the future; you will most likely need it again (pages 69-70).

CHAPTER FIVE

Become a stronger candidate

Nine ways to get out and involved

In this chapter you will:

- See what nonprofit hiring managers say impresses them most in a candidate.

- Explore ways to make yourself a stronger nonprofit job search candidate, including volunteering, internships, fellowships, term-of-service programs, board service, professional associations, industry publications, participation in mentoring, and a full array of education options.

- Learn some of the key ways to increase your appeal to nonprofit employers. Strengthening your nonprofit candidacy takes time, so start early!

What hiring professionals say they look for in a candidate

Idealist.org surveyed nonprofit hiring professionals from a range of large and small organizations to gauge their perceptions on the nonprofit hiring process. In one question, survey participants were asked to rank the experiences a candidate might possess, with 1 as the most valuable, down to 9 as the least valuable. The percentage of respondents selecting each option is reflected in the table below.

Table 1: Value of Various Life Experiences to Nonprofit Hiring Professionals (percentage of respondents ranking each experience on a scale of most-to-least valuable)									
	1 (most valuable)	2	3	4	5	6	7	8	9 (least valuable)
Board service	4%	4%	5%	2%	5%	7%	13%	13%	**36%**
Volunteer work with your organization	**30%**	15%	9%	9%	9%	4%	9%	4%	11%
Volunteer work with another org in a relevant field	11%	9%	18%	**20%**	16%	9%	9%	4%	4%
Internship in a relevant field	14%	20%	**24%**	8%	10%	8%	12%	4%	0%
Experience in the for-profit sector	**18%**	2%	12%	6%	6%	16%	12%	10%	20%
Participation in a term-of-service program	13%	8%	8%	15%	8%	**17%**	15%	8%	9%
Foreign language spoken by constituents in your program (not essential to the position)	4%	**18%**	10%	10%	8%	10%	16%	14%	10%
Graduate education or certificate program related to but not mandatory for the position	7%	9%	7%	**16%**	**16%**	**16%**	2%	**16%**	9%
Fundraising/Grantwriting experience	4%	15%	9%	11%	**20%**	11%	11%	15%	4%

Data from a survey of nonprofit hiring professionals in the United States conducted by Idealist.org in April 2007.

Volunteering

Nonprofit human resources professionals and others in hiring positions consider volunteering to be one of the best ways to make a professional transition into nonprofit work. Volunteering:

- **Expands your personal and professional networks**. Being "out there" and volunteering allows you to hear about opportunities and organizations that are hiring. Employees and other volunteers in the organization become your connection point to new opportunities. Later, your colleagues can serve as local nonprofit references for you as you apply for paid positions.

- Allows you to **work on new skills** as well as translate some of your preexisting skills into a nonprofit context.

- Gives you an **opportunity to lead a project**. Organizations often look for volunteer leaders.

- Lets you **explore possible career options and paths** without a long-term commitment. Many people find that what they think is their "dream job" turns out to be something they don't want to do for a living. Volunteering in your interest area first can help you see if it's something you want to explore further as a career.

- **Raises your visibility** within an organization. This can lead to the possibility of volunteers becoming staff members. You *should not*, however, volunteer solely because you think it will lead to a job, because it may not. There are always more volunteers than available positions. Your passion for the cause and desire to learn more should be your primary motivation for doing this work.

- **Demonstrates your commitment to a cause**. By turning your concerns and values into action, you demonstrate that you are engaged and willing to be a vehicle for change.

- **Improves your health**. Civic engagement and social involvement are actually good for you. (See the Corporation for National and Community Service research area for a report entitled "The Health Benefits of Volunteering: A Review of Recent Research" at www.nationalservice.gov/about/role_impact/performance_research.asp#HBR.)

With proper preparation, volunteering can be a win-win situation. You can fit meaningful volunteer work into just about any schedule and the reciprocity of volunteering means both you and the organization benefit from your time. When it comes to your resume, nonprofit hiring professionals may consider your volunteer work as significant as your paid work experience. You are developing and using skills that directly impact an organization's success, and although you are not being financially compensated, you benefit from personal and professional development. Nonprofit organizations leverage their capacity (i.e., are more effective at fulfilling their missions) through the contribution of your volunteer time.

The volunteering fast-track?

According to Laura Retzler, a nonprofit executive search consultant, volunteering in an organization's development department is the quickest way to a position. This is because development is such a vital, much-needed skill in any organization and there are very often positions open. Even if you don't plan to work in this area, having a perspective on development is of value anywhere in an organization. This is good to know if you are more interested in working for a specific organization or issue area instead of in a particular position.

If at first you aren't satisfied...

If you are interested in a role in the nonprofit sector but have had an unsatisfactory experience with a particular organization, consider volunteering in a similar role with a different organization. You'll then see whether your unsatisfying experience was just that a particular organization was not a good fit for you, or if it is the work itself that is not right for you. Given the diversity of organizations within the nonprofit sector, volunteering once in a certain capacity–for example, volunteer recruiting or event planning–does not necessarily mean that you know what that position is like in every organization. It may take a few experiences to get a fair representation of what a particular position can be like.

In order to realize the benefits that volunteering can bring, it is important to research your volunteer opportunities with the same diligence as you would a job or an internship (for tips on how to research organizations, see **Chapters Six** and **Seven**). Consider what you want in terms of the size of the organization, the work environment, the role or position, the time commitment, the mission, and what skills you hope to gain from the volunteer opportunity. While you may not need to analyze shorter, one- or two-day volunteer opportunities in as much depth as you would a longer commitment, a bit of forethought is always a good idea. Given the importance of networking, experience, and commitment to a cause, during a nonprofit job search your volunteer choices can make a huge difference in the success of your overall efforts.

Internships

Have some say over how you get yourself through the door...

An internship is a structured immersion in the world of nonprofit work. Whether paid or unpaid, an internship typically involves a combination of supervised project work and professional development components. Although there is never a guarantee that an internship will lead to a job offer, internships—especially intentional internships where you are both helping the organization and developing specific skills—are a great chance to show your value to a potential employer.

Interns are not the same as volunteers

Interns typically have a specific task, activity, or project to work on within an organization over a set period of time, all of which should be clearly defined from the beginning. Internship descriptions allow you to identify the skills you want to contribute to an organization, and help you make sure that you are maximizing your interning time. In contrast to internships, general volunteering may not necessarily mean that you can work on a specific project or in a particular role within an organization. Internships can involve assisting with broader organizational issues, and can sometimes be done independently and on your own schedule. This affords greater flexibility for people who want to be involved with an organization or cause but who need to hold down a job while preparing to enter the nonprofit sector. Additionally, "internship" has a more professional connotation (which makes sense as the word is borrowed from the business world) than "volunteer", which helps internships stand out on your resume. If you are at a place in your career where you are uncomfortable with using the word "intern" to describe your experience, see if your manager or supervisor would be willing to agree on another title for your work with the organization. Titles such as "assistant," "fellow," or "researcher" may be more useful instead.

Volunteerism's value: A personal story

Throughout my college years in St. Louis, I was peripherally involved with the campus Students for Choice organization. I cared about reproductive freedom and how the laws impacted doctors and their patients, but it wasn't until my second semester of senior year that I made the time to volunteer at a nearby Planned Parenthood affiliate. As a clinic escort, I spent Saturday mornings with a small team of people tasked with walking patients from their cars to the clinic door, showing quiet solidarity as they fought to ignore the words and shouts of anti-choice protestors outside the clinic.

After graduation I moved to Washington, DC and applied for an internship with the Planned Parenthood Action Fund PAC. The words "clinic escort" on my resume caught the eye of my future manager. In my interview, I was able to explain how escorting had cemented my commitment to the cause, and that I was ready to learn how fundraising and public policy work at the national level impacted clinics like the one with which I'd volunteered. The several Saturdays I spent as a clinic escort not only helped solidify my desire to pursue this type of work, but was also one of the main reasons I got hired at the national office.

–Julia Smith, Community Outreach Coordinator, Idealist.org

How do you find an internship?

You can use the same tools to search for an internship that you use for a volunteer or paid employment search: use your network to learn about opportunities, research locations of organizations, attend a nonprofit career fair, and conduct online searches. Idealist.org has over 1,000 U.S.-based and international internships opportunities (www.idealist.org/if/as/Internship). Many nonprofits list their internships on their own websites, and with colleges and universities; the career service office of your undergraduate or graduate program is a great place to start.

You may also consider approaching an organization that interests you and asking to create your own intentional internship. This gives you the opportunity to explore one of the lenses—issue, organization, role, or system (see the Four Lens Framework in **Chapter Three**)—in a way that is specifically catered to your interests and aspirations.

An all-too-common reality of internships is that you end up giving a lot more to the organization than you get in return. At the onset, be clear that you are excited about giving your time and energy to their cause and that you're also enthusiastic about gaining new skills and expertise through the experience. In other words, find out how the organization plans to help you hone preexisting skills in a nonprofit context or to develop new skills that you need to further your nonprofit career goals.

You would never take a job without knowing the benefits, and an internship should be no different. Interns deserve to get something in return for their dedication and this is best accomplished by advocating for yourself from the start.

Maximizing your internship time

Along with the opportunity to build your skill set in a nonprofit organization, there are several other ways to make sure you get the most out of your experience:

- Keep a running list of your achievements during your internship so that you have that information to use on your resume and in interviews.
- Take advantage of staff expertise in the organization by conducting formal and informal informational interviews with them. Ask them to recommend outside contacts you can interview.
- Attend all networking opportunities (fairs, lectures, community events).
- Build solid references by treating your internship with the respect you would a full-time position.
- Share with management any of your expertise that might be of use or interest.

Use the space below to note some ideas about local non-profits where you can inquire about internships.

"You would never take a job without knowing the benefits, and an internship should be no different."

Fellowship programs

Historically, the term "fellowship" referred to funding for graduate-level study or research. Today, however, the term is used in a variety of contexts and the definition has widened to include a large range of programs more aptly described as internships, scholarships, stipends, or grants—all of which can strengthen your nonprofit candidacy. Most programs that call themselves fellowships pair a monetary grant with some form of study, research, service, career exploration, or professional development. As well, most fellowships have a longer time commitment (often one year or more) and more autonomy than an internship or volunteer opportunity. Public service fellowships—the kind most likely to strengthen your nonprofit candidacy—cover a wide range of fields (for example, urban planning, leadership training, or medical research) and opportunities (like travel sabbaticals, working with other fellowship recipients in a laboratory, or a year off to complete a project), but all of them generally fall into one of these categories:

Fellowship opportunities
For a list of nonprofit and public policy fellowships, visit:
www.idealist.org/en/career/fellowship.html

Academic fellowship (or scholarship)

A monetary grant accompanied by a period of academic study, research, service and/or training, often with a public service focus. Historically, a scholarship referred to funding for undergraduate study and a fellowship referred to funding for graduate-level study or research, but this definition has widened. Now, these two terms are often interchangeable in academia, although "fellowship" maintains a more prestigious connotation.

Pre-professional fellowship (or internship)

A paid, selective, and often specialized period of service and career exploration in a public service field. Since these are often called internships, also consider internship listings when exploring pre-professional fellowships (see Idealist.org's internship search at www.idealist.org/if/as/Internship).

Social entrepreneur fellowship

A type of funding to create new public service organizations or ventures, paired with guidance and institutional support. Many of these fellowships look to support students and professionals interested in starting (or strengthening) their own nonprofit.

Mid-career fellowship

A form of subsidized career development for professionals, either to increase their capacity in their current public service role or promote their exploration of another professional field. These fellowships can include: training managerial sector-switchers to be leaders in a different field, supporting professionals by giving them a period of time to learn new skills applicable to their work, and travel or international work opportunities.

The breadth and scope of available fellowships means that most students and professionals can find a program that fits their interests and aspirations. Fellowships do take time to research and to apply for, but the potential gains—in new skills, knowledge, and networks—make them a very appealing avenue to explore for individuals entering the nonprofit sector.

Term-of-service program

What is a term-of-service program?

Some term-of-service programs such as AmeriCorps, Teach For America, and Peace Corps are well known. However, countless other programs also exist both domestically and internationally, and all are focused on connecting people with service organizations that need them. For someone wishing to enter the nonprofit workforce, participating in a term-of-service program can be a great starting place.

The beauty of many term-of-service programs is that, while they weren't designed to be entry points to the nonprofit sector, they are very effective at introducing people to the sector and giving them the skills, contacts, and experience they need to succeed. Through a term-of-service program, individuals with very little full-time work experience can take on positions in nonprofit organizations that have a great deal of responsibility, autonomy, and opportunities for training and professional growth. Additionally, professionals with years of experience in the for-profit or public service sectors can also take on term-of-service positions that immediately utilize their skill sets while focusing on a different bottom line in the nonprofit sector. Moreover, term-of-service programs often involve collaboration with area nonprofits and community leaders, which provides term-of-service participants with a great chance to grow their networks.

Benefits of the right term-of-service experience

As with any commitment, finding both a program and work site that fit your goals and personality is crucial. Interview at several placement sites just as you would in a salaried job search. It's advisable to ask yourself—and the organizations where you interview—realistic questions about the service you'll be performing, the training and support available to you, and the kinds of activities that will excite and challenge you daily. Questions to consider include:

- Will you provide direct service to clients, or will you be building organizational capacity through desk/computer-based work?
- Will you be starting up a project from scratch or continuing the work of the staff who came before you?
- What specific skills will you be able to transfer into another nonprofit position? Do these skills fill gaps in your nonprofit resume?

Benefits vary among different programs. In the United States, common benefits include a living allowance, a network of participants, training, and, at the end, an education award (money to use toward paying off student debt or continuing your education). Residential programs such as AmeriCorps*NCCC also offer group housing. Check with the programs you are interested in to find out what benefits are offered.

You'll gain a lot by participating in a successful term-of-service program while also adding new people to your network who want to help you succeed in your career. Your colleagues and supervisors may want to give you a strong reference or even hire you if a position becomes available. You will have great experiences to share during interviews, and your accomplishments can be reflected in your resume and cover letters. You will also have gained the skills and confidence you need to succeed, both in your service and in future jobs.

A term of service can be an ideal introduction to the nonprofit world for recent graduates, providing a great mix of structure, responsibility, and networking options. The low wages of a term-of-service program may turn some people off, but those who partake in such placements will eventually find themselves with an arsenal of skills, experiences, and networks to help them continue on their career journey into the nonprofit sector. And remember, many programs include an educational award or readjustment allowance at the end.

Eligibility, faith-based organizations, and resources

Eligibility requirements (i.e., age, education level, nationality, etc.) vary with each program, as do the participation requirements and time commitments (i.e., 10 months, one year, 27 months, etc.). Some term-of-service programs are faith-based. Participants aren't always required to be adherents to the faith, but should accept the diverse faiths and personal practices of peers while in the program. If you are interested in doing a faith-based term of service, be sure to ask any questions you have of the program director or site supervisor. Some faith-based programs are residential, allowing participants to live in a faith community as well as incorporate their values into their service to the community. Some of these programs will have an expectation that participants will share their religious beliefs with the clients they are serving, and you will have to determine whether doing so is your preference.

The tables on the following two pages offer a comparison of six of the best known term-of-service programs. Please note that there are many more term-of-service programs than the six in these tables. Idealist.org has a webpage devoted to them: www.idealist.org/en/career/oneyearservice.html.

 A term of service can be an ideal introduction to the nonprofit world, providing a great mix of structure, responsibility, and networking options."

Table 2: General Comparison of Six Well Known Term-of-Service Programs

	AmeriCorps* State and National www.americorps.org	AmeriCorps*VISTA www.americorps.org	AmeriCorps*NCCC www.americorps.org	City Year www.cityyear.org	Teach for America www.teachforamerica.org	Peace Corps www.peacecorps.gov
Focus areas	Direct service, in non-profits, schools, and government agencies.	Indirect service in nonprofits, schools, and government agencies. Emphasis on policy issues, ending poverty, and capacity building.	Residential, team-based, travel to sites throughout the region. Direct service.	Direct service, in non-profits, schools, and government agencies. Emphasis on youth and also physical service.	Education, specifically "eliminating educational inequity."	Education, community development, business development, environment, agriculture, health, HIV/AIDS, technology.
Location	United States and territories	United States and territories	United States and territories	17 cities throughout the United States	26-29 urban and rural areas throughout the United States	Urban and rural areas in developing nations in eight regions throughout the world.
Term of service	1700 hours, or about a year	One year	10 months	1700 hours in 10 months	Two years	24-27 months
Age and other eligibility issues	18+, U.S. citizenship or national/permanent resident status.	18+ (college degree helpful), U.S. citizenship or national/ permanent resident.	18-24, U.S. citizenship or national/permanent resident.	18-24, U.S. citizenship or national/permanent resident.	Bachelors degree, 2.5 GPA, U.S. citizenship or national/permanent resident.	18+ (college degree helpful), U.S. citizenship. Foreign language skills NOT required.
This program is best for...	People who want a career in direct service roles, such as teaching, case work, construction, gardening/farming, etc. Also for people who want to take a year to work before graduate school, or who simply want to contribute to their communities in direct ways.	People who are interested in a career in the nonprofit or government sectors, in affecting social change through public policy, and for people who work well independently (self-starters) and do not need to see the results of their labors right away.	People who thrive in a structured environment and work well (or want to learn to work) in a team setting. Good for gap year students, and for students who want to take a year off during college. Also good for people who want to learn a range of skills (from tutoring children to building houses), and love variety.	People who thrive in a structured environment and work well (or want to learn to work) in a team setting. Good for gap year students, and for students who want to take a year off during college.	People who are high achievers in academics, leadership, and work. Also for people who are passionate and want to learn more about public education in the trenches.	People who want to be informed U.S. citizens. Also for people who are high achievers in academics, leadership, and work; who have an interest in international development and/or public health, foreign service, international diplomacy, international business, etc.; and who want to master a foreign language, and to truly understand a foreign culture.

Table 3: Comparison of Education Benefits in Six Well Known Term-of-Service Programs

	AmeriCorps* State and National	AmeriCorps*VISTA	AmeriCorps*NCCC	City Year	Teach for America	Peace Corps
$4,725 Education Award (use towards qualified student loans and/or tuition at Title IV schools) at the completion of a full term of service	X	X	X	X	X	
Deferment or forbearance of eligible student loans possible	X	X	X	X	X	X
Cancellation of eligible student loans possible		X				X
Payment of accrued interest on eligible student loans during the term of service	X	X	X	X	X	
School partnerships offering Education Award matching grants	X	X	X	X	X	
School partnerships offering admissions deferments, application fee waivers, scholarship funding					X	
School partnerships offering fellowship programs for alumni					X	X Fellows USA
Service may count towards graduate degree						X Masters International

Table 4: Comparison of Pay, Health Care, and Other Benefits in Six Well Known Term-of-Service Programs

	AmeriCorps* State and National www.americorps.org	AmeriCorps*VISTA www.americorps.org	AmeriCorps*NCCC www.americorps.org	City Year www.cityyear.org	Teach for America www.teachforamerica.org	Peace Corps www.peacecorps.gov
Payment and other benefits	Monthly stipend (usually less than $1,000/month).	Monthly living allowance (usually 105% of poverty level in your region/state), child care benefits. Travel to orientation and service site provided. One year of noncompetitive status for a federal government job.	$400/month plus room and board	Weekly stipend, uniform, T-Mobile cell-phone, child care benefit.	Entry level teachers' salary in your school district, which can range from $25,000 to $44,000 depending on region. Government student loan deferral available and repayment of interest accrued during service.	Monthly allowance commensurate with local salaries. $26 monthly vacation pay and 2 vacation days per month accrue. Readjustment allowance at the end of your service (about $6,000). Language training and money to pay language tutors.
Health benefits	Basic health insurance (ask about coverage for preexisting conditions).	Basic health insurance (ask about coverage for preexisting conditions).	Basic health insurance (ask about coverage for preexisting conditions).	Basic health insurance (ask about coverage for preexisting conditions).	Health insurance comparable to other starting teachers.	Full medical coverage during service, and affordable health insurance for up to 18 months afterwards.

Board service

Board service is a fantastic way to get involved in the nonprofit sector from the inside. The structure of a nonprofit organization most commonly involves a volunteer board of directors who have responsibility for the overall conduct of the organization and a staff made up of employees, interns, and volunteers. Typically nonprofit board service is unpaid, but it can be a great opportunity to network with other community leaders, make important decisions, and utilize professional skills.

There are some broadly accepted standards about the way boards work, but certain requirements vary by state. Organizations have "charter documents" and other rules, directives, and manuals that dictate the legal and organizational duties of their board.

Board service typically involves meeting a set number of times per year (once or twice a year, quarterly, monthly, etc.) as a full board in addition to serving on committees, meeting with community members and potential donors, participating in conference calls and meetings with organization staff, and generally being a community advocate for the organization.

Boards are responsible for the overall health and effectiveness of the organization, including financial responsibilities that can vary based on the size of the nonprofit. Smaller nonprofits often require more financial oversight from the board as they cannot usually pay for a staff member or auditor to do the work. Boards carry out a variety of fiduciary responsibilities ranging from preparing receipts for donor contributions to filing the IRS 990 tax form required of all organizations with nonprofit "tax-exempt status."

Other key duties of many nonprofit boards are: establishing program goals and assessing performance, setting personnel policies, selecting and evaluating senior staff, approving and monitoring financial plans and results, and evaluating the board's own performance. Given the wide range of duties and issues that a board must oversee, a diverse talent pool is necessary for the success of the board and, ultimately, for the success of the organization. Furthermore, funders are increasingly assessing board diversity (age, gender, race, and other demographic information) as a criteria for determining their support for organizations.

There is often an assumption that the people who serve on boards are either wealthy or famous (or both!). However, as mentioned above, diversity is essential to the success of a board; organizations often seek out people who have a wide range of skills and experiences. While the ability to contribute financially to an

The board's role in finances

Board members carry a heavy stewardship responsibility in their service to an organization, as the board is responsible for overseeing the finances. Also, board members are typically required to contribute or solicit donations (this is sometimes called "give-or-get"). Some organizations, for example, have a set minimum contribution. Board members are also often expected to raise awareness of the organization throughout their network in order to increase the organization's visibility and funding.

Board service

Here are a few websites that can help you explore board service in more detail:

The Nonprofit FAQ
(www.idealist.org/en/faqcat/3-1) is a comprehensive source of information on many aspects of nonprofits. In particular, look at the link entitled "Board Basics" for an in-depth starter.

Board Café (www.boardcafe.org) features CompassPoint's Board Café newsletter for nonprofit boards. You can search for archived issues and subscribe to the e-newsletter here.

BoardnetUSA (www.boardnetusa.org) is a matching service for boards seeking new members as well as for individuals looking for board service opportunities.

BoardSource (www.boardsource.org) features a handy board FAQ in its "Board Info" section.

The **U.S. Department of the Treasury** (www.irs.gov/charities/charitable) includes required IRS forms (under "Filing Requirements"), links to the state nonprofit regulatory offices, and more FAQs.

organization is undoubtedly an asset, board members are expected to contribute in other ways, too. Board members who bring an understanding of law, finance, PR/ marketing, fundraising, or outreach are incredibly valuable to an organization. The requirements to be a board member are as varied as the different types of organizations in the nonprofit sector.

Board committees

Given the wide-ranging responsibilities of the board, many boards set up specialized committees to handle different aspects of their oversight. Some examples of committees are: Board Development, Budget and Finance, Executive, Fundraising, and Programs. Boards can also convene temporary task forces (i.e., a committee to search for and hire a new executive director, plan for a particular event, find a new office location for the organization, mediate an organizational problem) that meet for a finite period of time and then disband when the project is complete or the issue is resolved.

Professional associations

Professional associations are networks. Some are membership-based, with dues and considerable structure, including regular conferences, journals, or other services. Others are less formal networks of people doing similar work. Whatever your field or area of interest, professional associations offer an incredible number of benefits, ranging from a way to keep in touch with developments in the field to a means of connecting with professionals in the sector who have similar affinities. Many professional associations also publish newsletters, coordinate conferences, conduct webinars, host networking events, and manage listservs, among a variety of other activities.

Industry publications

Familiarity with key issues and experts in the nonprofit sector is an essential part of learning about the field. The following is a short list of organizations that have print publications and/or online editions available to view or download. These publications deal with general issues that affect the nonprofit sector. For more specific information, consider researching relevant professional associations to see if they produce their own publications. Many of these organizations also offer free e-newsletters or listservs to help you stay up to date on news that impacts the sector, such as political decisions or international events.

Professional associations
The NYU Wagner Graduate School of Public Service has a vast list of professional associations at: www.wagner.nyu.edu/careers/resources/associations.php.

This chapter's online resource page lists many more associations:

www.idealist.org/en/career/guide/ch5resources.html

Industry publications
Here are a few publications that focus on the nonprofit sector.

The Chronicle of Philanthropy
www.philanthropy.com

Nonprofit Online News
http://news.gilbert.org

The Nonprofit Quarterly
www.nonprofitquarterly.org

The NonProfit Times
www.nptimes.com

Nonprofit and Voluntary Sector Quarterly http://nvs.sagepub.com

The online resource page for this chapter lists more publications:

www.idealist.org/en/career/guide/ch5resources.html

Professional mentoring

One of the most effective yet elusive ways to develop yourself professionally is to have a mentor. "Research indicates that mentored individuals perform better on the job, advance more rapidly within the organization…, and report more job and career satisfaction," says Lillian Eby, professor of applied psychology at the University of Georgia. And if one mentor is this beneficial… having several is even better! Each mentor will be able to provide you with different perspectives on various aspects of your career. Similarly, if you have more than one mentor, you have the potential to connect to a broader range of people from your mentors' networks.

Mentoring can take on many forms, but in the most general sense, it is a relationship between a more experienced person and a less experienced one. In a professional sense, a good mentor will share skills, knowledge, professional contacts, and expertise; provide honest feedback; and act as a role model. Mentoring relationships take place over time, often spanning years and multiple job changes.

People find mentors through existing networks of family, friends, professors, or supervisors. Mentoring relationships develop on the job, in school, through volunteering, or through coincidental connections. Mentors typically evolve from personal relationships and so it is difficult to intentionally go out and seek a mentor. Nonetheless, there are deliberate steps you can take to begin the process of finding a mentor.

A mentor should be selected carefully. Here are a few tips on what to look for:
- It's not just a person's knowledge and contacts that are important, it's also their interest in mentoring and the fit or connection between the two of you.
- While strangers can become good mentors, the best potential mentors are likely to be those you know or those with whom you share some common ground. For example, potential mentors could be a manager or boss who supervised you in a professional environment, a professor or teacher of a class you took, or someone you know through friends or family.
- Don't limit yourself to just a specific professional field or area of interest; a mentor from a very different profession or background can also provide invaluable insights, career tips, and connections.
- Above all else, a mentor should be someone you admire. This respect is at the core of a mentoring relationship; it's hard to learn from someone you don't hold in high regard.

Find a mentor... and *be* one!

While you may be new to the field and probably not yet the best person to professionally mentor someone as you are just learning the ropes yourself, there are plenty of other opportunities for you to serve in this capacity. By mentoring someone, you will not only have the opportunity to make a difference in someone else's life, but you will learn about yourself and the nuances of a mentoring relationship.

National organizations like Girl Scouts, Boy Scouts, and Big Brothers, Big Sisters provide great opportunities to mentor someone in a non-professional capacity.

---

[1] Lillian Eby quotation from http://blog.penelopetrunk.com/2006/09/27/you-need-a-mentor-now-heres-how-to-get-one/

How to find a mentor

Here are three basic steps that can help you find a mentor:

1. Research

Read as much as you can about the position, issue, or organization in which you're interested. Make a list of people who are doing what you want to do or who are working in organizations or on issues that interest you. As noted earlier, ideally a mentor is part of your existing network. While you're researching, consider what questions you might ask these potential mentors. What is it about their jobs that makes them interesting or appealing to you? Consider what you would ideally want in a mentoring relationship with that person. If you have specific goals about what you want in a mentor, you'll be better positioned to reach them.

2. Make contact: start by requesting information

Draft, proofread, and send out an email with a few solid questions about specific issues or topics that are relevant to this person's experience. You could send emails to a few different people who you regard as potential mentors. While you may not hear back from everyone, there's a good chance someone will respond, even if you don't have a personal referral. This is partly because people love to give advice and feel flattered when someone (especially a person they've never met) asks for theirs. It's also because most people in the nonprofit sector love what they're doing and love talking about their work. If and when you get a response, try to get a dialogue going. Don't inundate the person with emails, but try to start an interesting email exchange with the person. If possible, after a few emails, ask if you can meet for coffee or a quick lunch. This can help establish (or determine if there is) the personal connection that is so important in mentoring relationships.

3. Evaluate the situation

Once you've met with or had a few conversations with a person, you'll most likely know if this is a potential mentor relationship or just an interesting dialogue. If they seem like they might be a great mentor, keep the relationship going through occasional emails, quick phone messages, or monthly coffee meetings. As you develop this relationship, remember to let the person know you appreciate their support; showing your gratitude will help a potential mentor realize how much you value their guidance. Mentorships rarely develop right away; just like any relationship, it will take careful cultivation and strategic planning. But it's absolutely worth it.

If you still aren't convinced, consider the potential situation. At worst, your email or phone call was ignored. At best, you have someone who seems like they'll be able to provide you with invaluable advice on your career, the nonprofit sector, and the myriad connections between the two.

MENTORS AND AGE

The ideal age of a mentor is debatable. A mentor who is within a decade of you, age-wise, may understand where you're coming from and what you're facing in the workplace better than a mentor who is three or four decades older. However, an older mentor often has more experience and connections, both of which are invaluable aspects of a professional mentoring relationship. What it will really come down to is finding a mentor who can help you learn and grow, and with whom you have a natural connection.

From informational interview to mentor relationship?

It's very possible that an informational interview could grow into a mentorship. After all, a mentor is someone who can teach you about a particular job, organization, issue area, or the sector as a whole; not to mention guiding your development of maturity, emotional intelligence, and leadership. Since you're looking for something similar from an informational interviewee, only on a more limited basis, the transition can be quite smooth. This should give you even more incentive to find interesting, exciting people who will agree to an informational interview. That said, your first meeting is probably not the best time to ask directly about a mentoring relationship--these need time to develop! Instead, in an informational interview, try asking if they have/had a mentor, how that relationship was developed, and any advice they can offer on finding a mentor --they may nominate themselves in the process.

Along with intentionally searching for a mentor, you can also make yourself a prime candidate as someone a professional would like to mentor. Here are some ways:

- **Work hard**: No one wants to help someone who doesn't look like they're willing to take the initiative and do good work.
- **Be a mentor**: This will not only connect you to new people and networks, but will allow you to understand what it is like being a mentor… and what can make or break a mentoring relationship.
- **Listen!** Ask good questions and engage professionals in conversation. Asking follow-up questions and showing interest may motivate someone to reach out to mentor you.
- **Take on leadership roles**: By taking advantage of opportunities like board service, volunteer projects, and roles within professional associations or organizations, you'll come in contact with other leaders in the sector, many of whom you wouldn't have met otherwise. These are some of the best potential mentors as you already have something in common with them and you are in position to draw on their experiences and advice as you develop your own leadership skills.

Keep in mind that you don't have to limit yourself to just one. Each mentor will be able to provide you with different perspectives on various aspects of your career. Similarly, if you have more than one mentor, you have the potential to connect to a broader range of people from your mentors' networks.

If you already have a mentor, are actively pursuing one, or are just thinking about how to begin this process, keep in mind that you will need to invest time to research, develop, and cultivate this relationship. However, with the perspective, advice, and connections you will potentially gain from such an endeavor, it is an important aspect of a job search, but an even more essential element of your long-term career planning.

Education

With the dramatic increase in the number of nonprofit-specific programs, certificate courses, and specializations, there is a broader range of education options than ever before for aspiring or working nonprofit professionals. This is a great indicator that interest and investment in working in the nonprofit sector is substantial and sustained. People looking to strengthen their nonprofit candidacy and their ability to do good work in the sector should consider taking advantage of this growing diversity of educational opportunities.

Furthering your education strengthens your candidacy for nonprofit positions because you will gain a broader and more in-depth perspective of the sector as a whole as well as of specific issue areas of interest. In addition, it demonstrates your com-

A MENTOR BY ANY OTHER NAME...

the GREAT DEBATE

When you find someone you think could be a great mentor for you, what is the next step? Do you sit down with them and ask them to be your mentor? Send them an email? Pass them a note with 'Yes' and 'No' checkboxes? If coming right out and asking someone to be your mentor feels awkward, a professional can still be your mentor without there being an official "Will you be my mentor?" discussion. After all, a mentor is someone who helps you grow and develop in a particular professional area. This kind of relationship often develops naturally without the need to put a formal title on it.

mitment to the work of the sector. While further education may not be for everyone, there are so many options that anyone can find a program to suit their goals. Because of this range of options, *education will be defined broadly in this chapter* as opportunities that provide specific competencies as well as theoretical, analytical, and/or practical knowledge about the history, current situation, and future needs in your specific field and the sector as a whole.

With such a broad scope of educational opportunities, there is often a desire to find a list of preferred options (this is frequently manifested in the dilemma of weighing programs that interest you against various rankings). However there is no *one* "best fit" for everyone—it's truly an individual choice. As you consider furthering your education, it is important to determine what works best for you, your situation, and your future goals and aspirations.

"There is no one 'best fit' for everyone when it comes to educational options–it's truly an individual choice."

Benefits of education

There are five primary benefits of education for people pursing nonprofit careers. Keep in mind that furthering your education can yield a variety of other personal benefits to you.

1. Building knowledge
2. Expanding your network
3. Gaining real-world experience
4. Strengthening your resume
5. Enhancing your professional opportunities

1. Building knowledge

While understanding the minutiae of nonprofit tax status, the history of the U.S. nonprofit sector, or the varying theoretical approaches to nonprofit work may not be a requirement of most jobs, having at least a general knowledge of the ins and outs of the sector and your issue area will be very beneficial. This can help you clarify where and how you see yourself fitting professionally, allow you to discuss issues with more depth and confidence, and assist you in recognizing professional connections and opportunities.

2. Expanding your network

Deliberately finding ways to connect to classmates, professors, administrators, guest speakers, teaching assistants, employers, and alumni expands your network and should be an intentional part of your education. Tapping your network is one of the surest ways to get a job, particularly in the nonprofit sector (see **Chapter Four** for more details on networking). The campus career service office can also help connect you to alumni working in positions, organizations, or issue areas in which you are interested. While taking a class, completing a certificate, or working toward a degree, relationship building should be a conscious priority alongside your coursework.

3. Gaining real-world experience

For nonprofit employers, evidence of real-world experience differentiates candidates who understand the actual day-to-day work of the sector from those who have book knowledge of it. Not all education options offer real-world experience. If this is important to you—especially if you have not worked in the nonprofit sector or in your field of interest—be sure to look for options that include internships or projects with local organizations, or other opportunities to get hands-on experience. Often, professors who work or consult with nonprofits have established ways to get their students accepted as interns at these partner organizations. An education that combines practical experience with theory will also help distinguish you from candidates whose exposure to nonprofits has been limited to the classroom.

Another way that educational programs offer practical, real-world experience is through service-learning, an educational technique that combines classroom study with field work. This is becoming increasingly popular and can provide specific project-based experience in just about any field. If, for example, you take a course on community development, a practical component could be designing and conducting a survey that maps community access to public transport. While this is coursework, it is also real-world experience and community service that you can (and should!) put on your resume.

4. Strengthening your resume

Many job postings will specify a particular degree, certification, or proficiency that is important (though perhaps not required) for the position. While these qualifications alone will not get you the job (unless they are required), they can distinguish you from other candidates. Even taking a single course on a subject can bolster your resume. If you are pursuing a position that involves a specific topic you've studied, including your coursework (briefly) in your resume can communicate your commitment to and intellectual engagement with that issue. See **Chapter Eight** for more information on writing resumes and cover letters.

5. Enhancing your professional opportunities

Statistics show that salaries are generally commensurate with level of education or certification: the higher the level of education, the higher the salary. While there is no guarantee that this will be the case in every situation, it is worth exploring which educational options have the best chance of increasing your earning potential and broadening your career options. Whether in regard to getting a promotion, switching organizations, or working in a different issue area, education can sometimes be key to movement within the sector.

Should you continue your education?

While the benefits of furthering your education are plentiful, doing so may not be the best option if it's only a default choice. If you're unsure of your next career move, in a dead-end job, or looking to switch sectors without any nonprofit experience, it's easy to say, "I think I'm going back to grad school" or "I'm planning on taking classes from my local community college" because you'll likely get nods of approval or pats on the back. This feels good, especially if you're unsure of your other options.

What do you want from your education?

For you, further education may:
- Be required for your desired professional field such as healthcare, law, teaching, and social work to name a few—fields where practitioners must have certification, licensure, or a degree
- Allow you to improve your career by bolstering your responsibility and/or income-earning potential
- Help you make a career transition from one role to another
- Serve to satisfy your intellectual curiosity and fuel your passion
- Get you the skills you need to do your job better
- Demonstrate to others your interest in and commitment to build new, necessary skills
- Help you test the waters before enrolling in a graduate degree program
- Help you complete pre-requisite courses that you'll need for grad school
- Let you refresh your knowledge in a specific area
- Give you an opportunity to look deeply at an issue area you care about
- Create opportunities for you to…

Spending time to assess your motivations for furthering your education will allow you to recognize what type of education will best help you reach your goals.

EDUCATION PROVIDES NO GUARANTEES As outlined in this chapter, there are a multitude of benefits to pursuing further education. One of the benefits may be increased professional options. However, education alone will not get you a job.

As you consider your educational options, keep in mind that a class, a certification, or a degree may distinguish you from other candidates, allow you to apply for higher level positions, and give you a greater understanding of the sector, but it will not automatically get you your dream job.

Plan ahead

While there are many benefits to further education, it is not a decision to take lightly. Plan ahead by assessing your goals, knowing your limitations, and researching your options.

1. Set goals

First, determine as specifically as possible what it is you're looking to get out of your educational experience. Try to hone in on particular knowledge and skills you hope to gain or strengthen. Do you want to better understand nonprofit management or financial accounting, the history of the sector, or a particular issue (i.e., education or international human rights law)? Do you want to develop skills in counseling, grantwriting, planning, or policy development? Are your professional expectations for learning in a particular course of study realistic (e.g., can you learn enough about accounting in a one-day seminar to take on certain tasks at work, or to impress an employer enough to receive a promotion or new position)?

Other reasons for advancing your education may include increasing your earning potential, shifting to a new specialty area, or expanding your network—just be sure to know your goals going in.

2. Know your limitations

Once you clarify your goals, realistically assess your limitations before researching your options. These limitations are mostly logistical but they can be helpful in focusing your research.

Financial

To assess your financial situation, you should have a sense for how much money you (and your family) will need to live on, what kind of financial safety net you need in case of an emergency, whether you plan to continue working while studying, or if you intend to go to school full-time to immerse yourself in the experience.

Begin by developing a budget for yourself. Determine your monthly expenses (housing, food, insurance, etc.), add in the estimated monthly cost of your intended education, and try to live on that budget for a few months. Also consider your eventual expenses once you graduate. Is it feasible? Regardless of how you go about assessing your financial readiness, be sure to make it a priority as it will undoubtedly impact your options.

Geographic

How flexible are you with where you can live? Can you move across the country (or another part of the world) tomorrow or are you firmly rooted in your community because of family, friends, a job, or other commitments? Understanding where you can go will be an important variable in assessing where you will apply. If you have no geographic constraints, wonderful—but recognize that it will make your search broader and a bit more complicated. If you're rooted in your area or need to stay in a specific city or region, your search will be more restricted at the outset. Be as open as your personal situation allows so you can take advantage of the broadest range of options possible.

Time constraints

What kind of time can you commit to furthering your education? Can you de-

HOW MUCH CAN YOU AFFORD?

Are you able to finance an entire degree or should you start by taking one or two courses? Would a $50 community course help you reach your goals, or do you need the credits that come with a $400 university class? Are you willing to take out loans, are you eligible for financial aid, or do you have enough in savings? If you are considering a degree program or certification that could take months or years to complete and requires a significant percentage of your annual income, it's advisable to assess your financial situation early in the process.

Financial self-assessment

Idealist.org partnered with the National Endowment for Financial Education (NEFE) to create a free guide to financial self-assessment called "Making a Difference: A Guide to Personal Profit in a Nonprofit World."

Find it here: www.idealist.org/en/career/financialadvice.html

vote two full-time years to an associates degree or a masters program, or will a class one night a week for two months be all you can balance? Whether you can take one Saturday class a year, a few courses at your local university each semester, or a full-time two year degree program, you can locate educational opportunities that will meet your goals and time constraints. This is an important consideration as you begin to identify educational opportunities, as it will help make your search a bit more manageable.

3. Research your options

Once you're aware of why you want to further your education, as well as your financial, geographic, and time constraints, you can start researching. In the following sections, you'll find resources for specific educational options, issues to consider, and general benefits of each option. As you are researching, keep in mind that these are very general considerations that do not take into account what you are looking for, where you are coming from, and what you will get out of any experience. Peruse the suggestions, do your research, and be ready (and excited) for the unexpected.

Degree options

If a formal degree is something you are considering, there are a few general options that you have, with a multitude of variables within each grouping. The common formal degrees are: associates, bachelors, and graduate degrees. Each is discussed below, and the accompanying "Learn More" sidebars offer additional avenues for research and exploration of these options.

Associates degree

Associates degrees are traditionally offered by community and junior colleges as well as vocational schools, but can also be an option at four-year colleges and universities. In general, they are applied degrees geared toward employment in a specific field that can be broken down into two categories: transfer and terminal (also known as career/professional). Transfer degrees provide a foundation for a bachelors degree by allowing students to complete general education requirements before transferring to a four-year university. Students in terminal degree programs are able to graduate with an associates degree upon completion of the required credits and are then qualified to work in specific positions, particularly positions within healthcare, education, and business.

There are a range of associates degrees, with the most common being Associate of Arts, Science, or Teaching. Full-time students typically complete associates degrees in one or two years. Given the following six factors, associates degrees can be an accessible option for sector switchers and people without a high school degree.

Degree options

For a more detailed discussion of each degree option, be sure to check out Idealist's Public Service and Graduate Education Resource Center. It includes information on issues such as taking classes on campus versus distance or online learning programs, being a full- or part-time student, and the pros and cons of working while getting a degree.

www.idealist.org/psgerc

Consider this if you're thinking about a nonprofit career:

1. Tuition tends to be lower in community colleges.

2. Many students receive their degrees within two years (full-time).

3. Associates degrees are highly sought after in health care and many business areas, as well as other fields where this is the educational requirement.

4. Community colleges tend to be more flexible in terms of time to complete the degree and course schedules (including night classes).

5. Community colleges have a strong connection to the local community and are likely to offer excellent networking opportunities.

6. In general, there are no prerequisites for students looking to earn an associates degree.

Good to know:

- Many community colleges allow people who have not earned a high school diploma to take college courses that fulfill high school requirements while simultaneously earning credits toward the college certificate or degree.

- Proprietary schools, also called "private career schools" can offer similar courses as community colleges, but are not always as regulated as community colleges. If you are considering taking courses at a non-community college institution, be sure to thoroughly research the reputation of the school, ensure that your degree will be recognized by employers, and compare tuition rates to other schools in the area.

Bachelors degree

A bachelors degree is an undergraduate academic degree awarded for a course of study or major that generally lasts four years. Today, the most common undergraduate degrees awarded are the Bachelor of Arts (B.A.) and the Bachelor of Science (B.S.). Many liberal arts colleges and universities award a B.A. for all degrees conferred, regardless of the subject (English, Biology, History, etc.). Often these schools only offer academic (rather than vocational or "applied") courses. Schools that offer pre-professional, four-year programs such as finance or nursing often award a B.S. degree.

Some of the larger institutions offer undergraduate courses that focus specifically on nonprofit-related topics, like Human Resources Management in Nonprofit Organizations, Introduction to Nonprofit Leadership, and Nonprofit Financial Administration and Resource Development. However, rather than focusing your credits (and time!) on nonprofit-specific classes, consider broadening your skills and knowledge during your undergraduate education. Nonprofit professionals often take on a diverse range of responsibilities within an organization and an undergraduate education is the perfect time to develop and hone a variety of skills and experiences. Take classes or find opportunities on and off campus to develop strong writing skills, a general knowledge of finance and accounting, leadership abilities, strong public

Associates degree

Most states have an Office of Community Colleges. These typically offer online, print, and annual guides to their state community colleges. Try searching for your state's name + "office of community colleges." This office is often based in your state's Board of Education.

American Association of Community Colleges (www.aacc.nche.edu) has a "Community College Finder" that is a clickable map with a quick-view breakdown of the number of tribal, independent, and public colleges in each state. If you click on your state, you can find a state-wide directory as well as a range of other statistics.

U.S. Two-Year Colleges (www.cset.sp.utoledo.edu/twoyrcol.html) offers a clickable map of over 1,000 two-year colleges across the country.

The "**Chronicle Two-Year College Databook**" is a directory of 2,488 accredited two-year colleges, public and private, with their major programs of study (over 900) leading to a certificate, diploma, associate degree, or transfer opportunity. It costs $25 but it's worth checking for this in your local public library to get a sense for the scope of two-year schools. (www.chronicleguidance.com/catalog.asp?prodid=423427)

National Center for Education Statistics provides a school search by geographic location, as well as statistics on enrollment and degrees conferred at a variety of educational institutions. (http://nces.ed.gov)

speaking skills, and then apply your knowledge in real-world settings. If you really want to take advantage of your college's nonprofit course offerings, then be sure to find time outside of class to apply and further develop these invaluable skills; you can also investigate whether your school has an American Humanics (www.humanics.org) program on campus that can help you prepare for work in the nonprofit sector.

Consider this if you're thinking about a nonprofit career:

1. Take a range of classes to deliberately develop the transferable skills that nonprofit (or any!) hiring managers are always seeking: communication, leadership, project management, collaboration, etc.

2. Take advantage of the campus Service-Learning Center to find volunteer and service opportunities. This will help you demonstrate your commitment on your resume, gain a sense of whether or not the nonprofit sector is a place you'd like to work, network with other students and community members, and gain valuable real-world experience. Find ways to get off campus and into the community!

3. Use your career service office to help you connect with alumni, professors, or people in the community who may be willing to give you 30 minutes for an informational interview (see **Chapter Four**), help you create an intentional internship or volunteer opportunity, or provide you with invaluable advice on a particular career path or position.

Good to know:

- The College Cost and Reduction Act allows students who serve ten years in a public service career to have their remaining student loans forgiven. The Act's definition of "public service" applies to employees of nonprofit legal advocacy groups and other IRS-recognized tax-exempt charities, as well as public school teachers, public health workers, and law enforcement and government employees. You can read the full bill at www.govtrack.us/congress/bill.xpd?bill=h110-2669 and a good summary of it at www.nasfaa.org/Publications/2007/G2669summary091007.html.

- Because competition for nonprofit positions is increasing, a bachelors degree is often the minimum education requirement for entry-level positions.

Graduate degree

For admission, graduate schools generally require an undergraduate degree in a related field or certain coursework that demonstrates knowledge in specific areas. There are two general types of degrees awarded in grad school: masters and doctorate degrees.

Masters degree

Masters degree programs typically focus more in depth on a specific field of study than bachelors degree programs. They generally take two years to complete (full-

Bachelors degree

For information on how to apply for and if you could qualify to receive loan forgiveness by going into a public service career, check out www.IBRinfo.org for details on the new legislation that will go into effect in 2009.

School rankings

There are plenty of ranking systems that are eager to tell you what are the best (without qualification) undergraduate colleges. These systems weigh criteria ranging from freshman SAT scores to campus dining halls to faculty salaries. *Washington Monthly*'s ranking takes a different approach. They framed their survey with the question: "What are reasonable indicators of how much a school is benefiting the country?" They decided on three criteria to answer this question: how well a school "performs as an engine of social mobility (ideally helping the poor to get rich rather than the very rich to get very, very rich), how well it does in fostering scientific and humanistic research, and how well it promotes an ethic of service to country."

To see a "best of" list that looks very different from the well known *U.S. News* ranking, see:

www.washingtonmonthly.com/features/2006/0609.collegechart.html

time) and may be course- or research-based, although they are often a mixture of the two. Many, but not all, masters programs require a thesis.

If you are considering a masters degree that will benefit you in your nonprofit career, there are a number of options. Below are five very general descriptions of masters degrees that are traditionally associated with nonprofit careers. However, other programs may be more appropriate to pursue depending on your career goals within the nonprofit sector such as Master of Education, Nursing, Divinity, or Public Health.

Masters of Public Administration (MPA): This degree provides students with an understanding of government and nonprofit management and is a good option for individuals interested in public service careers.

Masters of Public Policy (MPP): This degree provides students with a background in analyzing and evaluating information to solve policy issues. These programs usually emphasize statistics, finance, program evaluation, and economics coursework and can be applied in either government or nonprofit careers.

Masters of Urban Planning (MPU): This degree focuses on environmental planning; city revitalization; land use; housing, community, and economic development; and planning in developing countries. The career choices associated with this degree range from international aid organizations to local homeless shelters and housing agencies.

Masters of Social Work (MSW): This degree focuses on helping people and communities identify, prevent, and solve problems. It is often required for any mid to executive level social work position. The careers associated with this degree include child protection, hospice care, school social work, and mental health and substance abuse counseling.

Masters of Business Administration (MBA): This degree provides the option to specialize in a particular functional area or area of interest. It's becoming more common for MBA programs to offer a variety of nonprofit-focused specializations such as Social Enterprise or a concentration in Public and Nonprofit Management.

Doctorate degree

The most common doctorate is the Doctor of Philosophy or Ph.D., which typically demonstrates a person's competence in research, qualifies them to become a professor, and/or prepares them to play other roles (such as developing policy) in the nonprofit, public, and private sectors.

Graduate degrees

Idealist.org's **Public Service Graduate Education Resource Center** can help you consider how to link graduate study with your future public service career. It also offers no-nonsense advice on a full range of issues faced by potential graduate students. www.idealist.org/psgerc

National Association of Schools of Public Affairs and Administration (NASPAA, www.naspaa.org)

Seton Hall University has a catalogue of 186 graduate education programs with concentrations in nonprofit management which is searchable by degree and location. http://tltc.shu.edu/npo/list.php?sort=state&type=gr

Social Enterprise Reporter has an overview of MBA programs that focus on nonprofit management and social entrepreneurship. www.sereporter.com/?q=node/251

U.S. News & World Report provides a ranking of over 12,000 graduate programs in a number of disciplines. http://grad-schools.usnews.rankingsandreviews.com/grad

Net Impact's "Business as Unusual" is a guide to MBA programs that have a social and environmental focus. www.netimpact.org/displaycommon.cfm?an=1&subarticlenbr=2288

You may also be familiar with professional doctorates such as the MD (*medicinae doctor*) earned by medical school graduates, and the JD (*juris doctor*) earned by law school graduates. Numerous other doctoral degrees exist including practitioner's doctorates.

It takes between four and eight years to earn a doctorate degree, depending on the program, whether the student has already earned a masters degree (or is coming straight from completing an undergraduate degree), and the dissertation process.

Consider this if you're thinking about a nonprofit career:

1. Graduate degrees are often required for management level positions, particularly in social work, higher education, and medical fields.
2. Competition for nonprofit jobs is becoming more intense and, at times, a graduate degree can make the difference between two otherwise equally qualified candidates.

Continuing education options

Lifelong learning can take a variety of forms, from certificate programs to individual courses to community classes. These options can be great choices if you are looking to enhance your skill set, if you'd like to get a sense of a particular subject area before starting on a degree, or if nonprofit work is something you'd like to learn more about without committing a lot of time and money.

Certificate programs

There are many certificate programs offered through two and four-year colleges and graduate schools, but you can also work toward certification through professional associations, online degree granting institutions, management support organizations, and government agencies. A certificate program is generally a vocationally focused set of courses in a particular field that leads to certification status or license to practice. Prerequisites for certification can include any combination of the following: coursework, a degree, passing examinations, and/or successfully completing an internship or other experiential learning component.

Certificate programs
You can read more about certificate programs in the Idealist Public Service Graduate Education Resource Center at: www.idealist.org/psgerc

Certification can be an alternative to a graduate degree or part of your graduate education. Professional certification acknowledges to peers and potential employers that you have attained a certain level of expertise in your field. It may also enable you to legally practice in your state, enhance a skill set you are already using in your current work, and help you specialize within your field.

Professional associations, graduate schools, community education programs, and government agencies set the terms of certification. Coursework, examinations, and experience may all contribute to your eligibility for becoming certified.

Individual classes

There are a variety of reasons to take individual classes at a community college or university. Aside from life-long learning, participating in individual courses can help you prepare for a degree program, master material better and faster than simply reading on your own, discuss ideas with others, brush up on a subject, and understand principles in a field more clearly. They are also a useful way to test the waters in a subject without investing a lot of your time and money.

Community classes and workshops

Most cities and many smaller communities have organizations that offer nonprofit-specific classes and workshops. These classes are taught by local experts and also often take into account the local nonprofit landscape within the scope of the topic. Classes offered by community-based organizations range from traditional nuts and bolts of the nonprofit sector to topics that are relevant for all sectors. For example, an organization in Portland, OR—Technical Assistance for Community Services (TACS, www.tacs.org)—provides training and consulting resources for nonprofit organizations. They offer classes ranging from a clinic on tax-exempt status to a networking night titled "Safe Spaces: Conflict Resolution in Multicultural Workplaces."

Community classes
You can read more about the value of community classes in the Idealist Public Service Graduate Education Resource Center at: www.idealist.org/psgerc

Community classes are an ideal way to increase your knowledge in a specific area and meet people in your local nonprofit community while generally paying a lower fee than at a college or university. You can find out about community classes in your area by contacting your local nonprofit association. If you don't know your local nonprofit association, you can find it by going to the National Council of Nonprofit Associations (NCNA, www.ncna.org).

Beyond the classroom

As you consider how, when, and where to pursue your education, double check to make sure that you're doing it because you want to—not because others expect it of you. While it is great to be able to put courses, certificates, and/or degrees on a resume, real-world experience is often as (or more) highly valued than academic work in the nonprofit sector because of the hands-on nature of the work.

For this reason, your educational path shouldn't be limited to the classroom or coursework-based options discussed in this chapter. Experiential education opportunities such as term-of-service programs, travel adventures, or intentional volunteering projects can help you gain skills, knowledge, experience, and professional opportunities, as well as strengthen your network.

Conclusion

There are a multitude of ways to get involved with the nonprofit community in order to strengthen your job candidacy: interactive experiences like volunteering, interning, and serving on a board; more formalized opportunities like term-of-service programs, fellowships, and professional associations; and ways to expand your knowledge of the sector like reading industry publications and exploring further education options. No matter how you go about increasing the likelihood that a nonprofit employer will notice your application for a position, keep in mind that your ultimate objective is to not only appeal to an employer but also to make sure that you are intentionally engaging in activities that resonate with who you want to be and what you hope to accomplish. While nonprofit hiring professionals have identified key life experiences that they look for when making hiring decisions (like volunteer experience, internships, or fundraising skills), make sure that you are strengthening your candidacy for your own sake and not just for the sake of a particular organization. This holistic approach will help ensure that you are the kind of well rounded and intentional candidate that nonprofit organizations seek.

 Make sure that you are engaging in activities that resonate with who you want to be and what you want to accomplish."

SUMMARY

During your new career search, you need to explore several ways to make yourself a stronger candidate. Given the **statistics about what nonprofit hiring managers seek** in candidates, assess where your experiences and skills match their criteria and understand where you might have some gaps to fill (page 72). Then consider these **nine ways to strengthen yourself and your search**:

Volunteering. There are a myriad of benefits to volunteering, from connecting your passions and interests with action, to raising your visibility within an organization and the community. Nonprofit hiring professionals often look to the level of volunteerism as a way to gauge a candidate's commitment to a cause (pages 73-74).

Finding or creating an **internship** for yourself with an organization that interests you. Internships are useful for professionals of all ages as they allow you to work on specific projects and develop key skill areas. These kinds of experiences and skills will bolster your nonprofit appeal (pages 74-75).

Exploring **fellowship program opportunities**. A wide range of programs exist both domestically and internationally, and offer prestige, connections, and often a competitive stipend (pages 76-77).

Participating in a **term-of-service program**. For someone wishing to enter the nonprofit workforce, even at a mid-career point, participating in a program like AmeriCorps, Teach For America, or the Peace Corps can be a great starting place (pages 77-80).

Serving on a nonprofit **board of directors** is a way to get involved with a nonprofit from the inside. Board service is both a great networking tool and an opportunity to get a big picture perspective of nonprofit governance (pages 81-82).

Researching **professional associations**. These institutions are a part of the network you will need to build up as an emerging professional in the field (page 82).

Following nonprofit news through **industry publications**. Familiarity with key issues and experts in the nonprofit sector is an important part of learning about the field (page 82).

Mentoring relationships offer you a great opportunity to learn from someone with more experience than you in your chosen field. Mentoring someone new to the field is also a great way to pass on some of your accumulated knowledge (pages 83-85).

There are a plethora of **education options** which can give you theoretical as well as practical knowledge, as well as a wealth of personal and professional benefits. It's important to consider your personal circumstances as you think about continuing your education, while also being as definite as you can about what you want to achieve with your studies (pages 85-95).

CHAPTER SIX

Tools for the job search

Researching *all* the opportunities in your chosen location

In this chapter you will:

- Learn to use the internet's wealth of information to research and connect with people and organizations.

- Start your search by learning as much as you can about your preferred geographic area (even if you are searching locally).

- Continue your search by getting to know the local nonprofit sector. Learning about the major local players, consultants, networks and listservs, and other key aspects will better prepare you for the various types of interviews you may conduct.

- Consider a set of questions designed to weigh the pros and cons of relocating, if you are conducting a long-distance search.

- Explore the most effective ways to maximize your time visiting a new location.

- Think about other ways to make a long-distance transition, including tech tools that "shorten" the distance.

- Learn about the challenges of searching for career options abroad.

Using the internet as a job search tool (not a job search solution)

Simply put, a successful job search must involve getting offline and getting out in the community. Plan to meet many new people, make connections, and leave positive impressions! That said, you'll need tools to help you find those individuals, organizations, and resources that will help you to connect. This is where online search tools come in.

While the Idealist.org team hopes you find our website helpful, we also know that it's crucial to go offline and into the "real" world. The prevalence of internet usage has tricked some job seekers into thinking they can find their dream job by sitting in front of a computer diligently launching well crafted, individualized cover letters and resumes into cyberspace. And while that has its place, the savvy seeker must be more proactive. As you explore this chapter and learn some new ways to use the internet as a job search tool (but not a job search solution) keep this in mind: job seekers who shoot off numerous resumes every day are now a dime a dozen. In a

Job hunting is like car hunting

Think of your nonprofit job search the same way you might think about the process of buying a car. First, you go online to collect information: comparable car prices, current research, and available vehicles. After you've done your research, you typically seek out knowledgeable people in your network to ask about your purchase. This is your chance to confirm your notes and make sure that you've asked all the necessary questions. Finally, it's time to go and talk to the sellers, kick the tires, take the cars for a test drive, and make sure that what you see is what you want to get. This process of online, in-network, and on-site research is the same for the job search. And just as it's all about timing when you're buying a car (what's available compared to what you need), the same is true for the job hunt; both searches take time to find the right fit.

hiring market where at least 20 to 30 resumes can arrive in a hiring professional's inbox for every one open position, the odds quickly stack up against the job seeker who doesn't get offline to make personal contacts in the community. In other words, because of information overload, job seekers are victims of the information age as much as they're aided by the abundance of resources just a mouse click away.

The Search, Part I
Location, location, location

Searching for opportunities in the nonprofit sector is quite similar whether you plan to look in your current location or somewhere else. The key to local and long-distance searches is to learn more about the nonprofit sector in your target area in order to foster in-person connections.

Your first step, regardless of where you are looking, is to see how your preexisting network can help you in your search (see **Chapter Four** for more details on making the most of your local network). If you are considering moving to a new place, figure out how your friends, family, and alumni network can help by referring you to people or organizations in your target geographical area. Check to see if any alumni associations, professional associations, or interest groups that you currently belong to have a branch there. You should tap your personal and professional network well before you start doing online or text-based research on your new location; your network is truly your best asset when looking for a job in a new location.

Your next step is to learn even more about the community in which you are searching. In fact, even if you are looking in your current community, you should still strive to learn more. No matter how long you've lived there, you may never have thought to seek information from or interact with business organizations, local speakers series, resources at your library and city or county office, community college faculty, neighborhood associations, and even tourist offices.

If you are looking at moving to a new community, contact the county or city government office (you can start with their official website) as well as the local chamber of commerce to see what free resources they have available for people moving into the area. Many long-distance job searchers forget the simple fact that local businesses and government really want new people to move to town. New people mean more customers for businesses and a bigger tax pool for the government. There are usually a lot of local promotional materials and resources for people who are new to the area or considering a move.

Using my Japan and California networks... in Oregon

When my wife and I decided to move to Portland, OR after four years in San Francisco and two years in Japan, we felt pretty uncertain of our professional prospects in a new town. We both had some family in town but no one who worked in the industries that interested us. Fortunately, within a matter of weeks, most of our worries were completely dispelled.

As we started emailing friends and former colleagues about our intentions, we were inundated with replies consisting of variations on the same theme: "Portland is great. I have a good friend/colleague/old roommate who works at a nonprofit there. You should get in touch with them." Through our formal—and more significantly, our informal—networks, we were put in touch with more people than we had time to contact.

Between our newfound network of friends of friends (some of whom we had met previously at large social functions, like weddings), volunteering in several local nonprofits, and a few networking events (including the Portland Idealist Nonprofit Career Fair), we were able to start finding meaningful work within a few months—well before our savings ran out.

– Steven Joiner, Director, Career Transitions Progam, Idealist.org

The Search, Part II
Getting to know the local nonprofit sector

Your next step is to familiarize yourself with the local nonprofit sector—even before researching nonprofit job opportunities. Think of a local or long-distance job search first as mapping the organizational landscape. The following resources will help you to see what organizations are in your target region:

Idealist.org (www.idealist.org): Remember that you can use Idealist.org as an organizational search tool. From the homepage, click on the Organizations link and enter in your search criteria. At first, use "State or Province" and "City or Town" as the search criteria and choose "Within: 50 miles." The number of nonprofits that come up will likely surprise (and maybe even overwhelm) you. Depending on the size of the local population and the strength of the nonprofit sector in your location, you could end up with hundreds of results. Use these results to see which nonprofits are in the area and then make a list of the organizations that you'd like to contact for an informational interview. While this can definitely take a while, it is one of the best ways to gain an understanding of what's available in your target area. If you've completed the Self Awareness, Career Tracks, and Four Lens assessment activities in **Chapter Three**, you will have a good idea of which issue areas you can use as a search filter. Do this filtered search only after you've gotten a bit of perspective on the scope of the local nonprofit sector.

Once you have the list of nonprofits that interest you, you'll need to kick into networking mode. Set up a few informational interviews (see **Chapter Four** for more on this topic) or offer to volunteer (or intern) with an organization—you'll quickly find many more open doors and develop a much larger local network of people who know that you are looking for work. Even if the group you'd like to work with has no specific volunteer or intern positions open, you can propose a particular project or task that you think you'd be suited to help them complete. Consider your strengths and remember that nonprofit staff members are sometimes overwhelmed with things to do. Be sure to state that you're happy to scale your idea according to their needs and capacity to manage volunteers.

Additionally, make sure to sign up for Idealist's daily email alerts to learn about current jobs, volunteer and internship openings, events, resources (and more) near your target location. This will give you a sense of the breadth of issues and activities of importance in the local community.

GuideStar.org (www.guidestar.org): GuideStar is the best place on the internet to get a good sense of U.S.-based nonprofit organizations' financial picture. You

SO MANY RESEARCH OPTIONS

As you're researching organizations, either while looking for jobs or as you prepare for an interview, look in unconventional places! Using Facebook's or LinkedIn's search features, look for people in your network who may work for organizations you're exploring. Talk with people in your career center or alumni association to look for contacts in similar industries who may live close by. If you can still access your college library's online services, try using Lexis-Nexis to rapidly search articles in the press that feature nonprofit organizations. Business publications and local newspapers often cover the work of nonprofits you may not have heard of. A Google News search can also help with this. There is no such thing as too much information!

–Valinda Lee

Volunteering

You can learn more about volunteerism and strategies for volunteer management at these online resource centers:

Idealist Volunteer Resource Center
www.idealist.org/volunteer

Idealist Volunteer Management Resources Center
www.idealist.org/vmrc

can use GuideStar to search an organization's 990 tax forms and help answer a variety of questions about the organization: Are they growing right now? Did their budget go up and down significantly over the last few years? How much money do they pay top staff? Are they the kind of organization you've identified as wanting to work with in the Four Lens exercise (see **Chapter Three**)?

United Way (www.unitedway.org): Start by exploring groups supported by the local branch of the United Way. These groups have been vetted by the local staff and will have one additional source of funding via the United Way's local workplace giving program.

National Council of Nonprofit Associations (www.ncna.org): This is a network of 41 state and regional nonprofit associations that offers links to state nonprofit chapters and regional nonprofit resources.

Craig's List (www.craigslist.org): This popular website is one place to look for jobs in the nonprofit sector, but is indispensable for finding local events and community groups.

Charity Navigator (www.charitynavigator.org): While this site is intended to help potential donors evaluate charities, it can be a great resource to assess the financial health of over 5,000 U.S.-based organizations.

Universities and community colleges: If you've graduated from a college, contact your alma mater's career center; most campuses now also work with alumni. As well, there is likely to be a community college in your target location (near or far) along with area universities. Career centers (especially at the community college level) are usually open to people who want to ask a few questions about local opportunities or pick up some materials. Another great option is to find local community college and university professors who work on nonprofit issues. Professors and staff are often willing to meet and talk about local resources and networks. Also keep in mind that rural areas without a nearby college campus are not necessarily outside the realm of higher education. You should still look for the nearest colleges and universities to see if they partner with local nonprofits.

Local listservs and newspapers: Most urban areas also have a local nonprofit listserv or organization that works to support and promote nonprofits in the area. Many local newspapers (urban or rural) regularly report on the surrounding nonprofit community as well as featuring nonprofit opportunities in their Classifieds sections.

Further ideas on research
Research is a critical part of the nonprofit career search. You can find more research tactics in several chapters of this book:

Chapter Three has advice on researching your potential salary range.

Chapter Seven explains how to research and evaluate organizational culture, while **Chapter Nine** has tips on researching an organization before your job interview.

Chapter Ten includes useful advice on researching an organization's compensation package so you can negotiate more effectively.

THE OFT-FORGOTTEN PRINTED WORD
If you are exploring a new location, think about the wealth of print media that can help you get a good sense of your new home. See what regional history books or well-written memoirs exist to help you understand your location's history. Also see if your destination has a regional magazine as a way to explore the local food, arts, and culture. Consider looking for travel books (including camping, hiking, and other outdoor activity guides) written about your new location. Even if you are moving to town, you will find tourist resources invaluable for a long time after you arrive.

An internet search is one way to find these resources, but a more efficient way to locate local nonprofit resources is to ask during informational interviews (informational interviews are discussed at length in **Chapter Four**). Questions like, "Are there any local nonprofit resources that I should be aware of in town?" and "What local newspapers or e-newsletters should I read to get a better sense of the nonprofit community?" will uncover where the locals go.

As you are researching, don't worry whether organizations have jobs available. During this phase of the search, you are simply looking at the range of resources, organizations, and opportunities available to you in your target location.

From a distance: Finding a job or nonprofit organization "somewhere else"

Long-distance, remote job searching is tough work. Job searches can be stressful and frustrating, and the more distance you add to your search, the more difficult that search can get. This is not to say that long-distance searches are impossible or not worth the effort. Despite the inherent challenges in looking for a job remotely, people successfully relocate all the time. Keep in mind that, just as the level of difficulty increases for long-distance job searches, the level of planning and preparation should also increase. If you go about it deliberately, you may find yourself in a great new city with a great new nonprofit career.

If you are choosing to move

Look at several cities or regions that interest you and rank your destinations based on answers to some of these questions:

Which is more important to you: your job or your location?

Some people can be content almost anywhere if they like what they are doing. Others need to love their location, and job satisfaction comes second. Are you the kind of person who feels meaningful, fulfilling work is more important than where you are doing that work? Or are you the kind of person who would be miserable in a great job located in an area that you dislike? Should you move anyway and see what happens, or do you choose a location that interests you (maybe a bit less) but offers a chance to have a meaningful position?

If you move to a new town, are you willing to move again in a year or two if the job market doesn't offer you the kind of professional nonprofit opportunities you seek? Will your family or partner also find opportunities and happiness?

TAKE FIVE

The process of preparing to relocate can take months. However, it can be broken down into manageable parts depending on how much time you have to start your search.

What should you do if you only have five minutes to start searching? Start with an Idealist search and a Craigslist search. Got five hours? Do an organizational search on Idealist and identify five to ten nonprofits that you want to talk with. Head over to GuideStar.org to do a bit more research and, of course, make sure to look at the organizations' websites.

After five days of researching, you should have a few connections with professionals either in the nonprofits that interest you or with other individuals (college staff, the United Way, nonprofit support organization staff, etc.) and ideally have some informational interviews set up.

By five weeks, you should have gained a good sense of the nonprofit landscape in your area, conducted several informational interviews, added a few new individuals to your network, created a few intentional volunteer or internship experiences, and maybe even started applying for a few jobs.

What makes your target city a more desirable place than where you live now?

Are you falling into the "grass is greener" mentality? Or, are you accurately comparing your current location and the one you're considering? Some "desirability" considerations can be easily researched: for example, proximity to (or distance from) family, cost of living, professional opportunities, outdoor activities, commute estimates, and access to daily amenities. Other factors, like a strong sense of community, are harder to determine in advance. Decide if a geographic change is really necessary in order to accomplish your professional nonprofit goals. Consider asking locals about the drawbacks and opportunities they see for living in the region. You can even draw up a simple personal list of pros and cons (e.g., New York City. Pros: great arts scene, high salaries, good restaurants, many nonprofits. Cons: pollution, high rent, crowds, no personal contacts there).

How is the nonprofit job market in your target city?

You will find the greatest variety of nonprofit organizations in large cities, but these locations also have a higher cost of living and generally a more competitive nonprofit job market. More nonprofits mean more opportunities, but also a greater number of qualified candidates applying for available jobs.

Smaller cities and rural areas tend to have fewer nonprofits, so the competition for jobs is affected by the ratio of qualified applicants to these opportunities. A plus side of smaller cities and rural areas in general is a more affordable cost of living. That said, smaller towns and rural areas will likely have access to a less diversified pool of local funding as well as fewer support organizations. But, depending on your area of interest, rural areas may offer opportunities that cities cannot. If your secret passion is organic farming, you're likely to find some great networks outside big city limits.

What professional and organizational contacts do you already have in your target city?

Tap into your network. Ask around. Do research. You'll be surprised by how many people you are already connected to via your network.

Do you have enough savings to get by if you don't find a job during your first six months in your new location?

How much money do you need to save in order to afford housing costs, transportation, and other living expenses in your target city without a job for four to six months? Moving can be costly, so make sure that you can survive for several months while you get yourself acquainted with your new home. Are you willing to do part-time work of some sort while you search for the perfect next step? A

When both location and job matter

I am happy as a clam in a job that uses my skills, allows me to be creative, and challenges me to build new areas of expertise. Where my job is geographically located means much less to me. I can and have worked in less-than-desirable places where I have no friends at first, where I cannot ride my bike, where there is more pollution than is safe to breathe daily, and where the weather stinks. Yet, if I love my work, I can get used to minor inconveniences like daily smog and lack of bicycling lanes.

My husband, however, is happiest when he lives in the right place. He loves to commute by bike, so it is essential for him to have a bike-friendly location with wide streets, bike lanes, and comprehensive bike maps. He grew up in the Midwest, so now he prefers to live near the coast. He loves mountains, hiking, and camping, and is happy where we can access these activities easily on the weekends. He likes to live among people who are progressive, creative, and kind. He loves clean air. He has lived in cities he did not like, while doing work he adored, and yet was miserable. It's not that his career is unimportant to him. However, he is a teacher–a role that is in demand almost everywhere–so he can afford to be choosy.

His life's happiness is clearly anchored in place, while mine is anchored in work. I was happy to let him choose where we live now–Portland, OR. Initially, the long-distance job search was challenging. I found that hiring managers did not take my application seriously since I was out of state, and not available for in-person interviews. But I persevered and found a position as an AmeriCorps*VISTA Leader for a program based in Portland. After we moved here, my husband began his search for a teaching position. Now we both love working in a place that we love as well.

– Amy Potthast, Director, Service and Graduate Programs, Idealist.org

part-time or temporary job could cover your living expenses while you are networking to find your career position. Just be sure this temporary work allows you enough free time for networking and interviews for your new career position. This "hold it together job" will keep you from panicking and taking the first job that comes along.

Do you have a way out? What if your relocation does not work?

Luckily, in today's interconnected world it is easy to stay in contact with the people in your network. Be sure to stay in touch with former employers, colleagues, and friends who can help you transition back to your present location should your new location not work out. If it doesn't work out at first but you want to persevere, stay positive. Recognize that trial and error is often an important method for finding the best opportunity.

After identifying one or two regions where you'd like to live and which have viable career opportunities, begin the research phase of your search.

If you are forced to move

Perhaps your partner just got a new job in another city or state, or maybe you are moving to take care of a loved one. An involuntary move to another city or region can be extremely difficult: you are leaving behind friends and family, you may not be financially ready for a move, or you may be moving to a location that is less than desirable. In addition, job searches also come with their own challenges. The following advice will hopefully make the prospect of a "forced move" easier.

By starting your search as early as possible and by searching strategically—using preexisting networks, having a polished resume ready before you move, and researching the new job market in advance—you can help minimize the stress of the job search. You can also view this involuntary move as a unique chance to enter into new career path and embrace new career opportunities. Try to focus on the positive aspects of your move. Does your partner's new job pay for the move? Will the cost-of-living difference and a potential salary increase for your partner give you more time to search for a great position? At the very least, check into whether you can deduct your moving expenses from your taxes (see the "Benefits Glossary" section of **Chapter Ten**). If you are moving to care for a sick relative, will you be living with the relative for a while and saving on rent or mortgage payments? Will selling your current home change your economic outlook? Will this move give you a chance to experience a new part of the country?

There are many hidden positives, both for your lifestyle and your career, to a forced move. Keep them in mind (or keep a running list on your refrigerator) and stay

Financial self-assessment

Idealist.org partnered with the National Endowment for Financial Education (NEFE) to create a free guide to financial self-assessment called "Making a Difference: A Guide to Personal Profit in a Nonprofit World."

Find it here: www.idealist.org/en/career/financialadvice.html

focused on making a productive change. Also remember that research and planning will help ensure a successful move, be it voluntary or involuntary. Finally, it should go without saying that dwelling on the negative won't help your move go any more smoothly.

The visit

Once you have a comprehensive organization list for your location, it's time to start setting up informational interviews. Plan to visit your new location for at least three or four days, preferably both weekdays and a weekend. More organizations and other resources will be open during the week, and a weekend will allow you to explore the social scene. During the visit, you'll want to meet with people and discuss organizational opportunities, including volunteering and interning. You ought to be sure that the people who *should* know you are in town *do* know that you are in town—for example, nonprofit organization contacts, leads generated through your network, or local realtors. You can do this trip on a tight budget if you explore midweek airline deals (which often have cheap hotel and rental car packages), stay at budget accommodations (like hostels), and try to "eat in" as much as possible. Even better, consider staying with friends or family in town.

You will be taken more seriously by a potential employer if you demonstrate your intention to move by meeting with nonprofit staff members at the local organization before you start to apply for positions. Simply stating in your initial correspondence, "I am planning to move from Atlanta to Seattle at the end of this month" leaves too many questions and uncertainties for potential employers (Are you really committed to this move? Do you expect your relocation costs to be covered? Are you really committed to this organization or position?). However, if you've already met or spoken to someone at the organization, and you make sure to mention this in your cover letter, then those responsible for hiring are more likely to give your resume serious consideration.

Also, be aware that some nonprofit organizations have never hired outside of their region and are still not open to the idea. Unlike some for-profit companies, many nonprofits are operating with tight budgets and the thought of hiring someone who they perceive as unsure about moving to the area or uncertain to enjoy their new surroundings can feel very risky.

This may be for a variety of reasons:
- They have never needed to look outside of the local market.
- They place particular value on individuals with local expertise and contacts in the community.
- They cannot pay to fly an interviewee to their location.

JUST SHOWING UP COULD BE A BAD IDEA

So, you decide to just up and move, or maybe you had no choice, and now you have to see where you land once you hit the ground. If you do "just show up," make sure you have at least six months worth of living expenses in the bank or that you have a plan for an immediate "hold it together job" that will pay the bills once you arrive. Finding a job you know you don't want to keep for long is sometimes tricky, especially since you should strive to be honest with potential employer.

It takes several months to get acquainted with a new location before you actually move and usually another few months to establish your new networks. If you've not done any research, networking, or planning before you arrive, those "getting started" months are going to be even more necessary. With the wealth of information available on any conceivable location, there is no reason to delay building up knowledge and connections related to your new location months before you load up the moving truck.

- They cannot pay any relocation costs.
- They fear that your lack of an established community network may mean you will leave and return to your existing networks elsewhere.

Other ways to make a long-distance transition

As a job seeker, it is easy to forget about ways to get your foot in the door beyond the traditional approaches like networking, researching, and conducting informational interviews. Some other ways to make a shift include:

- Participating in a term-of-service program (AmeriCorps, Teach For America, Experience Corps) for a year (or two) to establish yourself, gain experience, and make contacts.
- Temping for a local nonprofit (or finding a temp agency that specializes in nonprofit placements).
- Going back to school for a masters degree, Ph.D., or another form of continuing education (see **Chapter Five**'s section on education options).
- Volunteering and interning in your new location to build a local network, demonstrate your interest in organizations, and avoid time gaps in your resume.

Going global

In today's world, international work experience is becoming a valuable commodity on a resume. Long gone are the days when work abroad was seen as a kind of "professional vacation." The linguistic abilities, cultural competency, and international perspectives that you gain working abroad are an asset in any position, international or domestic. So, sometimes it makes sense to go away... far away.

Realistically, starting a career in international nonprofit work will likely mean your initial opportunities are going to be unpaid. In fact, you often need to not only pay your own costs (transport, food, and lodging) but also a program fee that helps the local nonprofit ensure sustainability. Many job seekers frustrate themselves looking for that very elusive first paid international job opportunity. Therefore it makes more sense to begin your international job search by first conducting an international volunteerism search.

To help defray the cost of volunteering abroad, consider tapping your local network in advance (through fundraisers, donations, etc.) so that you can afford to get your foot in the door and, while abroad, begin to seek out paid jobs in the field. Many people also find a satisfying balance of working at a for-profit (teaching, working

THE REALITY OF NONPROFIT DISTANCE HIRING

Nonprofits rarely hire people without meeting them face-to-face first, and most nonprofits cannot afford to fly you in for an interview. This puts the responsibility on you to plan meetings before you move to a new city, especially if you are already applying for jobs.

That said, some professions regularly perform national searches and encourage people from faraway places to submit a cover letter and resume. For example, Student Affairs divisions of many colleges conduct national searches to find qualified candidates. When exploring a new nonprofit career path, ask professionals in the field if long-distance career searches are common.

Local vs. global organizations

Keep in mind while you are looking at international volunteer and work options that you have two opportunities: working with a local organization located in-country or working for an international organization (like the International Red Cross, Doctors Without Borders, the United Nations, or Oxfam) that has field workers in-country. Local organizations have a much more area-specific focus while international organizations offer their staff the opportunity to work in different regions of the world. You should be aware, however, that local organizations may have more difficulty hiring you (as a foreign worker) than they would accommodating you as a volunteer.

for a foreign company, etc.) while using their free time to pursue charitable ends. If you are looking to work abroad with a nonprofit (often called an NGO [for non-governmental organization] or charity), volunteering in a foreign country allows you to develop your professional network, language skills, and understanding of the local culture. Your unpaid work experience will undoubtedly help you enter the paid job market. You might consider your volunteer time as a flexible (and enjoyable!) way to "pay your dues" before you fully understand the lay of the land and can land your dream job. It's also just a nice way to try a variety of roles to see where synergy emerges.

Before you leave

Remember that it will be much more difficult to find work abroad while still at home. Though you are more likely to connect with work once you settle into a certain region, you can use time in your home country to explore the range of organizations located in your target country. Find out if there is a local networking organization in-country for foreigners, use your home country network to see if anyone knows of any international opportunities, and search for local resources (churches, cultural heritage festivals, or internationally oriented cultural and social groups like the Maltese Center in New York) already in your city or area.

The steps described earlier in the national/in-country long-distance search—using your network, researching the location, researching nonprofit organizations, and visiting (as a volunteer, on holiday, or to begin work)—apply equally to an international search.

Once abroad, it will be easier to identify sources of job information. Certain hotels or hostels have message boards where local organizations know to post job openings. Many community organizations act as clearinghouses for news and opportunities, and the local expatriate community can help expand your network.

Volunteering abroad takes a lot of logistical and financial planning. You should start saving money months in advance in order to cover basic expenses for the entire time you plan to volunteer. Hold a fundraiser to allow others to help support your cause. Contact family and friends and see if they can help you pay for your airplane ticket; maybe a relative has frequent flyer miles they can use to help you lower the cost of a ticket. The good news is that all these challenges will add relevant hard and soft skills to your professional toolbox.

Hold a fundraiser
Check out the International Volunteer Programs Association's guide to fundraising in order to help defray the costs of volunteering abroad: www.volunteerinternational.org/fundtips.html

Got a frequent flyer in the family?
Many frequent flyer programs will let members give a frequent flyer ticket to someone else (especially to relatives with the same last name). This is especially useful for frequent flyer members who are just a few thousand miles short of a free ticket and can't reach the milestone before the miles expire. By paying a "topping up" fee to bridge the mileage gap, those miles can help create an affordable ticket for a relative.

Wherever you go, be sure to take with you an openness to learning, comfort with the unpredictable, initiative to explore, and plenty of good humor. In addition, don't forget to pack or set up:

- A notarized copy of your diploma (It doesn't hurt to have diplomas for all your schooling, including high school, even if you've been out of school for years. Some employers require proof of education before they will hire you.)
- References from previous employers
- Writing or work samples
- The usual preparations for any trip abroad:
    * Your passport and any required visas, and a copy of your passport and visas (keep your copies separate from the originals in case your documents are lost or stolen!)
    * A plan to have access to or get emergency funds
    * Travel insurance (see what kind makes the most sense for you and your needs)
    * Vaccinations and other health precautions
    * A support network at home, including leaving a copy of your travel itinerary and contact information with friends or family
- Email electronic versions of any documents (as Word documents and PDFs of scanned materials) to an email account that you can access from any computer. This will ensure that you can make copies easily from any internet café or other public access terminals.

COMMON MISTAKES — **"RELIGIOUS GROUPS ARE ONLY FOR FOLLOWERS OF THAT RELIGION."**

Just because an international service opportunity is run by a religiously affiliated group doesn't necessarily mean that followers of that religion are the only people welcome to apply. While some programs have a faith component, many faith-based groups active in international civic engagement have programs that welcome all individuals looking to make a difference. Don't write off a program simply because it is run by a religious group different from yours without first exploring its structure, the qualifications for applicants, and the opportunities it affords.

Evaluating international volunteer opportunities

The following advice for individuals going abroad through a prearranged opportunity covers the basics, but consider a consultation with relevant officials in your target destination and your home country to discuss the legal, ethical, and political implications of your move.

Always thoroughly research the organization you will be working with before making a commitment. This is especially true when communicating or working with organizations based in another country. Many of the laws protecting our personal information, finances, and identity that we take for granted in the United States do not exist, or are not enforced, abroad. Also make sure to explore the ethical nature of the organization. You want to make sure that the organization is partnering with the local community, that your efforts will be sustained after you leave, and that the impact you have on the community is in fact the kind of impact you intended to have.

 Always thoroughly research the organization you will be working with before making a commitment."

Once you've identified an organization with which you may want to volunteer (either through personal connections or through Idealist.org or another search engine), be sure to thoroughly research the organization. Below are some tips:

Internet research

The first thing you should do is browse the organization's website:

- Try searching for the organization in a search engine, such as Google. What did you find? Did you find information from disgruntled volunteers or employees? Did any relevant news articles come up related to the organization? Was it good or bad news?

- Try adding relevant words to your search such as "Volunteer" or "Intern".

- Contact neighboring organizations that may be familiar with their work. You can find these through Google or by searching Idealist.org for organizations in the same city.

Contact them

You should always contact the organization for more information. Remember: Most reputable organizations will openly provide this information. Before you agree to volunteer with a particular organization on a particular program, here is a list of questions and considerations you should answer first through your research and then by contacting the organization.

- Where is the project?

- What tasks will you be doing both as part of the volunteer position and as part of day-to-day life? (For example, is cooking part of your duties during a homestay?)
  - What are your hours?
  - What are the costs?
    - What is included in these costs? (housing, transportation, insurance, meals)
    - Is there a budget or breakdown of how your money will be allocated and spent?

- What resources are available to you?
  - Language learning opportunities or classes? Is there a translator?
  - Timeline for the project. Is there a plan to sustain the project after you leave?
  - Why are international volunteers needed for this work? Why do they need the skills and experience you are bringing?
    - Do they involve local volunteers? This is important both for cultural exchange (working side by side offers many opportunities) and sustainability (local volunteers will provide continuity). It also ensures that the human capital developed by volunteers will stay at least partially in the community.
    - Is there time available to travel? Are there free days or planned excursions?
  - Is there access to transportation?

Jot your thoughts

Use the space below to note any additional questions you want to ask about an international volunteering position.

- What is the work environment like?
  * How long have they worked with international volunteers?
    - What is the average age of most volunteers?
  * Who will you be working with? A team? A manager?
    - How long have they been there? How old is the program? Is the staff local?
    - Do onsite staff speak English (or another language you know)?
  * How are they funded?
    - Relations with church? Government? Universities? NGOs?
  * Is housing provided?
    - If yes, what are the details (sharing a room, location of housing, type of facilities, etc.)
      * What should you expect? (plumbing, shower/toilet facilities, electricity, internet access, bedding, etc.)
    - If not, how do you set up housing (in advance or upon arrival, resources to assist with this process, expected costs, etc.)
      * Options for setting it up in advance or finding temporary housing when you get there
      * What are the local resources for finding housing?
  * Are there security or health concerns?
    - Any physical/cultural limitations? (e.g. gender identity, physical mobility, race/ethnicity, age, sexual orientation, etc.)
    - If you have special needs (dietary restrictions, mobility, allergies, etc.), can they be accommodated?
    - Does the organization have volunteer liability insurance?
  * How will you get to and from the housing or volunteer site?
  * Can they recommend local "survival guide" info? (how to use transit, find cheap eats, avoid unsafe areas, etc.)
  * Are you expected to bring any supplies?
  * What are they willing to put in writing about the program?
  * How do you plan to protect your information? (what to share, what/how to pay, what not to disclose, etc. to avoid identity theft or other scams)

The goal of contacting the organization is both to ensure that it is a good fit for you as well as to establish realistic expectations for your experience. If you feel that the organization is disorganized or unprepared, it may not be the right place for you to seek paid or volunteer work.

Your identity, visa, and money

There is an abundance of upstanding, quality international volunteerism organizations from which to choose. If you've done your homework well, you will get a

Books on international careers
Here are a few informative books you might want to read as you consider your international career options.

Alternatives to the Peace Corps: A Guide of Global Volunteer Opportunities by Paul Backhurst (Oakland: Food First, 2005)

How to Live Your Dream of Volunteering Overseas by Joseph Collins, Stefano DeZerega, and Zahara Heckscher (New York: Penguin, 2003)

Volunteer Vacations: Short-Term Adventures That Will Benefit You and Others by Bill McMillon, Doug Cutchins, Anne Geissinger, and Ed Asner (Chicago: Chicago Review Press, 2006)

Volunteer: A Traveler's Guide to Making a Difference Around the World by Charlotte Hindle, Nate Cavalieri, Rachel Collinson, Korina Miller, and Mike Richard (London: Lonely Planet, 2007)

sense of what kind of organization you are dealing with. Still, keep some of these points in mind as you finalize the logistics of your opportunity:

Personal identity: While it is reasonable for organizations to request information about future volunteers, be cautious about the type of personal information you release, and to whom. Disclosing the personal identification information in passports, drivers licenses, national identity cards, and the like can result in identity theft or scams, and should be handled responsibly.

Visas: Depending on your nationality and length of stay, you may or may not be required to have a visa to volunteer internationally. Since visa regulations can change quite rapidly, do not simply go by the information your organization provides; make sure to double-check at your host country's local embassy or consulate. The visa application process will vary depending on your host country and the type of visa that is required. For details on how to apply and required documentation, get in touch with your host country's local consulate or embassy. Also keep in mind that, in some cases, visitors with "humanitarian" visas may have access to locations that many international tourists cannot visit.

Since most consulates/embassies have their own websites, we suggest you search the web for the necessary contact information. You may also want to visit Embassy World (www.embassyworld.com) which is a website that provides contact information for embassies worldwide.

Money: Most often, organizations that require payment are typically working through placement agencies and those agencies will process your payment. If the application process involves making some sort of payment, try to go through an intermediary organization like Western Union rather than disclosing your credit card or bank account information. Also make sure you know the contact information for the person who handles this information on the organizational side. Before paying for anything, make sure to request a written agreement about what the money is being used for, what the refund policy is, and what kind of a guarantee you will receive by sending money. Although email exchanges are a useful way to get this kind of information, make sure to ask for something more than an email agreement. The organization you plan to work with should be able to send you a scanned file, or fax or mail you a copy of a signed agreement. Again, always try to get organizational references (ideally from someone from your home country) before sending any money. Another credibility check is whether the organization is affiliated with a well known and respected international NGO like Red Cross/Red Crescent, Unicef, Oxfam, or the United Nations.

PHOTOGRAPHY IN THE DIGITAL AGE

Be especially careful about sending photographs unless you know exactly what they will be used for (i.e., for a program ID card, an image gallery on the organization's website, or to help representatives from your host organization identify you at the airport). Bear in mind that photographs can be easily manipulated.

Going solo to volunteer in another country

While there are hundreds of volunteer-sending organizations in the world that will coordinate everything from housing and meals to the logistics of visas and travel, there are also many people that would just as soon go on their own. Whether this inclination to volunteer abroad independently is due to personal preference, a lack of knowledge about program opportunities, or for financial reasons (most volunteer-sending organizations do charge fees), the good news is that volunteering on your own is entirely doable.

First, a caveat: if you choose to volunteer internationally without the assistance of a volunteer-sending program, it is your responsibility to make sure everything is legitimate. With that in mind, here are two possible routes to consider:

Make arrangements from home

Start by determining where in the world you want to go: Will you be traveling in Argentina and want to volunteer along the way? Have you always wanted to visit China and think volunteering is just the motivation you need to finally get there? Next, figure out what issue you want to work on and what role you would like to play. Do you want to interact with young people at a local school or orphanage? Or are you more interested in working outdoors on environmental issues?

Once you know more about your preferences for the place, issue, and role, you can begin researching opportunities. To start, utilize sources like Idealist.org's global database of volunteer opportunities, connect with organizations you know and trust who offer global opportunities (e.g., Habitat for Humanity), or simply email or call international NGOs directly. One primary advantage of searching from home is that you can connect with former volunteers in your area to find out about their experiences and make more educated choices about where you serve.

Another possibility that you can explore from home is to gather a group of like-minded friends to create a cultural and volunteer exchange program with a contact in a foreign country. You can plan an annual trip with your friends where you work with the local contact for a period of time. These kinds of grassroots cultural and service exchange groups can operate without having nonprofit status and are often a more cost effective way to learn from, and assist in, a foreign community.

Find opportunities once you get there

Another option is to travel to your destination, get to know the area a bit, and then look for volunteer opportunities. With local contacts and a better understanding of the community, you'll likely have a stronger sense of where and how to volunteer.

Once you know more about your preferences for the place, issue, and role, you can begin researching your opportunities."

You may also find opportunities that will be hard to locate from home no matter how much searching you do online.

Once you've identified a few volunteer opportunities—whether from your home computer or via conversation with a new neighbor in a foreign community—it's time to start asking the same types of questions you would ask if going with an arranged program (see page 109).

When you're satisfied with the answers, put your understanding in writing. If both you and the organization are on the same page, you're ready to go! Have fun, revel in this adventure of your own making, and don't worry—if the experience turns out not to be what you'd hoped, you can always discuss changing your volunteer assignment within the organization… or simply look for another opportunity in your newfound community.

Back to the career search

After you've found the organization and project that you want to work with, start to focus again on your international job search. If you are intentional about your international volunteering (as you should be with any form of volunteering) you can use the time to develop your professional network, understand the local nonprofit community, work on your cultural sensitivity, and hone your linguistic abilities, all of which will assist you in your job search. Once you've "paid your dues" and figured out if you really do want to live and work in the community, you will be well poised to find paid work in either the geographic location or mission area of your volunteer position.

SUMMARY

Making sure to **research *all* the opportunities** in your location, be they local, national, or international, is one of the most important steps to a successful job search. Here are a few key points to remember:

While the internet is a great place to research opportunities, remember that you need to **get online to get offline** and meet people, make connections, and leave positive impressions (pages 98-99).

Strive to constantly **learn more about your location**. Continue to seek untapped resources and networks (page 99).

The internet has a wealth of sites that will help you understand the nonprofit opportunities in your area. Use sites like Idealist, GuideStar, Craigslist, and university and local nonprofit listservs as well as community college career centers to **conduct a targeted organizational search** (pages 100-102).

If you are **choosing to move**, ask yourself some important questions: What is more important to you–your job or your location? What makes your target city a more desirable place to live than where you live now? How is the nonprofit job market in your target city? What contacts do you already have there? Do you have enough savings to last a few months without work? What if your relocation is not successful? What's plan B? (pages 102-104)

If you are **forced to move**, there are many hidden positives, both for your lifestyle and your career. Keep them in mind (or keep a list on your refrigerator) and stay focused on making a productive change. Also remember that research and planning will help any move, be it voluntary or involuntary (pages 104-105).

The visit is a crucial part of a distance search. Start by learning more about your new location and then researching the local nonprofit sector. After you have an understanding of both the area and the organizations that interest you, plan a visit (pages 105-106).

If you want to explore **international career options**, consider starting out abroad in a volunteer position and using that time to develop a professional network, language skills, an understanding of the local culture, and work experience that will help you enter the job market (pages 106-113).

CHAPTER SEVEN

Does your work work for you?

Evaluating organizational culture

In this chapter you will:

- Understand how to recognize organizational culture and learn why it is an important consideration when choosing a job.

- Assess which elements of organizational culture are important to you.

- Learn how (and where) to research to evaluate a particular organization's culture.

- Recognize the opportunity that an interview provides to not only demonstrate your potential to the employer, but also to determine if the organization is a good cultural fit for you.

- Assess your fit with an organization based on your research, observation, and gut instincts.

What is organizational culture?

Organizational culture is best described as an organization's personality or "the way things work." Just as no two people have the same personality, neither do two organizations. This diversity makes it possible to find a great fit with an organization that matches your personality. The key to determining a good fit between you and an organization is understanding their culture. Since organizational culture can be influenced by elements such as expected work hours, dress code, and office layout, it can be hard to research and even harder to quantify. Especially in large organizations, different cultures can exist even among individual programs and departments. But, given the effect that a great cultural fit can have on individuals and organizations, it is worth spending the time to investigate and gather information. Like all aspects of the job search, the time spent learning about an organization's culture can be scaled depending on how much time you have and how much importance it has to you.

Organizational culture is created by a variety of factors:

- Organizational values (honesty, transparency, innovation)
- Work environment (how staff interact, degree of competition, mood of the office, collaboration with coworkers, time employees spend outside office with coworkers)
- Responsibilities (autonomy vs. structure, management opportunities)
- Work/life balance (hours per day or week, flex time, telecommuting options)

- Dress code (suit, business casual, informal Fridays)
- Office environment (cubicles, windows, display of personal items, gym or daycare facilities onsite)
- Training (emphasis on development, skill building, investment in your growth)

As you can imagine, most of these factors are hard to research and difficult to determine without actually working for the organization. In this section, you'll learn how to get a sense of culture before accepting or rejecting a job offer. You'll also determine how to prioritize the aspects of an organization's culture that are most important to you.

Why is a good fit important?

Both the employer and the employee benefit greatly from a good fit. For the employer, hiring someone who fits in allows the organization to maintain its current office culture, makes it easier for the new hire to transition into their new job, and reduces the possibility of conflict with other staff members. Additionally, if employees feel like they belong and are a valued part of the whole, they will feel a greater commitment to the organization and will be more productive.

Determining a good fit can be even more important to potential employees. Since you will spend most of your waking hours at work, a good fit can be the difference between doing work you love and dreading the alarm clock each morning. Also, with many nonprofit organizations, the work will be demanding; you'll need a supportive environment in order to make the job tenable. Finally, there are so many different organizational cultures that there is no reason not to find one that works for you. Begin your job search from the perspective that finding a great work environment is not a matter of luck, but of being strategic and deliberate in your search.

There are two steps in considering organizational culture:

1. **Know what you want in an organization's culture**
2. **Know how to evaluate an organization's culture**

1. Know what you want in an organization's culture

It's much easier going to the grocery store with a list that provides a clear picture of what you need to buy. With all of the distractions in the aisles, you have a better chance of staying focused if you know what you are looking for. Similarly, when you evaluate an organization's culture, it is also helpful to know what matters most to you in order to prioritize your interests. In the grocery store, you probably can't buy *everything* that you want. Likewise, when you're trying to figure out if an organization is going to be a good fit, you may not find all of the qualities you want. Hopefully,

 Since you will spend most of your waking hours at work, a good fit can be the difference between doing work you love and dreading the alarm clock each morning."

though, you can figure out if the organization can offer what is important to you in order to ensure a good match.

The other factor to consider is how the organizational fit compares to the rest of the compensation package. For example, once you've ranked your priorities in terms of organizational culture, go back to the big picture and figure out where organizational culture ranks in terms of salary, benefits, location, and so on. (See **Chapter Ten** for more on compensation and benefits, and **Chapter Six** for guidance on searching for a nonprofit job at a distance). While the value of finding a great fit is often underestimated, it is also relative to your individual situation: you may find the perfect job in terms of responsibilities and culture, but if it doesn't pay enough to support your lifestyle, it may not work.

What do you want?

Organizational culture is a complex equation made up of a variety of influences. In the sidebar at the right, you'll find these factors grouped by category. Within each category, consider which factors are most important to you and which aren't essential. While it is understandable to regard most of these aspects as important, try to prioritize them so that you'll be able to make your assessment of individual organizations easier. If there are any aspects of organizational culture that are important to you but are not listed, write them down at the bottom of the list (on page 118).

2. Know how to evaluate an organization's culture

Once you have a clearer sense of the aspects of an organization's culture that are important to you, there are two basic ways to find out if you'll mesh well with a particular organization: **research and observation**. As you've read in earlier sections, research is a necessity for all aspects of the job search process. It is essential to do research before you write and submit a cover letter and resume, before you go in for an interview, and especially before you accept an offer. While much of the research in these stages overlaps, this last phase of research is distinctive because you are considering whether or not the organization is the right fit for you, rather than demonstrating to your potential employer that you're a great fit for them.

Begin the "organizational culture" research as soon as the employer contacts you for an interview. When you're called about an interview, you know that, at least on paper, the employer has decided that you may be a good fit for them. This should give you confidence. Keep in mind that the process of evaluating the organization's culture is about whether the organization fits what you're looking for in your next opportunity.

SELF-ASSESSMENT CHECKLIST

Prioritize the following factors that influence organizational culture (the list continues in the sidebar on the next page, where there is also space for you to write factors that are important to you, but which aren't listed). After this exercise, you'll be ready to begin evaluating the cultures of specific organizations.

Organizational values

- Organization-wide emphasis on volunteering (paid time/organizational incentives to volunteer)

- Environmental focus/commitment to sustainability

- Embraces diversity and actively pursues it

- Seeks to collaborate locally, nationally, or internationally to achieve mission

- Values your long-term financial stability (401(k), other retirement plans)

- Emphasis on entrepreneurialism and innovation, or focus on established activities and time-tested programs

- Emphasis on metrics to measure success, both individual and organizational (number of clients served, increased donation levels, heightened outreach capacity, quotas met, etc.)

Work/life balance

- Expected work hours
- Flex time
- Compensation days
- Telecommuting options

[The list of factors continues in the sidebar on the next page.]

Research

Researching organizational fit should be done simultaneously with researching for the interview. This is because you want to know everything you can about the organization in order to use the interview as an opportunity to both show the potential employer your value and also to do some additional on-site exploration to see if the office is an environment where you really want to work.

Here's what to look for and analyze on an organization's website:

Look and feel

Most organizations have their own websites; this is the best place to start your online research. At first, just skim the site. Ideally, a website helps convey an organization through qualities like choice of colors, images, language, and tone. Keep an eye out for ideas, projects, or opportunities that the website is promoting. The look and feel of an organization's website are important indicators of the type of organization it is (or that it intends to be).

Mission statement

Once you've casually explored the website, narrow your focus and look for a few items that can give you some real insight into the organization's culture. The mission statement is a great place to start. What are the words the organization uses to describe its work? Is it casually written or does it use formal language? Is it expansive and broad or does it have a specific focus?

Staff/employee biographies

Next, look for employee/staff biographies. What information is revealed? Do the bios include strictly professional details or are there personal tidbits? Do all the staff have similar backgrounds? Are the photos relaxed, candid, posed, or formal? Can you tell how long the employees have been with the organization? Are all employees listed or only those with leadership positions? If there aren't biographies, this can also reveal information about the organization.

Annual report

An annual report is a great way to get a comprehensive summary of an organization because it often includes accomplishments, names and affiliations of board members, recent donors, organizational statistics, specific programs, and plans for the future. If an organization's annual report isn't on their website, see if you can find the various components elsewhere on the site. While these components are interesting by themselves (and great for interview preparation), collectively this information can give you an overview and understanding of the organization.

[continued from previous page]

Work environment

- Cubicles, offices, or flexible work spaces
- Extra facilities (gym, daycare, etc.)
- Rules about displaying personal items
- Use of light and space in office
- Common areas (mood, decor, postings for group events, etc.)
- Dress expectations (none, suit, business casual, informal Fridays)

Job description

- Variety is expected, change is rare
- Public and/or internal opportunities for acknowledgement
- Opportunities to express your creativity
- Autonomy vs. supervision/oversight by manager
- Opportunities for advancement
- Professional development/training (skill building, investment in your growth)

Coworkers

- Competition and/or collaboration is encouraged
- Interest in employees as people vs. strict rules of interpersonal engagement
- Clear hierarchy vs. more collaborative managerial structure
- In-office interaction among coworkers
- Collaboration between departments
- After hours camaraderie

Add other factors you value here:

Gut check

After you've reviewed the aforementioned materials, do a final gut check: if you were offered the job knowing just what you know from the above sources, would you be excited about taking it? Why or why not? While this is not a thoroughly educated answer, your instinctive feeling is still important in evaluating a subjective value like organizational fit.

Aside from the organization's website, here are some other avenues for research:

Personal experience/public opinion

This type of research depends on your network. Do you know anyone (friend, friend-of-a-friend, family member) who has worked with the organization as an employee, funder, collaborator, etc.? This person will be able to provide valuable insight into the culture based on their experience. However, remember that organizational culture is entirely subjective. What could be an ideal environment for one person may not fit with another's priorities, or vice versa.

Google search

This is the roulette of research; you never know what you'll find or if it will be useful. Your search may turn up a variety of news blurbs, community action project recaps, and probably even some blog mentions. Depending on the size and scope of the organization, you may be able to find all or none of these. Peruse and read the items that seem interesting or are likely to offer perspectives or information that you don't already have. Some of the key results to look for are: media releases, mentions of the organization's contributions to the community, and quotes sharing public opinion of the organization.

Questions for the interview

The final stage of your research is determining what you don't already know. Review your list of organizational culture priorities. What don't you know about the organization so far? Some of the elements you may value highly are aspects that you'll need to observe. For instance, coworker interaction and office layout are components to pay attention to at the interview. However, if you still don't have a sense of organizational culture (such as the amount of collaboration or the organizational structure), asking more about the culture during the interview is appropriate and demonstrates that you are interested not only in the work, but in the type of organization you would be joining. As you review your notes on the organization, come up with three to five questions to ask that will help you get a better feel for the culture.

Below, you'll find some sample questions to help you evaluate an organization's culture. As a word of warning, be aware that organizational culture is difficult to determine unequivocally; there isn't one question that will give you all of the answers, nor

CONTINUING YOUR EVALUATION OF AN ORGANIZATION

After you have gone through the organization's website, searched for information about them online, and sought out public opinion and personal experience stories, step back for a minute. Before you go into the office, meet the people, and get a feel for the atmosphere, think about what you're expecting to notice.

Write down:

- **three adjectives to describe the feel of the website**

- **three adjectives the organization uses to describe itself on its site**

- **three adjectives used by the press to describe the organization** (if you can find this)

Save this list of adjectives to refer to after your office visit. If the words you wrote down reflect what you saw in the office, great. If there is a discrepancy between what your research turned up and what you observed in your visit, consider the reasons for the disconnect. What is the culture in which you'll be working? Why is there a different feel between the organization's public face and their office atmosphere? Is the divergence attributable to the organization's efforts to achieve a new level of efficacy or growth, or are there indications that the organization is comfortable with its current level of achievement?

is there a single person who can let you know what it's like for everyone to work at a particular organization. However, organizational culture is something you can get a strong sense for by asking thoughtful questions and being observant.

Sample questions to ask at the interview:

- How are decisions made—and how are those decisions communicated to the staff?
- What role does the person who is hired for this position play in decision making?
- Does the organization emphasize working in teams?
- Can you tell me about the people who have had this position in the past, or about some particularly good work they have done?
- What are the organization's priorities (or aspirations) for the next few years?
- Are there established career paths for employees in this position?
- Can you tell me about the management style of the person who will be supervising this position?
- Are there opportunities for further training and education?
- Is there a dress code?
- Can you share the training schedule I might expect for the first week?

Observation

This second step of evaluating an organization's culture begins at your job interview. While you'll undoubtedly have plenty of things on your mind during the interview, the moments just before and after it are ideal opportunities to gather information. There are three ways to assess how well you may fit with the organizational culture: gut instinct, office observation, and observations during the interview. The best part about this stage is that whatever you observe and ask during the interview can contribute both to your knowledge of the organization and your success during the interview. For example, if you have the opportunity to ask what qualities are valued at the organization, you can answer questions highlighting how you exemplify those very qualities.

Gut instinct

When you first walk in for your interview, do a quick instinct check and ask yourself: "Is this a place I would want to come to work every day?" It's okay if you're not sure; you'll have plenty of time to gather more information. If you feel strongly either way, remember that feeling and, after the interview, see if your impression of the office has changed. Whatever your concluding decision, don't discount your initial impression; it's one of the more reliable barometers for assessing organizational culture.

INFORMATIONAL INTERVIEWS WHILE INTERVIEWING? Although informational interviews are a great way to get valuable, insider information about an organization, potential problems arise when you schedule an informational interview while you are engaged in the job interview process with the same organization. How much of a problem will depend on the size of the organization. If you are being considered for a position with a large organization, an informational interview with someone in a different office (or even a different city) than your interviewer(s) may not be an issue. However, requesting an informational interview with a staff member at a closely knit or smaller organization may be tricky; your informational interview could seem like an attempt to gain an advantage in the actual job interview.

Your decision will depend on the size and scope of an organization, your connection (if any) with the potential informational interviewee, and what you hope to gain. Once you've submitted your application, you might want to consider other ways to research the organization and make connections. Keep in mind that you never want to give even the slightest impression that you are trying to undermine or influence the job interview process. Before making any decisions, weigh the possibility of a negative impression against the potential positive outcomes of an informational interview and decide if it is worth the risk.

Office observation§

Your interview time in the office is incredibly valuable for collecting information to help evaluate the organizational culture. Before you go to the interview, have an observation checklist. This checklist may include:

- How are you treated by the front desk staff, interviewers, employees, etc.?
- Interactions between coworkers, management, etc.
- Do employees seem to be happy? Satisfied? Engaged?
- Physical layout of the office:
  * Cubicles/offices
  * Colors
  * Windows (natural light, plants)
  * What's on the walls?
- Overall mood of the office

§ *Please note that your observation should not even remotely resemble an inspection or a scene from a spy movie. In fact, any observation that you do should be from the couch, chair, or space where you are asked to wait for your interviewer. Do not wander the office making copious notes, try not to stare conspicuously at employees who are engaged in conversation, and avoid poking your nose into cubicles, kitchens, or other spaces where you have no need to be. Take advantage of the opportunity to observe but only to the extent that your observations are not visibly apparent and suspicious.*

During your job interview

This is the primary opportunity to get specific information about the organizational culture. However, you're also going to have to answer questions, make appropriate eye contact, remember names, and perform all of the other essential interview activities. Therefore, be sure to reflect on the interview immediately afterwards, recording your observations and impressions, and the interviewer's answers to your questions. If you prepare, it will be easier to answer questions well and remember as much information as you can. One way to prepare is to customize the interview worksheet (see page 123) with spaces for information that you're hoping to gain from the interview. This worksheet can be printed out and taken to the interview (for use just after you've finished) as a way to record observations and notes. If the sample interview worksheet does not work for you, consider finding another format that includes spaces for similar information.

Your observation at the interview has a lot to do with reading the staff's body language and interactions, and inferring as much information as you can from what they say to you. For example, while you'll be focused on answering questions, try to pay attention to what kind of questions are asked.

- Are the questions focused on your past experience, your future aspirations, or you as a person?

SHOULD YOU ARRIVE EARLY TO OBSERVE?

Some sources suggest arriving early for your interview so that you can get a better feel for the office and observe the employee interactions. A certain amount of extra time is understandable so that you can take a deep breath, use the restroom, or review your notes. If you do arrive early and can ask that the interviewer not be bothered yet, you may also gain a bit of time to observe. However, if you arrive too early, there may not be a receptionist to check in with and you may cause your interviewer to feel rushed to come greet you.

While extra time may give you a chance to prepare yourself before the interview and a valuable reconnaissance opportunity, too much time may start you off on the wrong foot with your interviewer. Keep in mind that whatever information you might gain by arriving excessively early may not be worth precipitating a bad impression of yourself (that you're impolite, or have poor time management skills), or a bad mood for your interviewer.

- How do the interviewers respond to your answers—are they skeptical, encouraging, or interested?

- Are the questions relevant to you, or are they fairly routine questions that might be asked in any interview?

- Do you feel like you're facing an inquisition, or are you engaged in a participatory conversation?

- Do your interviewers give away any indications about how aspirational the organization is? Are they satisfied or self-critical? Their verbal cues may indicate whether the organization is a work in progress (striving to get to a new level), or whether it's comfortable as it is (or perhaps even set in its ways).

Similarly, you can make notes on whether your interviewer is punctual and prepared, what the seating arrangement is, and, if there is more than one interviewer, how they interact with each other. (Again, do this just *after* your interview, not right in front of the interviewer!)

Final assessment

Once the interview is over and you've made notes on what you've seen and heard, compare your interview observations with the information you found out from your online research and by talking with people in the community. How does this information mesh with your organizational culture priorities? Will your priorities be met at this organization? Is this an office you'll enjoy going to every day? Do you feel like the organizational culture is a good fit for *you*?

Once you've thought about the many aspects of organizational culture and all of the clues and pieces you've gathered from research and observation, you should prepare yourself for the possibility of an offer. If you feel that you'll fit well with the organization, congratulations: you can then move on to evaluate the other aspects of the offer (see **Chapter Ten** for advice on how to evaluate compensation and benefits). However, if you have some unanswered questions about the culture, you can follow up with the employer to try to find answers that will help you decide to accept or decline the offer. Remember, by the time they make you an offer, they've committed to you. There is no better time to ascertain that not only is this a great job in terms of responsibilities, salary and benefits, and other attributes, but that it is also a great fit for you.

SAMPLE INTERVIEW WORKSHEET

Take the worksheet on the next page (or one that you've created) out for a test run. Use a doctor's office, the workplace of a friend, or even an institution that is open to the public like a hospital or university, and see what you can observe about the culture of the organization. What useful elements were not mentioned in the worksheet? What details do you really not need to pay attention to? Take this opportunity to customize the worksheet for your own needs, so that when you use it after an interview, you'll be confident that you're commenting on the important aspects of organizational culture in order to make the best decision when you're offered the job.

Sample Interview Worksheet

Name of organization: _____

Position interviewed for: _____

Date and time of interview: _____

Other position/organization-specific information:

_____

_____

NAMES/TITLES OF YOUR INTERVIEWERS:

List a few adjectives for each prompt.

How were you treated by the front desk staff, interviewers, employees, etc.?

_____

What interactions did you see between coworkers, management, etc.?

_____

Did employees seem to be happy? Satisfied? Engaged?

_____

What did you think of the physical layout of the office?

Cubicles/offices: _____ Colors: _____

Walls/windows: _____ Overall mood: _____

General notes from the interview:

_____

_____

_____

Any questions you didn't answer well at the interview, or responses you gave that you want to emphasize:

_____

_____

Specific information to mention in thank you note:

_____

_____

_____

SUMMARY

The process of **evaluating an organization's culture** should begin early in your job search. It can parallel your research for the resume, cover letter, and interview. And while culture can be an elusive element of an organization to evaluate, there are certain steps you can take to get a better feel for whether or not you'll be a good fit with the organization. The steps are:

Learning organizational culture and **identifying some of the factors that create it** (pages 115-116).

Understanding why **culture is important to evaluate**, for both you and the organization (page 116).

Assessing what you prioritize in an organization's culture (pages 116-118, including sidebars).

Understanding how to evaluate a particular organization's culture through **research and observation** (pages 118-122).

Evaluating whether or not an organization is a good fit for you (page 122 and worksheet page 123).

CHAPTER EIGHT

Presenting yourself on paper

Resumes and cover letters

by **David Schachter**, Assistant Dean for Career Services and Experiential Learning

at NYU's Robert F. Wagner Graduate School of Public Service[*]

In this chapter you will:

- Learn the importance of answering the three fundamental questions that any person making a hiring decision expects your resume and cover letter to answer: Can you do the job? Will you do the job? Will you fit in?

- Learn how to market your distinct skills to the nonprofit sector. Tailoring the language and relevance of your skills to the specifics of the nonprofit position you're pursuing will make employers take notice.

- Explore the various elements needed to craft a perfect, focused resume for the specific job for which you are applying.

- Understand that your cover letter is a persuasive piece of writing that nonprofit employers will use to measure your writing ability and your fit for the particular position.

There are few more humbling (and often frustrating) experiences than reducing your life's work and experience to a few pieces of paper. Furthermore, after boiling down who you are to a handful of pages, the person making a hiring decision will spend, on average, 15 seconds perusing your effort before placing you in the "yes", "maybe", or "no" pile. While presenting yourself through a resume and cover letter can be a challenge, there are several useful tactics that will genuinely make you and your potential value to the organization stand out.

As you prepare to send a potential employer your cover letter and resume, take a moment to get inside the head of the person doing the hiring. There are ultimately only three questions that a person making a hiring decision asks during those crucial seconds of analysis. They want to know:

1. **Can you do the job?**
2. **Will you do the job?**
3. **Will you fit in?**

---

[*] In this chapter on resumes and cover letters, the "Three questions", "Elements of your resume", "Focus of your resume", "What not to include in a resume", "Presentation", "Purpose of the cover letter", "Cover letter talking points", "Cover letter structure", and "Additional points" discussions are all by David Schachter. Grateful acknowledgment is made to New York University for permission to reprint excerpts from and adapt the work of David Schachter, Assistant Dean of Career Services and Experiential Learning at NYU's Robert F. Wagner Graduate School of Public Service © 2008. Reprinted with permission of New York University and David Schachter. http://wagner.nyu.edu. Some modifications to the original text have been made by the staff at Idealist.org

Let's delve into these three questions in a little more depth before moving on to drafting an effective cover letter and resume for a nonprofit opportunity, since these questions should shape how you frame, format, and phrase everything else.

1. Can you do the job?

In other words: Do you have the skills, experience, and education to be able to fulfill all of the requirements listed in the job description? Have you demonstrated that you were able to succeed in a similar role or under similar circumstances? Nonprofit employers want to see that your abilities match up as closely as possible to the qualifications and responsibilities in the position description. If you clearly show this in your resume, you are much more likely to get an interview.

Tip: Do not expect the employer to figure out how your past experience can be applicable to the position in question. Every bullet point and every detail listed in your "profile" should be a way to demonstrate what you could do if you were hired. Do this for each specific position for which you apply. Stop thinking of your resume as merely a way to show what you have accomplished; your resume is a way to demonstrate what you would accomplish for *this* particular agency in *this* particular role.

2. Will you do the job?

Are you committed to the mission and/or central issue of the organization? Have you demonstrated the work ethic necessary to succeed in this specific line of work? To nonprofit employers, your demonstrated commitment to and passion for the cause is important to your credibility.

Tip: Emphasize experience you have had with the mission of the organization, or its central issue—whether through volunteer service, work, or education. It's not necessary to highlight your commitment to other issues at this point. If you are hired, your involvement with other causes might be noteworthy.

3. Will you fit in?

Do you speak the language of nonprofits (i.e., do you say "organization" rather than "company")? Do you exhibit enthusiasm for this particular job at this particular agency? Do you use language that reveals your familiarity with the organization's mission? Does your sense of humor resonate with the prospective workplace? Employers want to know that you will feel comfortable working in the organization and that your colleagues will get along well with you. Similarly, you want to find out if you would like to work among the staff here, and if you'd be happy coming to work in this office every day.

Tip: Your ability to fit in with the organizational culture is not something you have a lot of control over. It's like dating—you and your date either have the chemistry to

MAKE YOUR EXPERIENCE CLEARLY RELEVANT TO A HIRING MANAGER

You may know that your work in Peace Corps overseeing the digging of 30 wells for a village shows project management skills, but few hiring managers have time to sit and figure out that connection. Be sure to spell out how your experience *directly* relates to the description of the position for which you're applying. Be explicit about how your management of the well digging exemplified your ability to organize, motivate, and stay on schedule. List the leadership skills that you developed while leading this project. Also highlight other positive aspects of your work: did you finish early or under budget, or recruit new partners?

Draw connections between past experiences and future expectations. Mention only the qualities that are relevant; you can leave out your dexterity with a shovel if it's not explicitly asked for in the job description.

continue, or you don't. It's never advisable to try to be someone you aren't in order to get the job. If you are passed up for a job that seemed perfect for your skill set, have faith that another job will come along that will be a better organizational fit for you.

Remember, your cover letter and resume are meant to attract hiring managers' attention and entice them to invite you (and not the other 100 applicants) in to get to know you better. The cover letter and resume are not meant to tell your life story. If you get the job, you should have plenty of time for that.

> After you draft your individualized cover letter and resume for the specific position you are applying for, reread both and **continually ask yourself if the information you've included answers the three questions**: Can you do the job? Will you do the job? Will you fit in? **If not, omit any irrelevant information**.

Marketing your distinct skills

No one has the exact same experiences and skills sets as you, so no one can answer "the three questions" the same way as you, either. But if you cannot communicate what you distinctly offer in the language of the nonprofit sector, your uniqueness may not shine through and your cover letter and resume may be doomed to the discard pile. This is easily avoidable, however, since marketing your distinct skills is a simple process that leads to a dynamic and engaging application—the kind of application that demonstrates a high level of self-analysis and the ability to communicate such personal understanding within the constraints of a job application process.

To market your unique skills in the nonprofit sector, you must take two steps. The first step is fitting your skills into broader categories that relate to working with people, resources, information, and systems; the activity detailed in the Imagine/Connect/Act sidebars beginning on this page will help you do this. The second step is to use the language of the nonprofit sector to convey these skills.

Step one: Skill categories

Professional skills can be broken down into broad categories that encompass all of the activities you do at work. These skill categories (based on a U.S. Department of Labor and Department of Education study of the skills necessary for workplace success in the 21st century) are universal throughout the professional world and are not sector-specific. The basic four functional areas that all of your professional skills should fit into are those you use to work with:

1. People
2. Resources
3. Information
4. Systems

YOUR SKILLS IN FOUR PARTS

List all of your professional experiences using action verbs, and then sort them into one of the four skill categories. This involves listing as many instances of interpersonal interaction, information management, resources management, and systems interaction that you can think of in your professional past.

After you have finished, review the four categories. Are some categories fuller than others? Do you have clear category strengths that you should emphasize in your cover letter and resume? Are there skill categories that you would like to improve? How can you start making those improvements?

1. People skills: This category refers to the social and leadership skills that you use in the workplace. Teaching, supervising, working on a team, negotiating, leading, communicating (speaking and writing), facilitating, interviewing, counseling, and cooperating are just a few of the skills encompassed in this category. "People skills" also include your own self-management, self-esteem, and sociability skills.

2. Resource skills: This category refers to the ways you handle available professional resources, including managing time (getting projects done before a deadline), money (working within a budget), materials (expertise with using expensive machinery), and space (utilizing physical space in the office, navigating page constraints in print advertising, and managing other instances where space is an issue).

3. Information skills: This category refers to how you collect, evaluate, organize, process, and maintain information. Your technological, problem solving, critical thinking, reasoning, decision making, and organizational abilities fall into this category as they are all related to how you handle information, data, and knowledge.

4. Systems skills: This category refers to your ability to understand and navigate the dynamic interplay between systems (knowing how social, technological, and organizational systems operate and intersect within a given workplace, as well as how to use them efficiently), see where processes can be improved (which involves monitoring and correcting systems), and design structures that will facilitate a smoother working environment.

You may notice an obvious overlap of these skill sets. For example, human resource professionals use people, information, resources, and systems skills. As you break down your professional skills into these four categories, note where you see an overlap. Skills and experiences that work across skill areas (for example, the ability to design a new information storage system for the office computer network) are especially valuable to both you, the professional, as well as to the organizations you want to impress.

Step two: Talking the talk

There are many elements of the nonprofit sector's language and vocabulary that are identical to the terminology of the public and for-profit sectors. But there is also language that is unique to the sector—language that you need to incorporate into your interactions with nonprofit professionals (see **Appendix One** for more on nonprofit vocabulary). At this point in your job search, you should hopefully already be more comfortable with some of the unique language of the nonprofit sector from reading job descriptions, organizations' websites, and industry publications, as well as from conducting informational interviews.

THE JOB SKILLS IN FOUR PARTS

Next, take the position description of the job you are applying for and assign the skills in the description to the four skill categories. Ideally, the categories heavy with skills for this position should be the same categories that you've identified as your main strengths. Emphasize these similarities in your cover letter and resume.

If there is a rather large difference between your skills and the job's required skills, you may need to consider whether this job is a good fit for you right now, or whether it's a position you can pursue in a few years when you have more relevant skills. If you decide that the connections between the position and your skills are strong enough to make you a viable candidate, be sure to emphasize the connections you do have with a given skill category so that the potential employer can see the same connections as you.

When marketing your skills to a particular organization, you should focus on the language they use to describe their work, their organization, their constituents, and their mission. The job description and organizational website are good places to start this process. If possible, read publications and press releases the nonprofit has produced and take note of the language they use to describe their work.

Below is a list of some common terms that nonprofits use (denoted by NP). When appropriate, their for-profit (FP) or public sector (GV) equivalents appear in parentheses next to the terms. Portions of this list come from "Sales Professional to Development Professional: A Workable Transition (A For-Profit Salesperson's Guide to Getting a Job in Non-Profit Development)" by Tony Ponderis (available online at www.raise-funds.com/071907forum.html).

NP: organization (**FP:** company, business/ **GV:** department, agency)	**NP:** fund development plan (**FP:** sales & marketing plan)	**NP:** fundraising goal (**FP:** sales quota, projected earnings)
NP: timeline (**FP:** sale duration)	**NP:** donors (**FP:** customers, investors)	**NP/FP/GV:** strong leadership, vision
NP/FP/GV: staff development, professional development, leadership training/ development	**NP:** mission-driven (**FP:** profit-driven, result-driven/ **GV:** mandate-driven)	**NP:** progress and tracking meetings (**FP:** sales meetings)
NP: constituency, stakeholders, partners (**FP:** market area, market segment/ **GV:** clients, constituents)	**NP:** suggested asking/ donation amounts (**FP:** fees, charges, price tags/ **GV:** taxes)	**NP:** building loyalty, cultivating stewardship, community ownership (**FP:** customer service/**GV:** responsive governance)
NP/FP/GV: capacity building	**NP/FP/GV:** quality product or service	**NP/FP/GV:** long-range strategic plan
NP/FP/GV: accountability	**NP/FP/GV:** budget	**NP/FP/GV:** competition
NP: case for support, promotion (**FP:** advertising & promotion)	**NP:** campaign committee (**FP:** sales force)	

It is easy for you to make sure that you demonstrate your distinct combination of skills and experience using some of the basic language of the nonprofit sector. Using the right terminology in your resume and cover letter cannot be overemphasized, as it is likely that a nonprofit employer will be put off by an application that doesn't show an understanding and competent usage of the sector's language. By grouping your skills into broad categories and then using the terms of the sector to convey those skills, you will demonstrate your own self-awareness in particular and your understanding of the nonprofit sector in general. Now that you can "talk the nonprofit talk", it is time to carefully construct your resume.

PUTTING IT ALL TOGETHER AND MARKETING THOSE SKILLS

Now that you have your skills (and the skills for the kind of positions that interest you) assigned to the four skills categories, it is time to "sell" those skills through your cover letter and resume. Your focus should be on highlighting your skills, and therefore yourself, as they relate to the nonprofit sector in general and the specific position within an organization in particular. Understanding the interrelatedness of a nonprofit position's skill set and your own skill set, along with the ability to speak the language of nonprofits, will make your potential contributions to an organization much easier to market and sell.

Nonprofits say the darndest things

For a further explanation of common terms used in nonprofit work, be sure to read this book's **Appendix One**, "Nonprofitspeak 101: A primer to the language used in the nonprofit world".

Resume building

Your resume is made up of a select group of facts that tell a focused story. Regardless of your background when entering the nonprofit sector, you need to focus your resume writing efforts on three key activities:

- **Reframing your skills and experience** to convince an employer of your potential value to their organization. Your keywords here are *transferability* and *relevance*—in other words, **Can you do the job?**

- **Answering** the second of the three questions: **Will you do the job?** For nonprofit work, a successful answer to this question will address your *passion for the mission.*

- **Dispelling preconceived notions** that others may have about you based on your past experiences: if you have a military background, you need rigidity and order; if you have a corporate background, you won't be comfortable if you aren't assigned an assistant or wearing a suit; if you are an athlete, you are more of a doer than a thinker... the list goes on—in other words, **Will you fit in?**

Your resume is obviously one of the most important components of your job search. It speaks both for and of you. It is your introduction and your personal marketing tool. With so much to do in so little space, it is vitally important that your resume is focused, concise, and compelling.

It is likely that employers will typically only glance at your resume for 10-15 seconds, so as you write your resume, bear in mind the perspective of an overworked and overwhelmed employer who wants to be impressed, but who can't be expected to decipher why you might be a possible fit for the position.

Elements of your resume

Your resume should always include:

- Name and contact information
- *Relevant* education and experience
- Volunteering and other forms of community involvement
- Information that indicates your viability as a candidate for a specific position: professional associations, languages, technical skills, awards, publications, etc.

Length of your resume

If you are entering the nonprofit sector for the first time, make your resume one page. That's right. One page. A one-page resume is much more likely to be concise and specific, so setting such a stringent limit on yourself will help you narrow the focus of your content appropriately. A one-page resume will help you spotlight

YOUR PERFECT RESUME

When job seekers sit down to work on their resume, they tend to stuff themselves into the confining, formulated language of "resume speak." Your true personality doesn't shine through and you miss the chance to write your "perfect resume." Before you begin to shape your resume, brainstorm what you would like to express about yourself to a potential employer. You should not worry about how to say what you want to say or about how to connect your self-expression to any particular job or particular employer. This is a time to simply express yourself.

Make a list, write a short paragraph, or even make a chart or graph that you feel accurately expresses who you are as a professional and what talents, skills, and enthusiasm you bring to the work about which you are passionate. Think of this description as your answer to the question, "What makes me the kind of person that other people want to work with?"

Survey says...

In a 2007 survey of nonprofit hiring professionals by Idealist.org, 23 percent said "Relevant paid work experience" was most important in a resume, and 20 percent said "Relevant unpaid/volunteer/intern experience" was a highly valued aspect of a nonprofit resume. Twenty percent of the respondents also said materials "Tailored to the specific organization" were key to being considered for an interview.

your skills and experience for a nonprofit position without having to fill space with irrelevant information.

Focus of your resume

Focus your resume elements (education, experience, professional affiliations, etc.) to show relevance and clearly defined transferability to the specific position, organization, and field of interest/issue area. While membership in organizations or volunteer experience can be important to highlight (because they answer "Will you do the job?"), your membership in the International Ventriloquists Association is not relevant to a development director position at a nonprofit. Membership in the Financial Planning Association, however, demonstrates your commitment to and understanding of long-term financial planning, which transfers well to the role at hand.

The following two focuses are ways to think about **your background** in order to give relevant structure and framing to your resume:

> **Examples of a focus on job function** are: program management, human resource management, policy analysis, administration, or fundraising. In a resume, this can be illustrated by:
> - Work and/or volunteer experience associated with a particular kind of job function. For example:
>   * Served on a board of directors: demonstrates governance and financial oversight.
>   * Very committed to a public affairs career: gained related work experience and talked to a variety of professionals in the field.
>   * Enjoy speaking before groups: provided campus tours and information sessions to prospective students and parents, presented to department managers at Sears, and offered teaching assistantship in public speaking course.
> - Relevant academic degrees, specializations, and course work. For example:
>   * Soon to complete B.A./M.A.
>   * Have liberal arts background with courses in writing, communication, and business.
> - Previous job titles and skill sets used to perform duties. For example:
>   * Related experience in marketing and public relations.
>   * Worked in sales and marketing last summer.
>   * Served as public relations and marketing intern—skills are very transferable to public affairs.
> - Appropriate managerial responsibilities for either entry-, mid-, or senior-level positions
> - Relevant foreign language and computer skills
> - Competent in handling market data. For example:
>   * Completed courses in Statistics and Survey Research.

MOVING FROM "THE PERFECT RESUME" TO "THE PERFECT RESUME FOR THIS POSITION"

As you craft the focus, content, and language of your resume, refer back to your "perfect resume" and begin to think about how much your resume for a particular position reflects what you said about yourself in your "perfect resume." It is easy to lose your ability to express your passion for the work as you get mired in content and language. You can express your personality and commitment through experiences and examples that you choose to highlight, while also crafting a resume with a particular reader in mind.

HOW LONG SHOULD YOUR RESUME BE?

There are various opinions on appropriate resume lengths. Here are a few to consider:

- Your resume should be no more than two pages unless you are applying for a senior-level position and have decades of experience.

- Your resume should be one page per degree that you hold.

- Your resume should be one page for every ten years of experience.

- Your resume should only be one page. No exceptions.

These opinions often take for granted that you are staying within your field of expertise when creating a resume. While there is no hard and fast rule, professionals entering a new sector should always err on the side of brevity.

Examples of a focus on field of interest are: access to education, public health care, the environment, prison reform, urban planning, and advocacy for an underrepresented group. In your resume, field of interest focus can be demonstrated through:

- Work and internship experience in organizations within your field of interest
- Volunteer work and community service with organizations in your field of interest. In many professional resumes, people neglect to address their volunteerism, even though volunteering is especially relevant for nonprofit work as it shows your personal commitment to and passion for an issue, implying "Not only will I do the job, but I used to do it well without getting paid. Imagine how committed I'll be with a paycheck attached."
- Relevant academic degrees, specializations, and course work
- Relevant group memberships and/or professional organizations
- Published articles (even if you didn't get paid to write them) related to the field of interest

As you focus your resume, regularly ask yourself if your information answers either or both of the "can you do the job?/will you do the job?" questions. Also, keep in mind the lenses of the "Four Lens Framework" (Issue, Organization, Role, System; see **Chapter Three**) that speak to you. Are you entering the field because of a belief in an issue or is there a specific role you wish to fill? Does your resume demonstrate this?

Content and language of your resume

Deciding what to include in your resume, as well as how you say it, should be dictated by the job for which you are applying. Highlight experiences that will be of value (including relevant volunteerism), and know that it is okay to de-emphasize or omit experiences that are not relevant. Where appropriate to the experience you are detailing, be sure to utilize the specific vocabulary of the nonprofit sector (see pages 128-129 and **Appendix One**). Remember that employers want to see:

Experience in the field (note: this doesn't say "paid experience in the field")

Doing an endurance event with Team in Training that raises money for the Leukemia and Lymphoma Society is a relevant example of fundraising experience. It also demonstrates your commitment to a cause.

Management level

Do you supervise others? Are you responsible for budget and finance? Do you set policy? Are you responsible for operations and oversight? Remember that your title may not fully express your managerial roles and responsibilities.

THE MASTER RESUME

If you create a "Master Resume" with all the responsibilities, skills, and accomplishments for every job you list, you can quickly draft a resume specific to each position you apply for. Simply delete irrelevant bullet points and then reorder your remaining points to align with the job qualifications essential to the position.

MAKING SURE IT IS ALL RELEVANT

After you draft a resume for a position, look back over your resume and put a "+" next to any elements that clearly align with the job description (these are elements in your resume that are absolutely, positively relevant to this specific employer's hiring needs), an "N" for elements that neither align nor are irrelevant to the description (these are elements that, while you would like them to be positively relevant to the employer, are at this stage not 100 percent related), and a "−" for any points that are clearly irrelevant and distracting to this specific employer. After a second draft, you want to have as many "+" elements as possible; see if you can reframe any "N" points so they become "+", and see if you can neutralize, de-emphasize, or delete the "−" elements. See the "Resume Worksheet" on page 142 for a way to dissect the position description and help shape the relevancy of your resume.

Skill sets

These are associated with a kind of job or a field (e.g., supervising, analyzing, budgeting, strategic planning, public speaking, motivating, researching, writing, fundraising, regional/demographic understanding, strong local network, fluency in languages).

Note: The above list of skill set examples consists of action verbs. Always use action verbs when communicating your skills (you can consult a glossary of action verbs on pages 140-141). While composing your skill sets, think about the kinds of universal skills that apply in any sector (i.e., transferable skills):

- **Multitasking**: the ability to do several tasks at once, switch gears quickly, manage several long-term projects simultaneously

- **Showing initiative**: starting a new program, solving a longstanding problem, asking for new responsibilities

- **Influence**: getting people to work with you despite not having direct supervision or control over them

- **Managing diversity**: working with people who have varying levels of qualifications and education within your organization. This also includes managing multicultural or multigenerational groups.

- **Working under constraints**: limited time, limited finances, limited staff (all of which are common in nonprofit work)

- **Flexibility**: changing project direction midcourse based on user feedback

- **"Pleasing the masses"**: making sure that everyone is happy, not just the people on your team… also known as stakeholder management

Quantifiable accomplishments and outcomes

These specify the result or impact on the organization and illustrate your contributions to the agency. Consider an activity to be an accomplishment if any of the following were satisfied:

- Planned or designed a program/training process to improve, reduce, or change outcomes (example: Designed and constructed a website that the organization immediately used)

- Improved quality, productivity, teamwork, etc. (example: Awarded a fellowship for excellence in service, work, and leadership.)

- Created an office environment through innovative management that made your team/division/section's work easier to accomplish or more efficient (example: Managed a team of seven colleagues located in three cities across the United States through biannual team retreats and telecommuting.)

- Achieved equal results with fewer resources. Nonprofits love when you can be successful on a limited budget. (example: Developed a promotional brochure which the organization is still using.)

- Achieved a measurable or specific goal or result for the first time (ex-

INADVERTENTLY REVEALING YOUR AGE ON A RESUME

the GREAT DEBATE

On a resume, any information or format that reveals your age may not be advisable, particularly if you are on the younger or older end of the spectrum. First, it can give an employer a reason not to hire you if you're outside of their preferred age range. There are a multitude of reasons why age can cause an employer to not consider you or your resume: lack or excess of experience, salary requirements, preconceived notions about your age group, etc. Second, even if age isn't a factor when an employer considers you for an interview, technically it can create a sticky position for the employer. For example, if you are not chosen for an interview, it could be perceived that it is due to your age, not any of the other factors that may have led to the decision.

While dates are often necessary to include on a resume, be aware of which ones might be possible to omit, particularly if you are either an older or younger job seeker. Keep in mind that for some employers, omitting dates can be as much of a red flag as if you included them. This may sound like a no-win situation, so just be sure you are deliberate about, and comfortable with, the approach you choose.

ample: Improved client return rate to over 75 percent for the first time in the organization's history.)

- Increased funding, revenues, resources, outreach, support, etc. Nonprofits love this, too. (example: Created alternative revenue streams through "Friends of the Opera" gift packages sold during intermission.)
- Reduced costs, turnover, problems, etc. (example: Helped decrease assembly line turnover rates by employing a job-sharing schedule and flex hours to accommodate line workers' requests for three-day weekends.)

Whenever possible, **present your accomplishments in numerical terms**, using percentages, monetary amounts, and numbers of clients served. Numbers jump off the page and help an overwhelmed potential hirer see your worth quickly and quantifiably. Examples include:

- Co-wrote a media campaign that increased sales by 37 percent
- Honored as "Top Salesperson of the Year" from 2002-2007 for bringing in an annual average of $3.5 million in new contracts
- Initiated winter series of workshops, which increased programmatic income 25 percent and helped solve organizational cash flow problems
- Increased revenues 15 percent by reviewing third-party payments for irregularities

Reread the job description again to identify key phrases and jargon. Incorporating some of this vocabulary into your resume is a quick and easy way to show employers that you have the education, experience, and qualifications they are seeking. However, do not directly copy and paste language from the job description or organizational mission statement and description; this makes it look like you are pandering and/or lazy. Use your thesaurus instead.

Formatting your resume: The chronological vs. functional debate

There is an ongoing debate about the merits of chronological versus functional resume formats. Resumes that are not in the traditional chronological order tend to raise suspicion since this is the format that most employers expect, but the chronological approach has its limitations. For mid-career professionals, a combination of chronology and functionality often works best. For a link to samples of each format, see the "Learn More" sidebar on page 135

Chronological resumes are straightforward and easy to scan. However, chronological resumes can give away your age and expose questionable gaps or other deficiencies in your work history. If you would like to stick with the chronological format to avoid suspicion, consider whether your education or your experience (including, as always, volunteer experience) is stronger. Place the stronger section first.

GAPS IN EMPLOYMENT

There is simply no way around the fact that gaps in employment or experience can catch an employer's attention, and typically not in a good way. It is impossible to know if someone looking at your resume will be more impressed with a steady employment record or the fact that you took some time away from your career to explore, travel, learn, etc. As such, it is generally a good idea to either avoid resume gaps or explain them clearly in your cover letter.

One way to avoid resume gaps is to omit months when listing employment history. For example, if you quit a job in February of 2006 and did not work again until November of 2006, you can smooth over the gap by simply listing the years worked: "Job X 2004-2006, "Job Y 2006-present." If you are going to omit months for one position, be sure to do so consistently throughout your resume.

If you plan to address the gaps in your employment, make sure to do so in the context of the position for which you are applying. For example, include any unpaid experiences during your employment gaps if they're relevant to the work you wish to do. Remember, relevant volunteer experience can be as valuable as paid work experience to most nonprofit hiring managers. You can also talk about how the experiences during your employment gap broadened your perspective on a certain issue or energized you to make a difference in a given community, or mention other tangible ways that what you did during your gap time relates to the passion and purpose that you hope to bring to an organization.

Functional resumes are organized by thematic skill areas or job functions and give you greater control over the organization and flow of your resume since you are not restricted by chronology. If you are looking to make a career transition, it may make more sense to organize your resume thematically in order to highlight your relevant skills and experiences as they apply to the particular position you are seeking. This also de-emphasizes recent irrelevant experiences. However, no matter how well you craft your functional resume, an underlying question for this format could be, "What are they trying to hide?"

A combination or hybrid resume can be a great solution for career shifters. This format begins with a functional overview of skills and follows with a chronological list of experiences. But beware: these resumes can be repetitious or too long if not carefully crafted.

Experience

This section covers both paid and unpaid experiences. Remember, when applying for a nonprofit job, relevant unpaid volunteer experience can be as highly valued as paid experience. As you format your experience section, consider how to best frame your work and volunteer experiences in order to make them as applicable and transferable as possible to the specific job you are seeking.

If your work experience is a greater match with a particular job description than your volunteer experience, list your work first. You can also divide your work and volunteer experience into separate sections and then give priority to whichever experience is more relevant. Thus, it is possible to highlight your volunteer experience first, your education second, and your work experience third.

Sample resumes

You can view sample chronological, functional, and hybrid resumes at the online resource page for this chapter:

www.idealist.org/en/career/guide/ch8resources.html

What if you don't have volunteer experience?

If you've racked your brain and cannot think of any times in your life that you've volunteered in any capacity, then it is time to start… slowly. While you may not have thought you had time in the past to volunteer, you should realize the old concept of setting aside several hours a week to do some sort of volunteering is now largely outdated. You can find an abundance of volunteer opportunities that you can do on your own time (and often from home). You can also find nonprofits near your home or workplace that you can help for short periods of time (a "lunch hour" during the day, an hour on your way home from work, a Saturday morning once a month). Yet another option is to make volunteering a social activity by volunteering where your friends volunteer, organizing a volunteer opportunity for yourself and your coworkers, or volunteering with your family.

Within both your Work and Volunteer Experience sections, use a reverse chronological format to list positions and, within each position, use bullet points to

the GREAT DEBATE

NOT DISTINGUISHING BETWEEN PAID AND VOLUNTEER WORK

While it is acceptable to not over-emphasize unpaid work (for example, by removing the title "Volunteer" from a job description heading), you do not want to mislead employers. The goal of incorporating unpaid work with paid work is to give these experiences–and the skills gained during the work–equal visual weight. Be clear within a job description when the work was undertaken as a volunteer. Failure to do so may come back to haunt you if a reference check is done and the potential employer learns that you were not wholly forthcoming in your work history. This does not, however, prevent you from emphasizing the personal and professional benefits you gained from all of your experience, volunteer and paid.

highlight the most relevant and substantial elements first. Look over the job description again to decide the order of relevance—the employer tells you what they consider most important based on the order of the job description bullet points.

Accomplishments

A key focus of your experience section should be on your accomplishments in each position. Use action verbs that highlight results to describe your accomplishments: implemented, created, tripled in size, transformed, invented, designed… Results speak more accurately to your skills as a professional and are often eye-catching to the reader (especially if the results have numeric values: "tripled the revenue stream from $250K to $750K").

Education

As with all other aspects of your resume, make sure to only include focused and relevant information in your educational background. Some points to keep in mind when writing the education section include:

- When listing educational experience, include **specialized trainings** and any **certifications** (military, professional, correspondence) that are relevant for the position for which you are applying.

- Make sure to explain **acronyms** and **program titles** for all your training so that employers unfamiliar with jargon from other sectors can clearly understand the relevance of your training and education. For example, if you talk about your experience with the Southeast Alaska Guidance Association (SAGA), define SAGA the first time you use it and then use just the acronym SAGA everywhere else.

- **Educational institutions:** List the full name of your graduate (if applicable) and undergraduate institutions in reverse chronological order (most recent first). Include relevant specializations, coursework, leadership positions, academic and social honors, and related research. If you are applying for work in the same geographic area as your school, consider including the names of professors who are active in the community, especially if they are active in your field of interest. Like numbers, familiar names quickly grab the attention of potential employers. If you choose to "name-drop" in this manner, just make sure that you left a positive impression on that professor during your studies. Also consider including relevant course titles and dates, but be aware that the more recent your studies, the more relevant these courses are likely to seem to hiring staff.

VERB TENSE

You want your verbs to be strong and active and to convey your ability to get results. Use present tense verbs ("design", "implement") for jobs or experiences in which you are currently employed/engaged. For all other experiences (work, volunteer, education, etc.), use past tense ("developed," "increased"). Avoid passive voice ("had attended") as it diminishes the strength of your verbs, and thus your impact.

HOBBIES AND INTERESTS

Including hobbies and interests in your resume can be valuable, but can also completely backfire. Employers may see this as unnecessary "filler" that detracts from the professionalism of your resume, or they may view it as a way to determine if you are a good fit for the culture of the organization. Hiring professionals' opinions vary widely about the relevance of hobbies and interests on a resume, so proceed with caution. You can decide if your hobbies and interests are relevant (interest in South American flora for an environmental education position) or likely to be commonly shared (keeping in mind that even broad-reaching categories have a good chance of not connecting you with an employer). For example, mutual athletic participation or favorite literary genres may or may not be a great icebreaker during an interview. Additionally, the likelihood of your interest in "collecting old TV Guides" or "staring contests" getting you an interview is pretty slim. In general, leave mentions of obscure hobbies and interests out of the resume, and keep mentions of common interest hobbies to a minimum.

Sample excerpt from education section of resume

SAN FRANCISCO STATE UNIVERSITY

Master of Business Administration

- **International Venture Capital Investment Competition Champion**
  - Analyzed real business plans for investment potential by interviewing entrepreneurs and conducting due diligence
  - Selected company to invest in, determined valuation, and wrote term sheet to mitigate risk
- **MBA Leadership Fellow**
  - Selected by MBA program to mentor incoming MBA students in leadership and communication skills
- **Center for Entrepreneurship, Business Plan Competition**
  - Net Impact – President, Marketing Club – VP of Finance
  - Created financial model of our product's business plan
  - Qualified for final round of business plan competition from a field of more than 50 entrants
- **Relevant Coursework**
  - Dr. Henry Jones, Management 416 "Archeological Methodology in Management"
  - Dr. Stephen Hawkings, Marketing 617 "Quantum Physics and Nonprofit Fundraising"

Additional information

The goal of this section is to provide any further relevant information that will cement your viability. This section can also include certifications or other non-degree training and development, professional associations, languages, technical skills, awards, or publications, if you haven't included these elsewhere in your resume. While this may sound simple on the surface, the additional information section can often be among the most challenging parts of a resume to write. This section, more than any other, can become the catch-all for anything that you couldn't fit into your education and experience sections. Avoid the catch-all tendency at all cost. Be selective!

Reread this section of your resume when you are done and be especially critical when asking, "Is this information relevant to this position?"

What *not* to include in a resume

- **Salary History or Requirements** (unless specifically requested): it is way too early for this (however, make sure to read the discussion of salary negotiation in **Chapter Ten**).
- **Grade Point Average**: unless you are recently out of school and had a 3.8 or better, leave it out. Even then, GPA is not vital information.
- **Any personal information**: height, weight, photos, or marital or health status. Although this information is commonly included in resumes in many other

A STATEMENT OF OBJECTIVE

One perspective is that your objective should be clear from your resume structure and cover letter; a carefully crafted, well-written resume should itself be a clear and concise summary of why you are a good match for the position. Why would you need a summary of a summary? However, a clear objective statement can frame the content and tone of your resume and, as such, can provide a "grab" for the hiring manager who is quickly perusing resumes. From the employer's perspective, a "Summary of Qualifications" or another such opening element that highlights the most salient aspects of your qualifications can frame what you have to offer much better than a statement of what you are looking for. (To see a sample resume with a summary, go the webpage in the "Learn More" sidebar on page 135.)

countries, the United States has a variety of anti-discrimination regulations that make it best to leave these details out of your resume.

Presentation

Your resume *must* be flawless. No pressure.

A single error in a resume can make employers assume that you are careless in your work. Proofread your resume. **Print it out and proofread it again.** Seeing your words on paper will help you catch small mistakes that you may not notice on screen. Remember that a printed version of your resume is likely what the potential employer will examine.

Now, read it out loud. Have at least two other people proofread your paper resume. Then, proofread your resume at least one more time. Now, read it aloud one final time to help you catch any remaining errors.

- Use **bold** or ALL CAPS (sparingly) to highlight positions and organizations.
- Use a slightly **larger font size for section headings**. For example, if your resume is in 12-point font, use 14-point font for section headings.
- **Use bullets**—employers prefer them. Bullets:
  * Give the eye a chance to rest and an opportunity to focus
  * Are a great way to highlight responsibilities, skill sets, and accomplishments
  * Allow you to easily re-arrange specific items so you can target your resume to a specific employer or sector
- **Use a standard font** like "Times New Roman" or "Arial". **Don't use a font size lower than 10-point**. A small font can be especially frustrating to readers with diminished eyesight and an employer may choose to discard the resume rather than trying to squint and read it.
- **Keep consistent margins**; margins should never be smaller than a half inch. You have a little room to maneuver when it comes to the vertical spacing between lines (decreasing the font size on an empty line to 4-point, for example) but having clean margins makes your resume all the more inviting to read. Also bear in mind that extra-wide margins may result in your resume not printing properly and it is obviously best to avoid this costly mistake.
- Keep lots of white space on the page—remember **it's the quality of what is written that matters, not the quantity**. A jumbled, cluttered resume will quickly end up in the discard pile.
- Use 8 1/2" x 11" (**U.S. letter size**) white or off-white, high quality paper if you need to mail in a resume. Use only white paper when faxing your resume. Use **black ink**.

MY RESUME IS THE PLACE TO DISTINGUISH MYSELF FROM THE CROWD!

There is no doubt that you will have to find a way for your resume to distinguish itself from the heaps of others that are submitted for any (and almost every!) position. And while using colored paper, fancy fonts, or (of all things) glitter and confetti in the envelope may get you noticed, it may be noticed in a way that will quickly send your resume to the "no" pile. There are few jobs where you will be hired because of your demonstrated knowledge of sans serif fonts or your choice of fluorescent paper. Hiring managers have precious little time to scan all of the resumes for the candidate who can clearly (and without bells and whistles) show themself to be able to fulfill all of the requirements of the position.

You can distinguish yourself by clearly demonstrating how your experience will benefit the organization, making your commitment to the organization's mission apparent, and following the directions for submission. You'd be surprised how distinctive that is to a potential employer.

The final look-over

Once you've got everything written out, organized, and proofread several times, print out a fresh copy and take a break. Give yourself at least half an hour away from the resume (though the more time you take, the better). With a fresh eye, come back and quickly scan your resume. Which elements, sections, or words catch your eye? Which elements take up the most space? Do these elements relate to the requirements of the position and how you will best meet those requirements?

Remember, you have control over what the reader will pay the most attention to and you obviously want the reader to spend most of their time on the pieces most relevant to the position. If one job or experience has more bullet points than another, the reader will naturally assume that the job with more bullet points is more important. Remember, the quality of the description matters more than the quantity of bullets.

> **You have control over what the reader will pay the most attention to in your resume."**

A cautionary tale: Revenge of the tracked changes

Like most people, you are probably drafting your cover letter and resume using Microsoft Word. In Word, you can choose the "Track Changes" option (which you can find under the "Tools" menu). This editing tool produces little marks that highlight each change you make to your document as you edit. "Track Changes" can be useful if others are helping to edit your work and you would like to track the modifications they make. When you are editing on your own, it is best not to track your changes.

If you have chosen the "Track Changes" option, you must "Accept Change" for each change you make to the document in order for the tracking mark to go away. Why is this relevant? Because your document could go out via email with "Track Changes" on and arrive in the hiring person's inbox with all the changes visible. This is embarrassing and unprofessional.

You can significantly decrease the chance of this happening by clicking the "Accept All Changes in Document" option (risky), accepting suggested changes one by one or making your document "Read Only" (safer), or sending as a PDF file (safest). Before you email a resume to a potential employer, run a test by sending a copy of your resume to another one of your email addresses or to a friend or family member to make sure that it arrives the way you intend.

After you've completed your final version, have a detail-oriented, brutally honest friend look it over and see if they can spot any structural problems (typos, ambiguous phrases, etc.), as well as identify the kind of skills you are aiming to highlight. A good way to go about this is to not tell your friend the specific qualifications asked for in the job description. See if they can deduce that information from your resume. If this information is apparent, well done. If not, discuss with your friend how you can shift the focus, wording, or content of your resume.

"Ring, ring"

People making hiring decisions usually have a very limited amount of time with far too many resumes to go through. Typically, they will scan the resumes quickly and pull aside 15-20 resumes to peruse more carefully. Assume this person's perspective when you look over your resume this final time. Pretend the phone is ringing, you have a meeting in 20 minutes followed by a conference call, and you need to present the Executive Director with the eight best resumes after your call. You have all of 15 minutes to weed through 100 resumes. As unfair as this may seem to a candidate, this situation is all too real.

Ask yourself, "Does my resume stand out enough? Can the hiring individual see my value to this position and organization in 10-15 seconds?"

Rework your resume (which usually means editing and shortening) until the answer is a definitive YES.

A glossary of action verbs

The verbs in the gray boxes on this page and the next can help you avoid formulaic "resume speak" and use vocabulary that describes your experience more dynamically. Of course, proceed with a bit of caution—be sure the verbs you choose really suit the activity you are describing!

Assuming responsibility, working, and creating results:

Accept	Coordinate	Gather	Prepare
Achieve	Describe	Generate	Present
Adopt	Design	Halt	Problem solve
Arrange	Develop	Handle	Process
Assemble	Dig	Implement	Produce
Assume	Dispense	Improve	Receive
Attend	Distribute	Initiate	Reduce
Audit	Double	Install	Repair
Build	Enforce	Integrate	Review
Carry out	Engage	Leverage	Sell
Chart	Establish	Maintain	Simplify
Check	Evaluate	Make	Transact
Classify	Expand	Network	Triple
Collect	Expediate	Operate	Update
Compile	Experience	Orchestrate	Use
Conserve	Fix	Organize	Utilize
Consolidate	Fortify	Overcome	
Construct	Garner	Perform	

Investigating, researching, and creating change:

Adapt	Discover	Initiate	Research
Analyze	Distribute	Inspect	Review
Assess	Establish	Interpret	Revise
Calculate	Evaluate	Investigate	Rewrite
Change	Expand	Monitor	Search
Compile	Explain	Observe	Solve
Compute	Experiment	Originate	Study
Conceive	Familiarize	Prove	Transform
Correlate	Find	Read	Verify
Decide	Improve	Reinvent	
Devise	Increase	Reorganize	

Working with and directing people:

Administer	Decide	Instruct	Recruit
Accommodate	Delegate	Join	Regulate
Advise	Determine	Lead	Resolve
Answer	Direct	Manage	Specify
Approve	Discipline	Mediate	Supervise
Authorize	Engage	Motivate	Support
Brainstorm	Evaluate	Negotiate	Team build
Coach	Facilitate	Notify	Train
Compromise	Guide	Order	Tutor
Conduct	Handle complaints	Oversee	Work on a team
Control	Head	Prescribe	

Communicating and interacting:

Advise	Counsel	Interpret	Present
Aid	Critique	Interview	Promote
Apprise	Design	Inform	Proofread
Build consensus	Display	Listen	Report
Clarify	Edit	Mediate	Speak publicly
Coach	Engage	Moderate	Suggest
Confer	Explain	Negotiate	Summarize
Consult	Express	Recommend	Synthesize
Contribute	Facilitate	Represent	Teach
Cooperate	Help	Resolve	Translate
Coordinate	Inspire	Participate	Unify
Correspond	Interact	Persuade	Write

Resume Worksheet

Use the categories below to dissect the position description and to help shape your resume. The organizations and workplaces that appear in the third column should comprise most, if not all, of the work experience on your resume. The bullets in the fourth column should be the only bullets you include on your resume.

Job detail, skill, or qualification	Have?	Where did I get this experience (including volunteering)?	What bullet points can I use to describe the experience?
Writing and communications	Yes	AmeriCorps/St. Johns Neighborhood Association Internship with Multnomah County Healthy Start	• Wrote six community newsletters and distributed them to 500 neighborhood residents, organizations, and businesses. Distribution list grew to 1,000 within six months. • Developed and implemented marketing plan for fundraiser. Through press releases, radio announcements, and public speaking, brought in $42,000 and funded the program for one more year.
Database management software	Yes	Internship with Idealist.org	• Using Salesforce, imported and managed 300 contacts; implemented an outreach campaign using mail merge. Enabled manager to reach out to 95% of clients from previous year.

Cover letters

The purpose of the cover letter

Cover letters are vital marketing tools that clearly define what you bring to the table. Additionally, your cover letter is usually one of the first pieces of information a prospective employer sees about you. If a busy hiring person is unimpressed with your cover letter, they may not even bother reading your resume.

Put simply, your cover letter is a piece of persuasive writing. Together with a resume, the cover letter should generate sufficient interest on the part of employers to make them curious enough to meet you. A good cover letter:

- Introduces who you are—your skills, experiences, education, background, and interests—as it relates to *this* job
- Clearly articulates why you are interested in working for *this* specific organization
- Does not exceed one page

Writing a good cover letter involves thinking about why you want this particular job and forces you to consider your qualifications. It is crucial that you understand what the employer is seeking, and then reflect that understanding through your cover letter. Be especially mindful of the specific terminology used in the nonprofit sector while preparing your materials (see pages 128-129 and **Appendix One** for more information on nonprofit vocabulary).

Nonprofit employers are interested in good communicators and your cover letter highlights (for better or for worse) your writing and communication skills. Poorly structured cover letters, or those with typographical, grammatical, or spelling errors, are used as quick criteria to screen candidates out of the process.

If you succeed with this "on-paper presentation" you have a greater chance of proceeding to the next step in the job search process, which is the "in-person presentation", better known as the interview. Bottom line: cover letters are much too important to take for granted.

Cover letter content

Talking points

Every job is defined by a unique combination of elements that the employer requires. Your work history, volunteerism, academic background, and even which issue areas you feel passionately about must all be presented in the context of what the organi-

 It is crucial that you understand what the employer is seeking, and then relect that understanding through your cover letter."

zation does and what they are looking for in a given candidate. For this reason, successful cover letters are *never* generic—they must be targeted to the set of required experiences and skills outlined in the job description. You can have several resumes ready to tweak and reorganize based on the position you are applying for, but you should write a new cover letter for each position. Experienced search committees can see right through a formulaic cover letter and will often quickly discard it.

Before you actually begin writing the cover letter, first identify the **required job elements**, and then consider which set of elements should be emphasized. Since cover letters should be just a few paragraphs long, deciding what to leave out will be easier if you put your energy into pinpointing what *must* be included.

In order to objectively extract talking points from a job description, you can approach the process analytically by taking the following steps:

Step one: Conduct research on the organization

The goal of this research is to develop *organizational talking points* to which you can refer in the introduction and conclusion of the cover letter. A few places to look when conducting your research are websites, brochures, marketing literature, annual reports, organizational directories, and trade journals.

- Explore the organization's mission—what they do, how they do it, and why they do it. Even if you are familiar with the agency, find out how they describe what they do. First and foremost, the mission defines a nonprofit, so it is crucial to quickly demonstrate your understanding of the context of their work.
- Determine how the position connects with the mission.
- Find out how this agency is different from similar organizations in the field. Be able to answer the question: "What makes this organization unique?"

Step two: Deconstruct the job or internship description

The goal of this step is to identify the raw description requirements and reduce them to manageable, refined description requirements. At this point, you should be able to answer the question: "What are the jobs, tasks, and responsibilities likely to be?"

- Identify and underline the required qualifications and skills in the description.
- Underline the responsibilities and task descriptions.

Step three: Consolidate and prioritize the key requirements you have extracted

You should end up with a list of five to ten refined position requirements that will allow you to write a cover letter emphasizing qualities the employer is seeking.

- Infer what the employer considers most important among the requirements outlined in the job description.
- Usually, employers reveal their priorities by listing the most important tasks and job requirements first, by repeating the same tasks throughout the job description, or by highlighting similar elements in different ways.

Step four: Plug yourself into the organizational and job requirements

Compare your background and draw parallels to the refined description requirements you have culled from the job description. Consider your relevant:

- Work experience
- Academic experience (degrees, program, specialization, and relevant coursework; other degrees; certifications; study abroad; etc.)
- Sector knowledge (your knowledge of: recent developments and trends in the nonprofit sector; the focus of organizations; influential people; etc.)
- Skill sets (managerial, financial, analytical, research, evaluative, public speaking, language, technical/computer, communication, team building, etc.)
- Beliefs/values (what commitments do you share with the organization?)
- Volunteer experience
- Leadership roles (awards, community organizations, work groups, etc.)

You should then arrive at a point where you can create a set of necessary talking points to use in the body of your cover letter that can also be used later during an interview.

If you follow these steps, you can objectively determine how qualified you will be in the employer's eyes based on the job description. It is unlikely that many candidates will have all of the required elements for a particular position. The closer you are, however, the better the fit.

Remember, like the resume, the cover letter should answer: Can you do the job? Will you do the job? Will you fit in? As a piece of persuasive writing, the cover letter is the primary place to convince the employer that the answer to all three questions is "Yes."

Cover letter structure

A cover letter should not exceed one page or five paragraphs, and it should be written in concise, professional language. When considering whether to be short and sweet versus sophisticated and expressive, let relevance to the position be your guide. Usually, four paragraphs is sufficient but three paragraphs are even better. Remember, your reader is busy and too many paragraphs can be a strong a visual deterrent.

"AVAILABLE UPON REQUESTS" AND SALARY

"References/Writing Samples/Additional Information available upon request": One view on these components is that they are obvious and unnecessary to mention; of course these items are available if requested. However, these statements, which occur toward the end of a cover letter or resume, can also be seen as a visual signifier that there is no further information and that this is "The End." If the job description has explicitly requested references or writing samples, you should include these in your cover letter or in a separate, clearly labeled section. As another alternative, you could include online links to your writing samples.

Salary History or Requirements: It is probably way too early in the game for this. This topic is best broached face-to-face during the interview rather than in writing. If the position description does not include a salary range, it is worth your time and the organization's time to make sure during an interview that the salary they are offering is one that you can accept. See **Chapter Ten** for more information on negotiating your compensation package.

For any and all aspects of your resume, be sure to consider both the position for which you're applying and your personal preferences. When it comes down to it, you're just not going to please every hiring manager with the multitude of style and content choices you'll make on your resume. The best you can do is be deliberate with your choices and try to make them relevant to the positions for which you're applying.

First paragraph: Introduction

- Introduce yourself by stating the position for which you are applying and where you heard about the position. If someone referred you to this organization, mention that person's name in the first sentence (assuming you have asked for, and they have given you, permission beforehand).

- Refer to your organizational and necessary talking points—communicating elements of shared interest can hold the attention of the reader.

- State that you have the requisite combination of skills to be an asset to the organization. Your challenge in subsequent paragraphs is to back this up.

Second paragraph: Professional and academic background

- If you anticipate your cover letter being longer than three paragraphs, it is important to concentrate on either your academic background or your professional background in your second paragraph. This will help you stay focused.

- Refer to your necessary talking points and highlight how you have the required skills to contribute to the organization. You should be expressing more here than stock sentences, like "I have strong research skills." Instead, explain how and what you have researched. For example, "My Fulbright research on volunteer management in Canada and the United States was incorporated into several articles published in major industry newsletters." You must draw a direct link between what you are referring to and what the employer is looking for. Give specific examples. Pull out a strong element or two from your resume. Remember, cover letters are not written in a vacuum.

- If you are writing a three-paragraph cover letter, it is fine to make this paragraph a combination of your academic and professional experience.

Third paragraph: Professional, academic, or "wildcard"

- Again, refer to the necessary talking points, and highlight how you have the required skills to contribute to the organization.

- This is also an area where you can speak to skills you possess that are not necessarily professional or academic—wildcard elements that may need to be expressed. They may be industry-related or stand-alone: technical and IT skills, regional understanding, languages, communication skills, etc.

- If you can include your "other" skills in your second paragraph without making it too long, do so and omit this paragraph.

Fourth paragraph: Synthesis/conclusion

- By way of conclusion, synthesize a number of elements already outlined

---

Additional points on cover letters

- A resume should always be accompanied by a cover letter, even if it is not requested.

- Whenever possible, cover letters should be addressed to the specific hiring person rather than "HR" or "Personnel." Pay close attention to spelling and job titles when addressing the contact person. A typo here could spell a quick trip to the trash for your application. When you cannot find a specific person to send your application to, it is still common practice to use the phrase "To Whom It May Concern" or "Dear Sir or Madam."

- Typographical and spelling errors can cost you a job. Use spell check as you type (but don't trust it), proofread your letter on paper at least three times, and ask someone else to look at it with a fresh eye.

- Don't forget to sign original letters and keep copies of all correspondence.

- Use good quality white or off-white paper for your resumes and cover letters.

- Make sure your name and phone number are on the cover letter in case it gets separated from your resume.

- If you are sending your cover letter via email, sending the letter as the text of the email message is acceptable. If sending your cover letter as an attachment, keep the text of your email message professional and brief. For example: "Attached are my cover letter and resume for the open ____ position with your organization. I look forward to hearing from you."

- Remember to attach your resume to the email. It is pretty embarrassing if you need to send two emails because you forgot the attachment.

- If possible, convert your resume and cover letter to PDF format to ensure that you are not sending a document with "track changes" leftovers from the writing process.

in your cover letter. Keep in mind that synthesizing and repeating are two very different processes.

- Stress your commitment to what the organization does or your high level of motivation.
- Mentioning the agency's stature in the field can be effective, too.
- You may also reinforce your professional and academic qualifications as they relate to the employer's needs.
- Tell them that your resume is enclosed.
- Include your telephone number and email address.
- Thank the employer for their time and consideration and state that you look forward to hearing from them.

Conclusion

Resumes and cover letters are the tools you use to market your distinct skills on paper. Since every employer and job opening is unique, your resume and cover letter must be customized and tailored for each position you pursue. By crafting resumes and cover letters that connect your *relevant* experience and abilities to those required by the employer, you can make your application materials "speak" to the people deciding which applicants to invite for an interview. The next chapter explores how to prepare yourself for an in-person presentation of the points you've made on paper in your resume and cover letter.

What if I don't hear back?
Be sure to give the employer several days to review your materials, and check the job announcement to see if they've indicated when they'll respond to applicants or announce a decision. If you don't hear anything from the employer after that time, feel free to send them an email (much preferred over calling) to inquire about the status of your application. Unfortunately, some employers don't have (or take) the time to keep applicants updated on the hiring process.

SUMMARY

Together, your resume and cover letter form the backbone of your job search. You should keep the following factors in mind while working on these essential nonprofit job search tools.

While creating your resume and cover letter, remember to **address the three questions** (pages 125-127): Can you do the job? Will you do the job? Will you fit in?

Market your distinct skills by addressing broader categories that relate to working with people, resources, information, and systems. Then use the language of the nonprofit sector to convey these skills to the employer (pages 127-129).

The **elements that every resume should have** are: name and contact information, *relevant* education and experience, volunteering and other forms of community involvement, and other qualifications that indicate your viability as a candidate for a specific position. These elements must be **tailored for the particular organization and position** you are applying to as well as for the nonprofit sector in general (pages 130-137).

Your resume should focus on showing the **relevance and transferability** of the aforementioned elements to the specific position, organization, and issue area (page 131, sidebars on pages 131 and 132).

Carefully consider resume attributes such as **length, format, and presentation** since these will help you present yourself in the most effective and concise way possible (pages 130-141).

An original, persuasive cover letter reflects your understanding of what the employer wants and how you are uniquely able to fill those needs. While there are clear parameters around a cover letter's structure, a cover letter should always be written specifically for the organization and position for which you are applying. They should never be generic or formulaic (pages 143-147).

CHAPTER NINE

Presenting yourself in person

Interviewing and first impressions

by **David Schachter**, Assistant Dean for Career Services and Experiential Learning

at NYU's Robert F. Wagner Graduate School of Public Service[*]

In this chapter you will:

- Learn the four keys to successful interviewing: know what the employer wants, be able to articulate how you can meet the employer's specific needs, behave in a way that convinces the employer that you fit into their organization, and prepare and practice.

- Understand the process of preparing for an interview.

- Consider how appearance and body language play significant roles in the first impression that people have of you.

- Learn the big interview dos and don'ts.

- Make sure you are prepared for the interview with the "Night Before Checklist".

- Recognize the importance of following up an interview with a thank you note. Every time.

Interview preparation

First of all, relax. It's easier than you think...

If you have prepared a quality cover letter and resume—a very distinct possibility since you have made it through round one into the interview phase—then you are nearly 80 percent ready for the interview. The potential employer has just weeded through a stack of resumes and pulled out yours. They have already committed time and energy to you and are hoping that you are a good fit. In other words, the employer is on your side and they *want* you to succeed during the interview.

Now, the hard part

Your interview will ultimately determine whether or not you get a job offer. Sadly, many candidates who looked great on paper flub the interview by failing to articulate their value to the employer. This doesn't have to be the case, since effective interview-

---

[*] In this section on interview preparation, the "Now, the hard part", "Preparing for the interview", "Interview dos and don'ts", and "Interview follow-up" discussions are by David Schachter. Grateful acknowledgment is made to New York University for permission to reprint excerpts from and adapt the work of David Schachter, Assistant Dean of Career Services and Experiential Learning at NYU's Robert F. Wagner Graduate School of Public Service © 2008. Reprinted with permission of New York University and David Schachter. http://wagner.nyu.edu. Some modifications to the original text have been made by the staff at Idealist.org.

ing skills can be learned. By knowing what to expect and being prepared, you greatly enhance your chances of receiving a job offer.

The four keys to successful interviewing are:

- Know what the employer wants
- Be able to articulate how you can meet the employer's specific needs
- Behave in a way that convinces the employer that you fit into their organization (especially significant for the culture-driven success of many nonprofits)
- Prepare and practice

Preparing for the interview

You should be very familiar with the job description and knowledgeable about the organization after finishing your cover letter and resume (see the discussions on resumes and cover letters in **Chapter Eight**). Be sure to print out or save a copy of the job description as they are often removed from the internet once the application deadline has passed.

For the first three steps of your interview preparation, you will be digging deeper into the same areas you explored when crafting your cover letter: researching the organization; creating job description talking points; and assessing your knowledge, experience, skills, and accomplishments to create desired talking points. The fourth and fifth steps of interview preparation involve developing answers to common interview questions and creating your own questions to ask the interviewer.

During the interview, your experience, career interests, and passions should all be presented in the context of what the organization does and what they are looking for in a given candidate—in essence, you want to focus on **the value you bring to the employer**.

In order to objectively extract talking points from a given job description, you can take the following analytical approach:

During the interview, you want to focus on the value you bring to the employer."

Step one: Conduct research on the organization

The goal of this research is to develop *organizational talking points* to use in the interview either as a statement or a well crafted question. Organizational talking points will also help you understand the context of the conversation that you will have during the interview.

- Explore the organization's mission—what they do, how they do it, and why they do it. Even if you are familiar with the agency, find out how they describe what they do. The mission first and foremost defines a nonprofit, so it is crucial to demonstrate your understanding of the context of their work.

- Determine how the position connects with the mission.
- Find out how this agency is different from similar organizations in the field. Know the answer to the question: "What makes this organization unique?"
- A few places to look when conducting your research are websites, brochures, marketing literature, annual reports, organizational directories, trade journals, and search engine results for press mentions and recent events.

Here's an example of incorporating organizational talking points into a question:

"I know your organization meets its mission by not only engaging in direct service at the local Teen Center but also providing resources for parents on its website. Are there other ways you plan to expand your outreach in the future?"

Step two: Create job description talking points

Deconstruct the job description in order to create *job description talking points*. Go back through the job description and highlight the qualifications and skills outlined in it. Underline the requirements and task descriptions. You should end up with a list of five to ten *refined position requirements* that will allow you to accurately describe the qualities sought by the employer. For these points, infer what the employer considers most important among the requirements outlined in the job description. Usually, employers indicate their priorities by listing the most important tasks and job requirements first, by repeating the same tasks throughout the job description, or by highlighting similar elements in different ways. For example:

"There is a clear emphasis on project coordination and leadership for this Construction Manager position with Habitat for Humanity. Can you give me an example of how these skills play out on a worksite?"

 Employers usually indicate their priorities by listing the most important tasks and job requirements first."

Step three: Assess your knowledge, experience, skills, and accomplishments

Draw parallels between the skills and experience you offer and the *job description talking points*. Ask yourself:

- "Where are there clear connections between the job and my skills?" Make sure that you can talk about these strengths with confidence. These are your major selling points.
- "Where are there clear differences between the job and my skills?" You will surely find some gaps between what the organization wants and what you can offer. It is unlikely that a candidate will have all of the required elements and this is especially true for mid-career professionals moving into the nonprofit sector.

There is a fine line between emphasizing transferable skills and claiming to have skills and experience that you really don't have. This is your chance to highlight—and *not* overemphasize—transferable skills.

The goal of Step Three is to develop *talking points to illustrate your matching skills*, i.e., talking points that you want to make sure to bring up during the interview. The talking points should show how your skills connect to the job description to ensure that the employer sees your "fit."

For example:

> *"I've led projects in my* **communications** *major for three different courses and helped to create better* **marketing** *plans for several campus organizations. As a result, I was responsible for increasing* **outreach** *for these organizations by an average of 20 to 30 percent in the first year of each new campaign. Since I bring diverse experience and an understanding of these best practices, I feel I will be very successful in fundraising and development. Plus, my experience as a project leader makes me comfortable managing others, including coworkers and volunteers, while working under a tight deadline."*

In this statement, the bold non-italicized words (communications, marketing, and outreach) are good examples of replacing business vocabulary—marketing, brand, and sales respectively—with the language of the nonprofit sector (see **Chapter Eight**'s "Marketing Your Distinct Skills" discussion for more details). It's important to use the language of the nonprofit sector, but if your interviewers do use business language or other specific vocabulary, you should feel comfortable using this terminology, too. It's a situation where you should follow and not necessarily lead.

Step four: Answering common interview questions

Now that you can talk about the organization, the job description, and how you fit into each area, it is time to make sure you can answer common interview questions:

Having strong *organizational*, *job description*, and *desired talking points* will help you ace most interview questions. At a bare minimum, be prepared to answer the following questions:

- Tell me about yourself. (See the "Elevator Pitch" activity in **Chapter Four**.)
  - * Do not assume that the interviewer remembers your resume.
- What do you know about our agency? Why did you choose this organization? Why are you interested in this specific position?
- What skills, experience, education, and training do you have that make you qualified for this job?
- Where do you see challenges in this position? Is there anything you don't feel qualified or comfortable doing?
  - * The answer to this should be humble without being negative: "I could use training with your database software but I know my strong computer skills will help me pick it up quickly."

- Why should we hire *you* in particular?
- How long do you plan to stay in the area? How long do you plan to stay at this organization? What are your long-term goals?
  - * Whether you are young or old, organizations like to know that you are reliable and have plans to stick around. Obviously, no one can predict the future but you can give a realistic outline of your plans without being overly committal or unnecessarily ambiguous. Frame your answer so that it is reassuring and shows commitment to your professional goals.
- What are your strengths?
  - * Answer this question as if they'd actually asked: What strengths of yours will benefit our organization/this position?
- What are your weaknesses?
  - * Answer this question in terms of challenges you've faced and what you've done to overcome them. How did you identify the problem and how did you work to solve it? Always end on a positive note.
  - * A good way to frame a problem and solution is by using the **PAR** method: What was the **P**roblem? What **A**ction did you take? What was the **R**esult? This technique can also be used to answer any questions regarding skills.
- A key part of this position is _____ and, from your resume, you don't seem to have a lot of experience doing this. Can you talk about that?

You should also be prepared to answer any of the following questions:
- What are your career goals? Where do you expect to be in your career in five years?
- How are your writing/analytical/people skills?
- Tell me about your supervisory/managerial/administrative experiences.
- What is your management style?
- Give me an example of your interpersonal skills.
- Give me an example of meeting a deadline.
- What motivates you? How do you motivate others?
- Why do you do volunteer work?
- What professional/social/academic associations do you belong to?
- Do you have any questions for me? (YES! See Step Five below)

Step five: Prepare your own questions to ask

Never leave an interview without asking at least two or three questions about the organization (but make sure it isn't information easily found online), the job and its duties (not already covered in the job description or interview—make sure to ask these early), or the professional background of the interviewer (how their po-

THE NIGHT BEFORE CHECKLIST

Roadmap

Don't leave things to the last minute!

Prepare your "toolkit" to bring to the interview on the night *before* the big day:

❍ Tissues or a handkerchief

❍ Cell phone or beeper (on *silent mode* once you get to the interview)

❍ Extra copies of your resume

❍ Breath mints (not gum!)

❍ Bottle of water

❍ Directions, suite or office number, and a contact phone number

❍ Any notes that you plan to bring (your list of questions for the organization, a list of strengths and weaknesses, anecdotal tales of achievements or successes, etc.)

❍ References in case they are requested during or after the interview

sition fits into the organizational structure, how they connect/interact with other departments, etc.). Asking questions gives the employer an opportunity to gauge your interest and curiosity about the organization, and also shows an extra level of interest in their work. Your questions can also highlight your ability and willingness to prepare for important conversations.

Here are some great questions to ask at the first interview:

- What do you think are the skills and attributes most needed to succeed in this position? (Ask only if they aren't clear from the job description!)
- What kind of support does this position receive in terms of human and financial resources?
- What are the initial short- and long-term projects for this position?
- How will my performance be measured here?
- If I were to take this position, what would you like to say about my work during my first annual review?
- What is the day-to-day office environment like here?
- In five years, where would you like to see this organization?
- What are the main challenges this organization faces in the future?
- Can you tell me why this job is currently open?
- How many people have held this position in the last few years? Why did they leave?
- Where are you in your hiring process and what are your next steps?
- What kind of training or training budget is available for this position? What is training like for new hires? (Be careful when you ask this question as it speaks more to what the organization can offer you instead of what you can offer the organization. This may be a better second interview question.)

Do not ask about salary, benefits, or vacation time until after the second interview, or until after they have made you an offer. See the sidebar on this page for more about subsequent interviews.

The next interview, and the one after that, and the one...

It is quite possible that, as a serious candidate for a position, you will be asked back for a second and even a third (and sometimes a fourth!) interview. Many organizations use the first interview to meet all the candidates who impressed them on paper and then invite a smaller number back who impressed them in person. This means that the first interview is a bit more of the "getting to know you" variety while subsequent interviews are meant for deeper analysis of candidates.

Interview rounds beyond the first can feature a skills assessment (creating an event calendar, promotional blurb, giving a short presentation, etc.) to answer the "Can you do the job?" question; a further discussion of the skills and eagerness that you bring, which answers the "Will you do the job?" question; as well as a cultural fit conversation that helps answer the "Will you fit in?" question.

Keep in mind that when you are invited back for another round of interviews, it is also your time to dig a little deeper into the organization. Subsequent interview rounds are also the point when you should feel more comfortable discussing the nuts and bolts of the job: compensation, professional development, and promotion opportunities. The organization is clearly interested in you and you need to be sure that you are equally interested in both it and the position for which you are interviewing. That said, this is *not* the time to start negotiating (that should only be *after* you are offered a job) but instead the time to fully understand the logistics as well as potential for the position.

A few points on first impressions

You have made it all the way to the interview with a strong cover letter. Now your work rests on the first 30 seconds to four minutes of the interview. First impressions are powerful, decision-making emotions that many of us discount. The truth is, first impressions form in only a few minutes and can influence the rest of the interaction. And while first impressions can be modified after repeated interactions, if you create the wrong first impression during a 30-minute interview, you are unlikely to get a second opportunity.

By following a few simple, straightforward rules, you can ensure that the first few moments after you walk through the interview door are entirely positive. After these crucial minutes, your interviewers will have a generally positive opinion of you and the remainder of your time together will naturally be more pleasant. If you make a poor first impression, it makes for an uphill climb to change opinions. With all of the questions and decisions you need to field, do you really want to start at a disadvantage?

Appearance

Unless the organization you are interviewing with says otherwise, dress professionally for your interview. You may end up going to several nonprofit organizations for interviews where you are the only person in the building in a suit. Just because many nonprofits have a more casual dress code, it does not give you license to arrive in jeans and a t-shirt. Your clean and neat hair and clothing should reflect your professionalism. Even if an organization tells you that it is a "casual office," still make sure to dress on the more professional side of casual, i.e., business casual.

The catch in dressing professionally is that the clothing can oftentimes be uncomfortable. Find two outfits (one for a follow-up interview) that look and feel good on you. Wearing a great looking outfit that you are constantly tugging and pulling defeats the purpose.

Similarly, too much "odor" (cologne, perfume, heavily scented soaps) is usually a deterrent. First, who wants to sit in a heavily perfumed room for 20-30 minutes while trying to concentrate on interviewing? Second, some people have allergies to heavy scents and making someone sneeze for 30 minutes doesn't leave a good impression. Finally, olfactory memories are particularly powerful and you never know when your cologne or perfume is the same as the interviewer's ex.

MANAGE YOUR DIGITAL IMAGE

Before you can begin to actively manage your digital image, you need to know what it is. Start by taking a critical eye to your Facebook or MySpace pages. Are there any parts of your profile or tagged pictures you're in that you wouldn't want a potential employer (or your parents) to see? Stricter privacy settings may help keep some of this away from those you don't want to see it, but they're not always foolproof.

Next, Google yourself. Assume that any potential employer will perform this search–is what shows up an accurate, professional representation of who you are? If your name is even a bit unique, consider setting up a Google Alert– you'll get an email every time your name is found on the internet. This may not be as useful if your name is a more common one like "Jane Smith".

To enhance your digital image, you might consider creating a LinkedIn (www.linkedin.com) profile, listing internships in related fields that you've had, and professional associations you may be a student member of (like the American Psychological Association). Don't forget to include related volunteer activities, majors and minors, or anything else that may pique a potential employer's interest.

Finally, if you see something you don't like, a kindly worded email to the website manager is often all you'll need to get it removed. If that doesn't work, find ways to push more professional information about yourself to the top of the search results: write an article for the student newspaper, comment on a career-related blog, or start your own website or blog.

–Valinda Lee

One final note on dress for those who subscribe to the "I wouldn't want to work at an organization that judges me by my clothes" school of thought: first impressions based on how you dress for an interview aren't about proving your uniqueness or reaffirming your independent streak. Instead, it is a simple psychological fact: people have immediate reactions and form instant impressions, and those reactions fundamentally influence their decisions about, and interactions with, you. Dressing appropriately also shows your ability to adapt to a fairly traditional professional environment, which may be a necessary skill for this position. Let your unique sense of style show *after* you get a job offer. This means covering tattoos, taking out some piercings, not wearing overwhelming cologne or perfume, and so on. You want your interviewer to pay attention to what *you* are saying, not what your appearance seems to be saying.

Body language

You have walked through the door in appropriate and comfortable professional attire and have already begun to help your interviewers form a positive impression of you. Now your confident body language needs to shine. Look everyone in the room directly in the eyes and smile. Shake hands with everyone in the room and make sure it is a good handshake. Don't give the "dead fish" handshake (a limp, effortless grasp without any pressure), nor should you grab the fingertips and squeeze. If you are uncomfortable shaking hands, practice with friends until your motions are fluid and natural.

Continue to make solid eye contact as you field questions during the interview. If making eye contact is difficult for you, practice this simple exercise while going over your interview question preparation:

> Line up a set of objects (vases, cups, a baseball, photos, etc.) on a flat surface in front of you and, as you eloquently answer your practice Q&As, look at each object for a few moments before moving on to the next object. Do this repeatedly until you start to find natural segues in what you are saying (a pause, an emphatic point) to shift your eye contact to your next object.

By shifting your point of focus, you will naturally make eye contact with everyone in the room, thus making your interviewers feel included in the conversation. You can even take "eye contact breaks" while you are thinking and formulating answers. Looking someone in the eyes and saying their name (writing down everyone's name at the start of the interview will help you remember who's who) is a simple yet effective way to create a positive first impression.

NICE DOESN'T MEAN EXPENSIVE

Appearance matters in interviews. If your interviews necessitate a suit, you're going to want to invest in one that looks good. In general with suits, you get what you pay for. However, you can choose what type of "quality" you spend your money on. If you don't have several hundred dollars to spend on a suit that's made of a quality fabric and fits you well, you can buy a less expensive suit and have it tailored to fit. The fabric may not be the best, but the fit will. For $20-$50, you can turn an inexpensive suit into one that will reflect the confident, high quality image you want to convey.

EYE CONTACT ERRORS

A common eye contact mistake is to look at the person who asked you a question and speak to them as though there is no one else in the room. Aside from excluding the other interview participants, this can have the additional negative impact of making the questioner feel uncomfortable under your steady gaze. Another common mistake is to talk to the person who appears to have the most authority. Not only can this alienate anyone else present at your interview, but your perceptions of authority may be wrong, too.

After mastering handshakes and eye contact, the last body language point to be aware of is nervous tics. Controllable physical nervous tics (clicking pens, bouncing your leg, tapping on flat surfaces, etc.) are as irritating and distracting as verbal tics ("umm," "like," "and all"), and both can be avoided. Controllable physical and verbal tics are usually caused by nervousness, so by practicing your answers, taking a few moments to think, and fighting the urge to simply keep on talking, you can break any habits you have. Also, try to practice getting comfortable with verbal silences. You can do this during conversations with your friends or family, at social events, or even when you're conversing with someone at the grocery store. To avoid the temptation of physical tics, remove potentially distracting items from your immediate grasp (pens that "click" or small items like erasers that you fiddle with) and either keep your hands still or use them while talking. Keep both feet firmly on the ground if you tend to bounce. By sitting up straight and not slouching or reclining, you will be more likely to remain alert to your own physical actions.

Jot your thoughts

Use the space below to note any nervous habits you are prone toward. Respond to each thought with an idea on how you can control for that habit.

Roadmap

THINGS TO DO AT AN INTERVIEW

DO...

- Research the job and the organization to develop *required talking points*.
- Practice giving clear and concise answers to common interview questions as they relate to the specific job for which you are interviewing.
- Practice your 30 second speech (consult **Chapter Four** for advice on developing an "elevator pitch").
- Prepare to ask relevant, sophisticated questions.
- Dress conservatively. It is always better to be overdressed.
- Arrive at the interview at least a few minutes early to ensure you will not be late, collect your thoughts, go to the restroom, and familiarize yourself with your surroundings.
- Know the name of the person with whom you are interviewing, and how to pronounce the interviewer's name (subtly write down the name of everyone interviewing you at the start and refer to the names when addressing each person's question or statement).
- Greet the interviewer with a firm handshake, eye contact, and a smile.
- Ask for clarification if you do not understand a question.
- Ask if you have answered a question sufficiently.
- Enjoy yourself. Relax. Remember, they want you to succeed.
- Show confidence. You are interviewing them, too.
- Send a thank you note ASAP that addresses specific and relevant issues that were discussed during the interview.

Enjoy yourself. Relax. Remember, they want you to succeed."

THINGS NOT TO DO AT AN INTERVIEW

DON'T...

- Interview without doing your homework on the organization and the job.
- Assume the interviewer sees your qualifications as clearly as you do, or that they even remember your resume.
- Talk incessantly. Instead, be substantive but concise; if you feel like you are rambling, you probably are.
- Discuss salary, benefits, or vacation time unless it becomes necessary (i.e., the interviewer brings it up or there is a natural segue to the topic).
- Complain about a former or current employer (but be prepared to be honest about employers you don't use as references).
- Plead how much you need a job.
- Look at your watch during the interview.
- Wear (too much... or any) perfume or cologne. Scents can trigger strong emotions.
- Dress or behave too casually.
- Assume the interviewer knows all the right questions to ask.

Interview follow-up

The simple act of sending a thank you note can be extremely powerful. A thank you note expresses thoughtfulness, initiative, and attentiveness—attributes that may be the final deciding factor between two candidates. Moreover, sending thank you notes after an interview is now so commonplace that you will stand out (negatively) if you don't send one. In other words, sending a thank you note is not optional.

Within 24 hours of your interview, send a thank you email or mail a letter. Your email should be sent to everyone with whom you interviewed. If you are mailing a letter, address it to everyone with whom you interviewed and try to send it the same day as the interview to ensure the note arrives as quickly as possible. Considering the fact that many hiring decisions are made soon after the interview, it may make more sense to send an email instead of a letter. Your note should thank the interviewers for their time, articulate again some of the relevant skills and value you would bring to the position, emphasize how you would address their specific needs, and express your continued (and even heightened) interest in the position after the interview.

When crafting a thank you note, reflect on the conversation and questions brought up during the interview. If they talked about a specific problem, project, or responsibility during the interview, you should address this again in your letter.

THANK YOU NOTES: EMAIL, TYPED, OR HAND-WRITTEN?

the GREAT DEBATE

Many career search guides insist on typed, business-style thank you notes. Others underscore the personal touch that a handwritten note sends. Still others espouse the view that as long as a thank you note is sent, it doesn't matter if it's emailed, typed, or handwritten. All of these perspectives are valid; it just depends on the situation. If you've just finished with a formal, suit-and-tie interview at a large nonprofit, a typed note may be appropriate. After your second interview (since you'll have already mailed a thank you note after the first interview), an emailed thank you note might be fitting. To follow up on a relaxed interview at a smaller nonprofit, a handwritten note would be perfect. For any situation, just be sure to make a choice about which format feels most appropriate given the people, the interview, the organization, and your own personality. There is no absolute truth in thank you notes... except that you absolutely must send one!

Here is a common thank you letter structure. Remember, keep it brief and to the point.

First paragraph: Express your appreciation for the interview

- Thank the interviewer for meeting with you.
- Re-emphasize your interest in the position.

Second paragraph: Remind the employer why you are a good candidate

- Write about your skills and strengths as they relate to the position.
- Refer to something specific that the employer mentioned during the interview and address the needs you may be able to meet for the employer.
- Mention any additional points you would like to make that you did not mention during the interview, or that you would like to re-emphasize.

Third paragraph: Reiterate your enthusiasm

- Thank the interviewer again.
- Add that you look forward to hearing from them.

ADDITIONAL POINTERS ON INTERVIEW FOLLOW-UP

Your interview process isn't quite over when you leave the interview! There is still time to make a favorable impression that can help you land the job. Keep these interview follow-up points in mind. They really can make a difference.

- When sending a hard copy of your thank you note, print (or type) your letter on the same standard size, high quality paper that you used for your resume, and use a good quality printer.
- Sign original copies of your letters in blue or black ink.
- Refer to your notes so you can reference what happened during each specific interview.
- Use a professional tone.
- Keep the thank you note to two or three brief paragraphs.
- Do not attach requested references or writing samples to a thank you note. Let the thank you note stand alone and send these other items separately if requested.
- Proofread the letter carefully.
- Double-check spelling of contact names and titles.
- Don't procrastinate. Write your note while the experience is fresh in your mind, and send it soon after the interview.

SUMMARY

Once you've gotten an invitation to an interview, you've already impressed the potential employer... on paper. While you've undoubtedly conducted serious research and put in significant effort up to this point, you're now at the most important part of the process: convincing the interviewer that you are the perfect candidate for the job through your interview and the first impression you leave. To **present yourself well in the interview** and **leave a good first impression**, you should:

Understand **the four keys to successful interviewing** (page 149): know what the employer wants; be able to articulate how you can meet the employer's specific needs; behave in a way that convinces the employer that you fit their organization; and prepare and practice.

Prepare for the interview (pages 150-154) by conducting research; preparing your talking points; assessing your knowledge, experience, skills, and accomplishments; knowing how to answer common interview questions; and preparing your own questions to ask.

Prepare your "toolkit" the **night before the interview** (sidebar, page 153).

Understand **how to influence people's first impressions of you** by being deliberate about your appearance and body language (pages 155-157).

Be aware of the **interview dos and don'ts** (pages 157-158).

Recognize the importance of always following up an interview with a **personal thank you note** (pages 158-159).

CHAPTER TEN

Closing the deal

Understanding benefits and the art of negotiation

In this chapter you will:

- Understand the variety of benefit options and find out how to uncover what benefits an organization offers.

- Decide which benefits are important to you.

- Consider six reasons to negotiate your offer and understand how to go about negotiating a better offer.

- Learn when you should begin the negotiation process.

- Assess whether or not an offer is acceptable for you.

- Plan out a negotiation process that works for you.

You got an offer! Congratulations!

Because of all of your preparation, your resume made an impact, you had a great interview (or two), and you are the one they want to work with. This is definitely time to celebrate—be sure to make time to acknowledge your hard work and success.

But before you accept the offer, take some time to reflect, and assess whether this job is going to meet your professional goals, whether those goals are a better work/life balance, a job you can create from scratch, a sustainable salary and benefits, or anything else that you are seeking from your job at this point in your life. The roadmap at right can help you consider these points (some of which are also discussed in this chapter!).

Understanding benefits

Once an offer is made, it is a common mistake to consider only the salary in determining if an offer is good enough. However, while salary is undoubtedly important, it is only one part of a compensation package. It is important to take all of the benefits into consideration when deciding if a job is a good fit for you. All too often, though, with the complexity and variety of insurance plans, reimbursement programs, and other elements of a compensation package, benefits can become an afterthought: "Well, if they give me *some* kind of health care, what more do I really need?"

BEFORE YOU ACCEPT OR DECLINE AN OFFER...

Before you accept or decline an offer, here are a few things to take into account:

- Don't get caught up in the moment

- Be sure to consider organizational fit

- Recognize that salary is only one component of the compensation package

- Make sure you understand all of the details of the job offer... including benefits

- Don't forget to negotiate–carefully

Think of understanding benefits as a three-step process:

1. **Understanding benefit options**
2. **Deciding which benefits are important to you**
3. **Finding out which benefits the organization offers**

As with anything else, the more information you have, the better the choices you can make and the more control you have over the outcome.

1. Understanding benefit options

Benefits fall into three basic categories: insurance, reimbursement/bonuses, and time off. Due to the tendency toward organization-wide insurance plans, you will probably find the most flexibility in the benefits that fall into the latter two categories. This is also where you will find the most variation from one compensation package to another. At the end of this discussion, on page 164, you'll find a mini-glossary of some of the major benefits with brief descriptions and points to consider for each of them. Please note: most compensation packages will offer only some of these options.

2. Deciding which benefits are important to you

Benefits Checklist: Rank the following benefits in order of importance to your personal situation, with 1 being the most important and 11 the least important. Consider both benefits that you need now, as well as benefits that you anticipate needing in five years. For insurance plans, bear in mind that there can be major discrepancies in costs and coverage level; not all plans are the same.

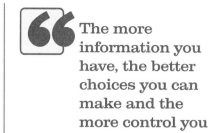

"The more information you have, the better choices you can make and the more control you have over the outcome."

As you fill out the Benefits Checklist, be sure to record your thoughts on the importance of each benefit.

Benefit	Now	In five years
Health insurance with coverage for partner and children		
Vision and dental insurance		
An insurance plan with a good mental health program/employee assistance program		
Specific, recurring medical needs (prescriptions, allergies, physical therapy)		
Assistance with child or elder care costs		
Vacation time		
Flexible schedule/telecommuting/shortened workweek		
A retirement plan/401(k)/403(b)		
Education reimbursement/job training/conference fees		
Moving/relocation reimbursement		
A portable computer, PDA, or other job equipment		
Other:		

While you just ranked the benefits in order of importance to you, you shouldn't have to choose any of these benefits over another. Before you accept a job offer, know what benefits are offered, and compare those to the benefits you need. This will also be important when it comes time to negotiate your compensation package. As with all aspects of finding a job that is a good fit for you, be sure to know what you need, as well as what is being offered.

3. Finding out which benefits the organization offers

It is important to communicate to the organization that, while you are glad to have received an offer, you need to make sure their compensation package is viable for meeting your long-term needs before you can commit to taking the position. After you have convinced the organization of your worth, you need to make sure that the opportunity is a worthwhile one that will provide you with the support you need to do your best work.

Know how to find this information

Many employers now list their benefits plans online so check their websites first. Also consider asking to read an organization's benefits handbook once you've been offered a position. Check to make sure the benefits handbook is current. Alternately, if you have friends who work for the same organization, you can ask them specific questions.

There may not be a lot of room to negotiate, especially for entry-level candidates."

Know what questions to ask about specific benefits

One of the more important details to find out is when you become eligible for the benefits, especially when it comes to health insurance. If you won't be eligible for benefits for the first three months of employment, it is important that you have some other kind of insurance in place during that time. For example, you may be able to continue your insurance coverage from school or a previous job through COBRA (see www.dol.gov/ebsa/faqs/faq_consumer_cobra.html for more on COBRA).

Other key considerations: how much money, if any, you need to contribute to the cost of the insurance premiums (nonprofits often cover more of their employees' premiums to compensate for lower salaries); how much the co-pays are for doctor/dentist visits, as well as coverage for dependents or partners; and if benefits are taxable. You could also ask for details about a retirement program, and whether the organization matches employee contributions.

Know what benefits are negotiable

There may not be a lot of room to negotiate, especially for entry-level positions. One of the areas you may find some flexibility, though, is time off. Many organizations have a waiting period before new staff can request vacation days. If you already have a vacation planned during that waiting period, you may be able to ask them to waive the waiting period. Another example is the use of flex time. Organizations may be willing to negotiate flex time more openly since it is a largely internal issue.

Benefits glossary

Child/Elder care benefits: Child care and elder care are becoming more prevalent in benefits packages. If these issues affect your life, find out what the employer offers either in terms of payment or referrals.

Compensation time: While few nonprofit employers offer overtime pay for exempt staff, many do offer "comp time." Comp time means that for every extra hour you work overtime you can take up to an hour off. This may be a formal system that requires you to keep careful records, or it may mean that you have the flexibility to come in late or leave early; there may also be a cap to comp time.

Flex time: Perhaps the employer can't be flexible about your salary, but they may be flexible about your work time. Could you reduce the number of hours on the job? Could you work alternate hours that would allow you to pursue other opportunities (whether paid or connected to other passions)? You could also ask about job sharing, compressed workweeks (e.g., working ten hours a day for four days), and telecommuting.

Health insurance: This is one of the standard benefits that organizations usually offer full-time employees, but most internships and part-time jobs will not provide health care benefits. This is also one of the benefits that will probably not be open to negotiation because of laws requiring employers to provide consistent health benefits to all employees. However, you should still find out the specifics of the health care options that each position offers.

Options: Some organizations offer several options of health care plans from which to choose (Preferred Provider Organization [PPO], Health Maintenance Organization [HMO], Point of Service [POS], etc.). There should be an HR person (or someone in Operations or Administration who acts as a Benefits Coordinator) in the organization who can explain the pros and cons of each option. This is a particularly complex part of your compensation package and you should inquire about the plan's details and costs.

Structure: Medical services have gradually changed from traditional fee-for-service organizations into health maintenance organizations (HMOs). HMOs receive a fixed premium each month, and in exchange offer a range of services. HMOs provide many services under one plan, while fee-for-service providers operate less centrally and allow members to choose which medical practitioners they use. With these plans, there may be different pay scales for doctors outside a network.

Disability accommodations
While there are some federal laws governing disability accommodations, regulations vary state by state. If you need accommodations in your workplace, you should make sure you know your state's regulations about what employers are required to provide. Also, be sure to read up on if, when, and how to disclose your disability. For more information on disabilities and accommodations in the workplace, here are some resources that may be useful:

• **Definition of a disability**
www.jobaccess.org/ada_definition.htm

• **Americans with Disabilities Act**
www.usdoj.gov/crt/ada/

• **Handbook of your employment-related rights under the ADA**
www.eeoc.gov/facts/jobapplicant.html

• **Job Accommodation Network**
offers articles and resources on a variety of ADA-related topics, searchable by federal, state, local regulations; by disability; by specific legislation; and other criteria. Resources include "Pre-Employment Testing and the ADA", "Health Benefits Plans and the ADA" and many others.
www.jan.wvu.edu/links/atoz.htm

For additional resources on disability accommodations, visit the resource page for this chapter:
www.idealist.org/en/career/guide/ch10resources.html

Mental health services/Employee assistance programs (EAPs): Some employers offer employee assistance programs, typically set up with an outside contracting agency, to provide confidential counseling in dealing with stress, substance abuse, relationship problems, and family issues and/or personal concerns.

Other services: If you have specific, recurring medical needs (physical therapy, allergies, prescriptions, etc.) check to see that your treatments are covered by an employer's plan. Do so as discreetly as possible (see the sidebar on page 166).

Dental and vision insurance: With some health plans, dental and vision coverage is included, while in others it may be only partially covered or not covered at all. Consider whether preventive care and surgical care are covered and to what extent (deductibles, co-pay, and annual and lifetime maximums).

Job resources: Does the organization have the resources (equipment, office space, personnel, budgets, software, policies) that would make your work life easier? Is there a budget for other things that you need to do a good job? Some employers are willing to make adjustments or investments to accommodate your work needs. Consider if you need any other information about your work environment and the resources that will be at your disposal to evaluate the job offer properly.

Life and disability insurance: Life insurance usually affords a certain amount of basic coverage for employees with the option of buying additional coverage for employees and their families. Disability insurance provides a percentage of lost wages in case the employee is unable to work due to a non–work-related injury or illness. The period and cost of this kind of coverage varies from plan to plan, and is above any disability coverage required by the state. Please note that Worker's Compensation is another form of insurance that most employers are legally required to carry for injuries that happen while on the job.

Professional development programs: Professional development reimbursement is an incredibly valuable part of a compensation package because, if you are someone new to the sector, you have much to learn about the field. Be sure to ask about opportunities to attend conferences or national meetings. Even the smallest nonprofits often see the value of networking and development. Expressing interest in these opportunities at the outset will make it clear that you are interested in growing with the organization.

Relocation expenses: If a position within an organization requires a move, sometimes an employer will help pay for your moving expenses. Employers can help defray the cost of a move in many different ways. Some employers will pay a percentage of your salary as their contribution to moving expenses; others will offer a flat contribution; still others reimburse an employee for the exact

A reasonable accommodation...

is any change or adjustment to a job or work environment that permits a qualified applicant or employee with a disability to participate in the job application process, to perform the essential functions of a job, or to enjoy benefits and privileges of employment equal to those enjoyed by employees without disabilities. For example, reasonable accommodation may include:

- providing or modifying equipment or devices,

- job restructuring,

- part-time or modified work schedules,

- reassignment to a vacant position,

- adjusting or modifying examinations, training materials, or policies,

- providing readers and interpreters, and

- making the workplace readily accessible to and usable by people with disabilities.

An employer is required to provide a reasonable accommodation to a qualified applicant or employee with a disability unless the employer can show that the accommodation would be an undue hardship–that is, that it would require significant difficulty or expense.

[Source: The U.S. Equal Employment Opportunity Commission, www.eeoc.gov/facts/ada18.html]

cost of the move. If relocation is necessary for the position, it is worth asking if compensation for relocation expenses is an option.

In certain circumstances, some relocation expenses that are not reimbursed by your new employer may be deducted when you file your income taxes. These expenses include the cost of transporting household goods and personal effects as well as travel and lodging costs. For more specific information, please see IRS Publication 521: www.irs.gov/publications/p521/ar02.html#d0e1163

Retirement plans: The most common retirement plans are Sections 403(b) and 401(k). These plans allow employees to deduct a portion of their pre-tax salary and put it into a fund for their retirement, which can help employees fall into a lower tax bracket. The money is invested while in the account and cannot be taken out of the fund (without incurring penalties) until an employee reaches retirement age. An employer may contribute or match a percentage of the employee's contribution; whether or not your employer does is an important question to ask. Most nonprofits offer 403(b) retirement plans that mainly differ from a 401(k) plan in how they are administered. For all practical purposes, the benefits of these two types of retirement plans are comparable. Some nonprofits offer defined benefit plans (a pension plan with guaranteed payouts).

Sick/personal/parental leave: The Family and Medical Leave Act (www.dol.gov/esa/whd/fmla/) requires that most organizations with 50 or more employees provide up to three months of *unpaid* leave for personal or family illness and parental leave for the birth of a child. Some employers only offer what is required under the FMLA, while others provide some form of *paid* time off for similar reasons.

Tuition reimbursement: These programs help support an employee's continuing education. Reimbursement can range from a single workshop or a college course to a full degree program. Larger organizations are more likely to offer a formal plan, although smaller organizations are often willing to negotiate time away from work for educational purposes, even if they can't help with the cost. Also keep in mind that many education-focused nonprofits (like private universities) offer scholarships to partners, spouses, and children of employees.

Vacation time: This is one of the more flexible and variable benefits. However, there are often specific guidelines on vacation days. For example, vacation days may be limited during an employee's first year (or first few months); they may not begin accumulating immediately; and there may be a cap on the number of days an employee can take consecutively or during peak periods when time off is discouraged. Similarly, be sure to find out if and how the organization delineates between vacations, personal days, paid holidays, mental health days, and so on.

AVOIDING RED FLAGS

While it's important to get as much information as you can about the benefits package offered, please don't feel obliged to explain your specific reasons for inquiry. For example, if you are thinking about having a child down the road, you don't have to divulge that kind of information to a potential employer.

The best way to learn about the organization's full benefits package is to ask to see the Benefits/HR/Personnel policy manual. That way, you can get a full picture of the benefits they offer and learn more about the ones that matter most to you. Some employers will readily supply this, while others may not.

Benefits

You can find many more resources, including links to salary surveys and benefits descriptions, in the online resource page for this chapter. Visit:

www.idealist.org/en/career/guide/ch10resources.html

Negotiating your compensation package

According to a recent Idealist.org survey of nonprofit hiring managers, only *2 percent* of candidates actually negotiate their compensation package. The same survey showed that the majority of hiring managers are open to discussing compensation with a candidate. This information suggests that there are plenty of lost opportunities for candidates and employers to work together to improve compensation packages.

As you consider negotiating, remember that once you have an offer, you have already proven your value to the employer. Similarly, once you accept, you've missed your initial chance to negotiate, but you should be able to return to this topic after you've been on the job for a while. If you're still unsure about negotiating, here are six reasons why you should:

1. **It's okay to ask for what you're worth.**
2. **The first offer is often not the best possible one.**
3. **A higher starting salary means higher raises (in this or future jobs).**
4. **Salary is not the only part of a compensation package that you can negotiate.**
5. **Asking for a more competitive salary/benefits package does not suggest that you only care about money, or that you do not care about the mission of the organization.**
6. **Negotiating shows that you are confident in and can advocate for yourself and your abilities.**

1. It's okay to ask for what you're worth.

While the job will undoubtedly benefit you, don't underestimate the benefit that you will bring to an organization. Whether this is your only job offer or one of many, your first job out of school, or a position for which your skills are perfectly matched, you are a valuable asset to the organization. Your future employers made you an offer because they recognize your value and they'll do what they can to bring you into their organization. If done correctly, negotiation is a way to ensure that you're being compensated fairly for all that you will bring to the job.

2. The first offer is often not the best possible one.

There is no reason to expect that the first offer an employer makes will be the best offer. One reason for this is financial constraints. Thus, you may find more flexibility to negotiate aspects of your compensation package that are less intrinsically tied to the organizational budget (such as flex time and telecommuting options). In any case, it's fair to assume that they may not be making you their best offer and that negotiating could lead to a better offer. If you don't ask, though, they won't offer!

NEGOTIATING IS ALL ABOUT NUANCE

Whether it's due to nerves or misperceptions of the negotiation process, some job seekers end up creating a situation that is more confrontational than it really needs to be. Negotiation is a nuanced art; it is never an ultimatum. Whenever you engage in a discussion about negotiation, use caution: you've come this far, the employer is invested in you (but may still be looking for warning signs), and you don't want to put their back against the wall or create ill will. Beware of your tone and the language you use. As you start negotiating, be sure to begin with mutual respect, an awareness of other perspectives, and an understanding that the end result isn't victory or defeat, but an agreement that allows both sides to come away satisfied.

NEGOTIATING AN ENTRY-LEVEL POSITION

While some degree of negotiation is appropriate for any position, negotiating and renegotiating for an entry-level position can be a risky move. Some hiring professionals have little to no tolerance for negotiating for entry-level positions, while others are open to the idea. Since you have no idea what kind of hiring professional you are dealing with, it is better to approach negotiations for an entry-level position with limited expectations and a shorter list of "must haves."

3. A higher starting salary means higher raises (in this or future jobs).

Say you take the employer's first offer of $30,000 a year and that every year, you get a 5 percent raise. Below is a chart that shows the difference that a salary increase at the beginning can make over a few years.

Years with the organization	$30,000 starting salary	$35,000 starting salary	$40,000 starting salary
	Yearly salary with 5 percent raise		
After one year	$31,500	$36,750	$42,000
After three years	$34,729	$40,517	$46,305
After five years	$38,288	$44,670	$51,051
Net difference in yearly salary after five years	$8,288	$9,670	$11,051

As you can see, the difference at the end of five years is significant. If you can negotiate a higher starting salary, it will become exponentially worth it each year.

4. Salary is not the only part of a compensation package that you can negotiate.

Negotiation should always take into account other benefits. Before you negotiate, be sure to know as much as possible about what is offered in the organization's benefits package as well as what your priorities are in terms of benefits (both in dollars and peace of mind). Ask which benefits might be flexible if the salary is non-negotiable. In particular, flex time and professional development opportunities are often areas where an organization has some flexibility. However, keep in mind that benefits such as health and life insurance will probably not be negotiable, because organizations need to offer uniform benefits for the entire staff. Also, an entry-level candidate may find less flexibility when negotiating. This doesn't mean you should forgo this step!

Here are some other components of a compensation package that you should be sure you understand:

- Salary increases: know when they happen, how a raise is determined, the schedule for reviews
- Health benefits
- Time off: vacation, sick days, personal days, holidays, family leave
- Flex time
- Family/domestic partner benefits
- Pension/retirement plan
- Student loan forgiveness or subsidization programs
- Signing bonuses or other incentives
- Moving expenses
- Professional development

WOMEN AND NEGOTIATION

Women make up approximately 70 percent of the nonprofit workforce[*], but men working in the sector earn salaries that are 28 percent higher than women[**].

A study from *Women Don't Ask*[***] analyzed salaries of students graduating with masters degrees from Carnegie Mellon University. Men's starting salaries were, on average, 7.6 percent (almost $4,000) higher than women's starting salaries. Of these same students, 57 percent of the men had negotiated their salaries while only 7 percent of the women had done so. The study also found that, on average, students who negotiated were able to increase their starting salaries by 7.4 percent, or $4,053. Interestingly, the initial salary disparity between men and women directly correlates to the percentage increase received by those who negotiated.

With statistics like these, negotiation should be an essential part of everyone's job search process.

[Sources: [*] Cryer, Shelley. "The Next Generation of Nonprofit Sector Leadership" (NYU Wagner, 2004).
[**] GuideStar. "2004 GuideStar Nonprofit Compensation Report" Available at: www.guidestar.org/news/features/2004_comp_findings.jsp
[***] Babcock, Linda and Laschever, Sara. *Women Don't Ask.* (Princeton: Princeton University Press, 2003)]

- Education reimbursement
- Travel opportunities
- Your title or responsibilities
- Performance-based advancement opportunities

While the benefits above are essential elements of an offer, be sure to also evaluate the less quantifiable benefits of working for a nonprofit organization:
- Sense of connection with the mission of the agency
- Opportunity for professional development
- Increased and varied responsibilities
- Chance to transition into a new field
- Opportunity to develop new skills
- Implications for your life outside of work

5. Asking for a more competitive salary/benefits package does not suggest that you only care about money, or that you do not care about the mission of the organization.

The organization has made you an offer because you've demonstrated that you're passionate about the work, have the skills to do the job well, and are committed to the organization. By negotiating your offer, you are not negating any of this. You're negotiating because you want to make sure that you're being compensated fairly for the work that you will do for the organization. If you don't feel you're being compensated fairly, you are less likely to be a happy and productive member of the organization in the long-term. Since the employer has decided that you are the candidate of choice for the job, it is in the organization's interest to work with you to develop the best possible offer to allow you to thrive and remain in your new position.

6. Negotiating shows that you are confident in and can advocate for yourself and your abilities.

By the time you negotiate your salary and benefits, you'll already have a job offer. By negotiating for yourself, you demonstrate your confidence in your skill through your ability to advocate for yourself. Since many nonprofit organizations do some sort of advocacy, this latter quality will be welcomed by savvy employers, as people who can advocate for themselves are often excellent at advocating for other issues or people, too.

When should you negotiate salary?

Always after you've been offered the position and before you accept. After an offer has been made, you are in your strongest position. You know the employer wants you, the value that you'll bring to the organization is apparent, and you have

---

Sealing the deal: An example of self-advocacy's importance

Lauren became so frustrated with her current position that she quit without having another job lined up. She took two weeks to recharge and then jumped back in to the job search.

Within a month of beginning her search, she had applied to several jobs, interviewed for a few of them, and received an offer for a great job with a child advocacy organization. When the hiring manager called to offer her the position and tell her the compensation details (which included a 10 percent raise from her previous job), she thanked him and asked for a chance to think the offer over.

She called back two days later, thanked him again for the offer, and then said that while she was excited about the job, she wanted to know if he was open to discussing a higher salary. Lauren outlined several of her performance and skill-related qualities to justify this request, gave a ballpark figure of what she had in mind, and then waited.

The hiring manager paused for a moment before saying, "I'll have to ask HR about a salary increase, but I just want to tell you that I could not be happier that we've offered you this job. You just did such a marvelous job of advocating for yourself, I can only imagine what an incredible advocate you'll be for the kids our organization serves. Let me see what I can do to meet your request."

been chosen over all of the other candidates. All of your hard work researching, preparing, networking, and interviewing has paid off and finally you have an offer. Congratulations! Now take some time to think about it.

This is not a game, nor is it a stalling tactic. It is an opportunity to spend some time making sure that the offer is fair, the position is what you thought it would be, and the organization is the right fit for you. Up to this point, you've been working hard "selling" yourself to the employer; now it's time to step back and make sure that they've sold themselves to you.

As soon as you get an offer, before you accept or decline it, be sure to:
1. Thank the employer for the offer.
2. Let them know how excited you are about the prospect of working for them.
3. Ask them when they need to know your decision and, if necessary, negotiate a day and time (one to three days is a reasonable range).

To negotiate or not to negotiate?

What makes an offer acceptable is an entirely personal decision. There are a number of factors that can make an offer acceptable to you. However, a decision of whether or not an offer is acceptable should be based on *your* research, *your* financial needs, and *your* knowledge of what will help *you* thrive in a work environment. Any of the components of your compensation package could make an offer unacceptable, but as we've mentioned above, many may not be negotiable. This is particularly true if you are an entry-level candidate; employers often have more flexibility when it comes to more experienced candidates.

For some, salary will be paramount on the list of priorities. For others, the responsibility and opportunities for leadership will be most important. In a recent survey, undergraduates ranked what an ideal employer would offer. For these students, the top priority was "flexible working conditions."[1] Competitive compensation was way down in fourth place. This is not to say that you should reconsider how essential flexible working conditions or salary are to you. Rather, be sure you're considering the offer in regard to what is important to *you* and not what you (or others) think *should* be important.

When you are considering an offer, be sure to also consider the realities of the organization, the specific position, and your experience level. Take the time to compare your salary and benefits to comparable positions, examine your financial and personal needs, and consider the unquantifiable benefits of the position and organization (in-

---

[1] Sass, Erik. "Undergrads Link Brand Preference to Employment Packages" *Marketing Daily* 15 May 2007.

What if they offer you the job but don't mention what the salary or benefits are?

While it is irresponsible for an employer to neglect to mention salary or benefits when making a formal job offer, it becomes your responsibility to ask if this occurs. If the person with whom you are speaking does not know either salary or benefits information, ask to be put in contact with someone who does. This information should be offered up front; you should not feel awkward about asking for it.

SALARIES A FEW CLICKS AWAY

Having accurate salary and cost of living information is an essential component of salary negotiation. While manners keep us from asking people what they make, salary resources compiled at Idealist.org (see Learn More box on the next page) can begin to give you an idea of what you can reasonably expect to make in different positions in your area. If you're considering relocating for your job, you'll also want to know how much you'll need to comfortably live in your new city. $40,000 will mean very different lifestyles in Fort Smith, AR and New York, NY. Use salary calculators like the ones at CNN Money, CB Salary, or Bankrate.com to help you calculate the differences. There are a few nonprofit-specific salary surveys you should check out, both national and city-based (see "Learn More" box next page). However, be aware that they may not offer particularly specific information, but rather will provide a salary range that may be helpful in your search.

–Valinda Lee

cluding networking opportunities, professional development options, and work environment). Weigh the pros and cons of all aspects of the position, including fit! If the cons outweigh the pros, decide if you want to negotiate, and if so, what needs to change for you to accept the offer.

How do you negotiate?

Before you negotiate, you need to know how your position is funded and the value of your skills and experience in the marketplace. Ideally, you should be able to find this information before or during the interview process. If you haven't done the research or the employer hasn't provided the details, it is entirely possible that you won't know this information by the time you get an offer. However, it is essential information for you to have before beginning the negotiation process.

Where is the funding coming from?

Positions with nonprofit organizations may be funded by several different sources. It may be a grant-funded position or it might be covered by general operating costs. You will want to dig a bit deeper on the grant-funded positions. You should know how long the grant lasts, whether a plan is in place for when the grant runs out, and what deliverables are required for the specific grant that funded your position. You may ask about this during the interview process or after an offer is made.

Know what you're worth.

Once you know the salary and benefits that you've been offered, compare it to your previous research about your worth-on-paper (see the section on researching your salary range in **Chapter Three**). Keep in mind your level of experience, the size and budget of the organization, the geographic region in which the organization is located, and what the current job market climate is.

If possible, find out what the general nonprofit salary range is for the specific position you've been offered. Salary information can be found online in a variety of places, although most are not nonprofit-specific. However, the information (either nonprofit or for-profit) should give a good frame of reference with which to begin.

The sidebar at right mentions some free online resources for gathering salary information. However, two of the best places to find salary information are offline:

- **Your college career center**: Many career centers have subscriptions or have paid for their students to use premium salary calculators. Be sure to check here first for best resources.
- **College alumni working in similar fields**: These connections can be great resources for finding out salary information, not to mention expanding your network while you're at it!

Salary information

Here are some free resources where you can find salary information. Many salary calculators offer free services, but charge a fee for their premium services.

Occupational Outlook Handbook: (www.bls.gov/oco) is a comprehensive site with information on a variety of careers and the education or training needed, the salary, projected job prospects, key position responsibilities, and working conditions.

Salary.com: (www.salary.com) is a website that offers free salary and cost-of-living calculators as well as benefits and job evaluation tools.

CBSalary: (www.cbsalary.com) This is a free salary calculator by Career-Builder.com. Enter a job title, city, state, and education level to view positions with the same or similar job titles. Some notes on usage:

- To search their nonprofit positions, type "non-profit" with a hyphen.
- The salary calculator takes you to a sponsored page after you enter your search criteria but you can simply click the "No thank you" tab to continue to your search results.

For additional salary information resources, visit the online resource page for this chapter at:

www.idealist.org/en/career/guide/ch10resources.html

Convey your value

A negotiation should be based on what you bring to the organization and not what you need. While you've undoubtedly spent time assessing your financial situation and are probably thinking about your student loans, your rent, or your travel budget as you consider negotiating your offer, these are *not* reasons for an employer to consider your request. Instead, you should be able to clearly explain the value you will bring to the organization. This is what employers will be willing to pay more for. To prepare, sit down with a list of the responsibilities and qualities listed in the job description. How do your skills and experiences match up? Are there any areas where you have particularly deep experience or specifically relevant skills? These points should be the basis of your negotiation since they are what the employer can recognize as the unique assets you will bring to the position.

In practice, this means avoiding needs statements like "I have a lot of financial responsibilities, ranging from my student loans to my car payments," and focusing your negotiations on statements like, "I feel that my educational background and experience running a campus volunteer program should be taken into account while we discuss compensation."

Know what you want

Once you've evaluated all aspects of the position, if you see more negative aspects than positive ones, you need to figure out the main reasons why the offer is unacceptable. Is it salary? Vacation time? Insurance? Flexible work hours? If you have a long list of issues that you'd like to negotiate, the position just may not be right for you.

Write out all of the specific aspects of the offer that you find unacceptable. Next, narrow your list of aspects to negotiate down to one or two that are the most important to you. Bear in mind that you'll likely find the most room for negotiation in areas such as salary, flex time, telecommuting, and willingness to cover your dues for membership in professional associations and pay for fees for trainings and conferences. Organizations usually have far less leeway to negotiate with individual employees over their insurance offerings and reimbursement policies. Finally, develop specific, proposed solutions for each aspect you'd like to negotiate. Be sure these proposed solutions are realistic based on the organization, the position, and your experience. Once you've done this, it's time to begin the negotiation process. Before you begin, remind yourself one more time that the organization really wants you.

The negotiation

There isn't *one* right way to negotiate. While there are a number of steps you can take before the negotiation (wait for an offer, research benefits, prioritize which elements of an offer are most important to you), there isn't a foolproof script to follow. Instead, try to figure out what will make you the most comfortable. It is better to approach this

CHOOSING A JOB FOR ALL THE WRONG REASONS Making the decision to take a job based on salary, the priorities and pressure of family and friends (it's "what everyone else wants you to do"), or because you "have nothing to lose" or "don't have any other options" can all put you on the fast track to dissatisfaction. Money really isn't everything. The friends and family members pressuring you to take a job do not actually have to go to the job and do the work. Do you really solve anything by taking a job that you know you will hate?

As you explore the possibility of taking a given position while negotiating, make sure that you are advocating for your long-term happiness and satisfaction. It is a common mistake to not negotiate more than your monetary and security needs. Job satisfaction, comfort level, and dedication will, more than the money or "having a job," determine your overall happiness and workplace commitment.

as a problem solving activity with both sides trying to reach a common goal rather than viewing it as a battle. Also, remember that this is not personal. Particularly if you are an entry-level candidate, there may not be much flexibility for your position. Even so, if the issues are important enough to you, you should certainly consider explaining this to your potential employer. In doing so, just be careful to not appear as though you're being inflexible or dampen an employer's excitement about hiring you.

As you negotiate, also be mindful that you are not obliged to answer questions the employer may pose about why you are particularly interested in a certain benefit (especially if the reasons relate to a personal situation concerning yourself or a loved one).

POSSIBLE WAYS TO START THE NEGOTIATION

The following is an excerpt from the resources developed by David Schachter, Assistant Dean for Career Services and Experiential Learning at NYU's Robert F. Wagner Graduate School of Public Service. This script should not be used word-for-word when you're negotiating with a possible employer. Rather, it should be viewed as a possible approach that can be customized to fit your needs and the negotiation situation.

Before the date you must get back to them, call the employer and say:

- "I'm still very interested in the position, and I believe I can bring _____, _____, and _____ to your organization. I'm wondering, is it possible to enhance the offer in terms of salary (or vacation, benefits, opportunities for review, etc.)?"
- Shut your mouth! Bite your tongue! Do not fill in the silence! Let them speak first. See what they have to say.

Yes: If they give you what you want, thank them and tell them you'll get back to them by the deadline.

Maybe:
- If they say they'll have to get back to you, ask when you should be hearing from them or when you should call them back.
- If they ask you what you had in mind:
  * Ask them, "What do you think is possible?" or
  * Give them a range of what you're looking for.

No: If they say no, say, "Okay, thanks, I'll still get back to you by _____."

If possible, get it in writing

Although most employers will not offer you a written employment contract, often they will provide you a summary of the offer in writing. Review this document

THINKING OUTSIDE THE SALARY RANGE BOX

Salary negotiation is tricky for employers, too. As you decide how to proceed, it's worth considering potential perspectives of the staff with whom you'll be negotiating.

Say you are fully qualified for and excited about a particular job, but you are also looking for a position that pays significantly more than the stated salary range. If you decide to apply and are invited in for an interview, this is one of the few instances where discussing your salary requirements before you receive an offer may be beneficial. If you wait until an offer is made to tell the employer that your salary requirements are well out of the stated salary range for the position, employers may rightfully feel as though you've wasted their time because the organization just cannot match your salary needs.

Bringing up the fact that you are excited about the job but are looking for a higher salary requires significant tact and careful timing. For example, in the first interview, the employer may not yet understand what value you would bring to the organization. However, if you wait too long, you could cause frustration and hard feelings. During the second interview, the employer should be aware of the value you'd bring to the organization. However, the process hasn't progressed so far that the employer won't have any alternative if your request isn't something the organization can accommodate.

carefully. If you and the employer negotiate and agree to amend the offer, politely ask that the written summary of the offer be revised to include the changes you've agreed upon. But be aware that many nonprofits will not offer a written summary of the benefits package (although this information may be included in the benefits/HR/personnel policy manual). While it's certainly preferable to have such a written summary, it is not necessarily a norm.

What should you do if asked about salary history or requirements before an offer is made?

It is not unusual for job announcements to ask you to include your salary history or salary requirements with your application. The request is made in earnest; many organizations need to know what kind of compensation you require to see if you are within their budget. If you indicate a salary that is too high, you may not even be considered for the position. If you cite a salary that is too low, you may undervalue yourself and not be offered the salary that the organization was willing to pay.

When these types of requests come early in the interview process (especially in the job posting!), they are difficult to handle. You have several options:

- Explain that you'd be happy to discuss salary once you have a more detailed sense of what the position requires.

- Indicate that your salary requirements are negotiable and flexible (but do this only if you are, indeed, flexible). Many people say something like, "My desired salary range is $_____ to $_____ but I am flexible for the right opportunity."

- State your salary history (if applicable) or desired salary in a broad enough range so as not to knock yourself out of the running or set the offer lower than what the organization expected to pay.

- Ignore the request. (This can be a risky tactic to use as no one likes to be ignored. If you decide to ignore the first request, be ready to use one of the above tactics if they bring the topic up again. Do not ignore a salary request more than once.)

There are three reasons why it is unwise to discuss salary prematurely:

1. In the beginning stages of the interview process, you will probably not have a clear idea of what the job is worth. Discussing salary too early could cause you to place an incorrect value on the position.

2. The interview process is all about helping the employer recognize what you can offer. Even if your salary expectations are higher than the employer intended to pay, the interview can help convince an employer what an incredible asset you'd be to their organization, and that you are worth every penny they can afford.

3. You could make your salary expectations known and undervalue yourself. An employer may have a much higher estimate of what the organization is willing to pay you for your work. If you start too low, you may be offered a much lower salary than the employer initially intended.

LEVERAGING ONE OFFER AGAINST ANOTHER

Imagine this: you've had a few interviews at different organizations and two, in particular, went smashingly. You get an offer from Organization A right away, but you really want to work for Organization B.

In this situation, you can contact Organization B and let them know that you're really interested in their position, but that you've received another offer. Tell them your timeline (when you need to either accept or decline the first offer), reiterate your interest in their position, and ask if they'll be able to let you know their decision in time for you to evaluate both positions.

Remember why it is worth negotiating

Negotiation is rarely anyone's favorite part of the job search. However, be sure to keep these reasons for negotiation in mind once you've gotten over the euphoria of being offered a position:

1. **It's okay to ask for what you're worth.**
2. **The first offer is often not the best possible one.**
3. **A higher starting salary means higher raises (in this or future jobs).**
4. **Salary is not the only part of a compensation package that you can negotiate.**
5. **Asking for a more competitive salary/benefits package does not suggest that you only care about money, or that you do not care about the mission of the organization.**
6. **Negotiating shows that you are confident in and can advocate for yourself and your abilities.**

Conclusion

It would be ideal to receive all of the benefits mentioned in this section, but the reality is that your job offer is unlikely to include every one of the compensation elements outlined here. This is why it's crucial to define your benefits priorities and do what you can to find a job that offers those benefits that matter most to you. It's also important to keep in mind that if you do get the job, your opportunity to negotiate is not over, nor is your compensation package set in stone. In fact, negotiation—and the gradual enhancement of your entire compensation package—should be an ongoing part of your career.

As you settle into your new job, remember that your employer wants you to succeed and to stay with them. This means that some of the benefits you may have been unable to obtain at your hiring could become attainable once you and your employer have developed stronger bonds of trust based on your performance and dedication. It's common to negotiate for a higher salary after you've been on the job for a while, but don't forget that other benefits offerings can also be improved. While some benefits (especially in the area of insurance and reimbursement) are likely to be fixed as a result of the need to offer standard benefits to all employees in an organization, other aspects of your compensation package can (and should!) be revisited and enhanced the longer you work with an employer. Moreover, if your organization is able, it may begin offering new benefits that were previously not part of your compensation package. Keep your benefits priorities in mind as you progress in your career, and remember that negotiation doesn't stop at the start of your new job.

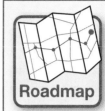

THE FIRST 100 DAYS: TIPS FOR A SUCCESSFUL START

- Don't be unprepared for your first day; go back and review all of the research you did on the organization

- 90 percent listen, 10 percent talk is a good initial rule of thumb

- Ask if there are any new colleagues who will be particularly beneficial to talk to early on–people who know your work area well or have specific institutional knowledge to share

- Seek out a mentor within the organization (see **Chapter Five**)

- Have a frank discussion about any unwritten rules or expectations. Also feel free to seek clarification of performance metrics and expectations.

- Be aware of (but avoid getting caught up in) the always present office politics

- Don't go in thinking you'll "fix" everything.

- (In the beginning), it's okay to not know where the bathroom is. Or the kitchen. Or the fax machine. Or...

- Pay attention to office conventions and abide by them, at least until you understand the environment. Even relatively informal offices may still have some taboos about dress codes or the manner in which staff address one another–give yourself a chance to learn these often unwritten "rules"

- Taking vacation during your first few months may not be allowed, and is probably not a good idea if you can avoid it.

- Be conscious of potentially annoying habits like gum-chewing, mobile phone ring tones, long or loud phone calls, and pen-tapping.

SUMMARY

Once you've been offered a position, be sure to take a moment to congratulate yourself for all of your hard work. However, make sure to remember the last, essential part of the job search process: closing the deal. This involves **understanding benefits** and **the art of negotiation**. In these stages you will:

Understand the variety of benefit options that could be included in a compensation package (pages 161-166, mini-glossary pages 164-166).

Decide **which benefits are important to you** based on your personal situation (pages 162-163).

Learn **what benefits a specific organization offers** by doing research, asking questions, and knowing who to talk to at the organization (pages 163-164).

Consider **several reasons why you should negotiate** your compensation offer (pages 167-169).

Know how to figure out **when you should begin the negotiation process** (pages 169-171).

Understand how to go about **negotiating a better offer** (pages 171-174).

Assess whether an offer is acceptable for you based on the priorities you determined through your assessment of your needs (pages 170-172).

Remember that **negotiation should be an ongoing aspect** of your career (page 175).

CHAPTER ELEVEN

Staying ready

A career search doesn't end when you get a job

> **In this chapter you will:**
>
> • Understand that getting a job is an important milestone, but it's not the end of the road. Even if you love the work you are doing, you are still on the career continuum–it pays to be ready!
>
> • Consider six ways you can keep yourself poised and prepared for the next time you need to search for a job.
>
> • Learn how to efficiently stay ready for a future job search.

Congratulations! The good news is that you've made it. You have a great (even "dream") job and you are on your way to connecting your profession with your passion. The "bad news" is that this is not the time to stop the activities that made your job search successful. Given the fact that most professionals today follow a nonlinear career path, your new job may be the first of many positions you'll hold during your career. As well, your recent travails should be a fresh reminder of how difficult and often unpleasant the job search can be… whether your job search was well planned and meticulously executed, or a stressful experience that often left you scrambling to make it to the next networking opportunity with your newest resume straight out of the printer. By staying "job-search–ready," your next job search will be a lot less difficult. Thus, this bad news isn't all that bad: being prepared for your next career move is easier than you think.

After reading some, or hopefully all, of this book, you should realize that your career is an ongoing continuum. This means that you are never completely done. Dream organizations change and the perfect job can become something quite different over the course of even a few years. Beyond the fact that we change as individuals, with our passions and goals following suit, the world around us is ever changing. This inevitably impacts the organizations and individuals with whom we work. In short, it pays to stay ready! Below are six steps you can take to strengthen your current position and stay primed for a future job search, if and when that becomes necessary.

Step one: Repay and then bolster your network

Everyone loves a success story. So, as soon as you get acclimated to your new position, make a point of setting aside enough time to reach out again to the network of individuals who (in any way) helped you to connect with your current role. Since they were essential in helping you find your current position, let them know that you appreciate all their assistance and insight. Articulate your eagerness to stay in touch (make sure they have your professional contact information!) and be sure to offer yourself as a resource in your current role. Find out what they need and how you can help them. You can share with them the mission and programmatic focus of your new organization. Encourage them to send people to you for information and assistance. Finally, let them know that you continue to view them as an invaluable resource and one who can help others who may come to you for assistance.

Ideally, you can also start connecting with individuals in your network to collaborate on projects you take on as part of your new position. This will not only help you to do the best work possible in your role, organization, and community, it will also help you strengthen your network for use in the future. If you can run workshops, collaborate on events, co-create materials, or otherwise strengthen your professional network connections, you will show those who helped you (maybe even without necessarily knowing your work ethic and professionalism) that their faith in you was justified and you will also quickly expand your network to include other individuals who know your skills and personality. Fostering these kinds of collaborations can allow you to try out new roles within your organization and connect with members of your network whose work doesn't directly relate to your role. For example, if one of your contacts works in printing and advertising but your new role focuses internally on direct service, talk with your outreach director or other staff in charge of your organization's "public face" to see if you can play a (small) part in working together with your contact's organization.

Step two: Establish new ties

While you are repaying and bolstering your network, begin to think about ways to create new contacts and connections. Your new role should put you in touch with contacts already established by your organization—ask your colleagues about their professional networks and see how you can get connected. These networks may even have a professional angle to them: associations, local leadership councils, and policy advocacy groups focused on passing legislation to help your organization's mission. Seeking out new contacts will allow you to do your job better (which helps your organization) while also improving your standing in professional circles. Being asked to speak at professional events or representing your organization during policy and planning meetings are ways to grow professionally and should also improve the standing of your organization.

Keep in mind, however, that networking *at* work is not limited to networking *for* work. New networking possibilities also include social and recreational circles. Maybe a new coworker is involved in an art club and you've been looking for a chance to break out the watercolors again. Maybe you can do a fundraising event with a colleague's walking group. If you focus on what networking really is—building relationships—you will find limitless opportunities to continue creating a strong network that can help you do good work, try fun new activities, and assist with any professional career shifts in the future. In the meantime, enjoy the camaraderie and new friends!

 Focus on what networking really is–building relationships– and you will find limitless opportunities to continue creating a strong network."

Step three: Keep track of accomplishments

As you start your new role, be sure to recognize your accomplishments: how you contribute to projects, complete tasks, and learn new skills. It is a lot easier to keep track of these skills and accomplishments as they happen rather than trying to reflect back on years of work when you need to get your resume ready for a new job search. Regularly setting aside time to update an "Accomplishment List" is the best way to capture your achievements.

Most organizations have a three-, six-, and/or twelve-month review process to help your supervisor (in particular) and the organization (in general) stay abreast of what you've accomplished in that time as well as to develop a strategic plan for the next few months. Use this as a valuable opportunity for self-assessment. Take time to benchmark what you've done, consider what you would like to do before the next review, and reflect on your current role and responsibilities. See the review process not as a critique of your work but as a chance to reflect and grow. This regular check in with yourself and your supervisors can help ensure that you are still in a job you're passionate about, still growing professionally, still doing work that excites you, and still with an organization that inspires you. Keep an electronic version of these reviews so that you can easily copy and paste your accomplishments into your master "Accomplishment List."

If your organization doesn't have a formal review system, ask a supervisor to sit down and offer feedback or start your own personal review cycle quarterly or twice a year. This process shouldn't take you more than an hour and can be split into two parts. First, create a list of projects and tasks you've completed since you started or since your last review. Be sure to note the various skills you used to get the job done. For example:

Promotional Material for the Organization's Tenth Anniversary Fundraiser
- **Teamwork**: Coordinated with Executive Director, Outreach Director, and special Board of Directors "Anniversary Subcommittee" to agree on design and wording.
- **Computer Skills**: Used Photoshop Pro to create professional, distribution quality materials.
- **Budgeting**: Worked with outside vendors for printing and distribution of promotional flyers. Able to come in under budget by $12,000 and still increase volume of distribution by 20,000 individual mailings.

Internal Needs-Assessment Intake Forms for New Clients
- **Research**: Looked at recent studies to decide key assessment areas for new clients. Conducted interviews with several leaders in the field.
- **Team Management**: Coordinated four planning meetings with a team consisting of Head Clinician, Intake Coordinator, HR Director, and all seven Counselors to ensure that intake tool was valuable and appropriate.
- **Editing**: Took old intake assessment tool and incorporated new research and planning meeting feedback to create a stronger organizational tool.

Now make a list of the pros and cons of your current role. Is the balance still tilted toward the positives? Does your job still challenge you? Do you still feel satisfied when you fulfill your responsibilities? On the other hand, have things changed (including your needs and interests) enough that your job is no longer the exciting opportunity it once was? If this is the case, you'll want to again tap into your network so that you can be aware of any opportunities that may be a better fit than your current role. This process of self-reflection can also help you structure a conversation with your current employer about what might need to change in order for you to stay with this organization.

Since it is easy to get swept up in a new position, set aside a dedicated amount of time (and make sure to put it on your calendar!) for self-assessments. This will help you to begin tracking your accomplishments as they happen. If this assessment is a regular part of your routine, you will eliminate gaps in your memory later on. It will also allow you to continue to assess whether your job is the one you want now and still satisfies your needs. Furthermore, performing these assessments regularly will make your next active job search significantly easier. Finally, maintaining a self-assessment process will allow you to fix problems as you proceed with your work, as opposed to having them build up to into situations that could cost you your job.

Step four: Continue to update your "master" resume

Many professionals treat working on their resume with the same level of enthusiasm they bring to going to the dentist, balancing the checkbook, preparing tax returns, or any one of a million "necessary evils" in life. It doesn't have to be this way. Your resume should be a living document that serves as a reminder of your constantly growing list of accomplishments, skills, and experiences. Most people who "hate writing a resume" feel this way because they wait until a resume update is absolutely necessary. "Absolutely necessary" tends to coincide with another major stressor: a job search. This addition can make the process of resume writing seem even more tedious and unpleasant.

While it is unrealistic to think that anyone has time to update their resume on a frequent basis, if you do even a marginal job of keeping track of your accomplishments over the course of a year, an annual "resume redux" is a simple task that takes less than an hour. Simply copy and paste your accomplishment list into your master resume and then format accordingly. This is a good time to consolidate old position descriptions, academic information, and personal information to make room for current accomplishments. And, yes, this is even the time to delete some of your older jobs that are no longer relevant to your professional future.

As you rework your resume, remember that this working document can be a bit longer and more descriptive than one you would send out in a future job search.

STAY INFORMED

Even when you have a dream job, it is essential to stay up-to-date with what's going on in your field as well as what's happening in the nonprofit sector. Idealist.org makes it easy for you to subscribe to **RSS feeds and email alerts** that will keep you informed of new blog entries, groups, volunteer opportunities, or jobs on the site. See these links:

• Idealist.org RSS feeds www.idealist.org/if/idealist/en/RSS/RSS/default

• Idealist.org email alerts www.idealist.org/if/idealist/en/My-Idealist/Register/default

You can also search other career related sites (including local nonprofit job resources) and subscribe to feeds that relate to your specific interests.

You might also want to search for (and comment on) **blogs** that relate to the nonprofit causes that you're passionate about. Finally, save yourself time by setting up job search agents at career websites so that you will be automatically notified when new opportunities become available. Check with your college career center to see if they have RSS feeds or job search agents you can use to stay in the loop.

–Valinda Lee

In other words, this master resume should contain more information about all of your skills, experience, and accomplishments than you would necessarily use in a resume that you are sending to a potential employer. (See the **Chapter Eight** for more information on crafting the exact resume for the exact job for which you are applying.)

As is the case with networking, making time to keep your resume updated can have professional benefits even if you are completely satisfied with your current position. After all, resumes aren't just for job seekers. Your resume is also a tool that can demonstrate why you would make a great speaker at an event, member of a nonprofit board, or author of an article for a publication in your field. It doesn't take much effort to ensure that the story your resume tells about you is classified as "current events" rather than "ancient history."

Step five: Keep your options open

When it comes to job inquiries and offers from other professionals, the old adage, "It is better to have it and not need it than to need it and not have it," rings especially true. While you may feel as though you're being disloyal toward your current employer if you don't flatly state your disinterest in other job opportunities, you are really only doing yourself a disservice. There will likely come a time when you will need to contact your network to let them know you are actively beginning a career search. Another option is to be clear that you are always open to new opportunities so that people in your network will think, "Edgar might find this interesting. I'll call him," rather than, "Too bad Edgar would never think of taking another job because this opportunity would be great for him."

 A time may come when you need to contact your network to let them know you are actively beginning a job search."

Walking the fine line between letting others know you are completely satisfied with your work yet still open to hearing about new opportunities is best done by being straightforward (and a small dose of humor never hurts). A statement like, "Thanks for letting me know about that. To be honest, I'm really enjoying my work right now and not looking elsewhere, but you never know when that will change [pause for chuckle] so please keep me in the loop," conveys this sentiment concisely.

Finally, being open to hearing about new opportunities will help you regularly and honestly assess your current situation. This means keeping a realistic understanding of where your current role, organization, and salary fits into what is available to you elsewhere. Just as you should transmit opportunities to folks in your network, you should never stop looking at what's out there for yourself.

Step six: Continually self-assess

Remember that the career process is an ongoing part of your life that you should continually re-evaluate. Make a commitment to periodically do a self-assessment (for many ideas on self-assessment, see **Chapter Three**). This can mean staying open to new roles, objectives, and skills as well as assessing past experiences to use in the future, asking for ongoing feedback, and periodically checking to make sure your "inspiration tank" is not running on empty.

You should never stop asking yourself if this job is really what you want to do. Remember that you started this journey in order to connect your passion with purpose. You may find that what you thought you wanted when you took this job is no longer where your interests lie, and you should not feel like it is inappropriate to continually reassess what you want to do with your life.

Get real. Who has time for this stuff?

Sure, we are all busy people with social, professional, and family obligations that constantly pull us in different directions. So how can someone realistically live their life and do their job while simultaneously staying ready for new opportunities or the possibility of another job search? The answer to staying ready is the same for the job search as it is for so many other tasks in life: break it down into small, manageable pieces.

- Consciously incorporate networking into your daily work life and create new ways to connect with people you know and people you'd like to know.
- Create opportunities and take the time to attend events to stay visible in your community so that people think of you first when something new comes along.
- Set aside 30 minutes a few times a year to update your "Accomplishment List" and resume.

When all is said and done, staying "job-search–ready" and keeping aware of how your current position fits in with who you are now and where you want to go shouldn't take more than the equivalent of one to two days of work per year. Considering the alternative—a frustrating and time-consuming scramble to get up to speed while real financial and application deadlines breathe down your neck—a few days of intentional work is a very small price to pay. You may even find that maintaining fruitful relations with established contacts and meeting new people, enhancing your skills and trying new roles and responsibilities, and taking some time to reflect on your successes is actually… enjoyable!

SUMMARY

It is important that you avoid the temptation to put your resume, network, and other job search tools on hiatus after starting a new job. Continuing to stay job-search-ready doesn't take a lot of time and can really pay off. Use these steps as a way to stay ready and avoid some of the pitfalls of a future job search:

Repay your network by contacting everyone who helped you in your search. Actively create ongoing ways to collaborate with your network in your new role (pages 177-178).

Continue to **create new ties** in order to strengthen your preexisting network and allow you to do the best work possible in your new position. Ideally, these new ties will help you expand the scope of your work and may help you in a future job search (page 178).

Regularly **keep track of your accomplishments**. It is easier to recall the details of your work as they happen rather than months or years down the road. Use organizational review processes or create your own review schedule to benchmark your accomplishments (pages 179-180).

As you track your accomplishments, **keep updating your "master" resume**. Even setting aside time once a year to perform a "resume redux" will help ensure that you don't have to scramble to update your resume when new opportunities arise (pages 180-181).

Always keep your options open. Just as you should share opportunities with people in your network, make sure to stay abreast of opportunities your network may send your way (page 181).

Make self-assessment an ongoing part of your professional life. Interests, lifestyles, circumstances, and your level of satisfaction can all change over time. Self-assessment is necessary to make sure that the professional choices and opportunities you pursue still fit in with who you are and who you aspire to be (pages 181-182).

If you **make a little time for these tasks on a regular basis**, it is easy to stay job-search–ready. That way, you'll be well prepared for your next move along the career continuum (page 182).

CHAPTER TWELVE

Nonprofit hiring practices

The challenges of the job market

In this chapter you will:

- Learn about the three key nonprofit hiring practices that contrast to those of the public and for-profit sectors.

- Understand five factors that make the nonprofit sector job market challenging.

- Consider five reasons why seeking meaningful work in the nonprofit sector is a challenge worth undertaking.

How nonprofit hiring practices differ from other sectors

Do you have the skills? Do you have the passion?

When it comes to evaluating an applicant for a job opening, nonprofits look to an applicant's resume to answer the same initial question as those hiring in other sectors: Does the applicant have the necessary skill set to do this job? Put another way, they want to see if the person is qualified for the job. After that, there is a question unique to nonprofit hiring practices: Does the applicant demonstrate a passion for the mission of the organization? Keep in mind that if your resume does not clearly show you are *qualified* to do the job, then you likely will not make it to the second question—no matter how well you demonstrate your passion for their work.

Nonprofit employers share the same interest in strong cover letter writing as employers in other sectors. Furthermore, since many nonprofit employees fill several different roles in an organization, they need to have transferable skills. One of the most important of these skills is the ability to write well. Your cover letter is the first place that most nonprofit employers look to see a demonstration of your writing skills. Candidates who take the time to write a non-generic, thoughtful cover letter with clean grammar and spelling will naturally rise to the top of the applicant pile.

During interviews with nonprofit HR professionals conducted by Idealist.org in 2007, all interviewees said they would consider an applicant with all of the skills mentioned in a job description but with limited civic engagement *over* a candidate with ample civic engagement experience who lacks some of the necessary job skills. That said, passion for the mission (demonstrated through volunteering, board service, internships, etc. See **Chapter Five**) will set two otherwise equally talented applicants apart.

What if you cannot demonstrate your passion?

If you are interested in applying for a position with an organization but you lack a track record that clearly demonstrates your passion for the organization's mission, you can refocus the attention of the employer to your other examples of passionate engagement to a cause. Your cover letter is a good place to discuss your passion for one cause and how the experience of, for example, working with homeless teens translates into transferable skills and wisdom when it comes to, say, working with adults with developmental disabilities. Make a case for your commitment to a cause and then connect that cause to the organization's mission, or show why your passion has shifted from your earlier focus to the mission of the organization in which you are now interested (perhaps a change in your family situation, a traumatic experience, or new knowledge sparked this shift).

Three key differences from other sectors

Decentralized job postings, an unusual hiring cycle, and a close-knit community

The logistics of nonprofit hiring differ in three key ways from public and for-profit hiring practices. First, since nonprofits usually have a limited budget for job postings and recruitment, nonprofit openings are harder to find. Second, unlike other sectors, nonprofits don't usually recruit and follow a hiring calendar. Third, nonprofits often look internally first and then to other nonprofits in the community next when hiring for new positions. This means that many job openings are never publicized.

While it is harder to find a central nonprofit job posting location, it is not impossible to stay up-to-date. Many nonprofits (especially smaller ones) only post on their own websites, on local free job sites, and in local newspapers. Larger nonprofits utilize resources like Idealist.org, as well as their own organizations' websites and local free job websites. A lack of centralized job posting locations makes it all the more important to know the local nonprofit community (organizations, networking contacts, and local resources).

While many nonprofits do not follow a hiring calendar per se, there are definitely busier hiring times to keep in mind. According to Daphne Logan, Vice President of Human Resources for America's Second Harvest, some organizations assess their hiring needs at the end of their fiscal year and then do a wave of hiring for the start of the new fiscal year. If you are interested in a particular organization, learn when their fiscal year begins (look at Annual Reports or their IRS 990 forms on GuideStar.org) and keep close tabs on them during this period. Other organizations may not hire on a fiscal cycle but may be influenced by other factors. Jenny Estrada, former Director of Human Resources and Security for Planned Parenthood of the Columbia/Willamette, notes that organizations like Planned Parenthood are attractive to professionals between undergraduate and medical school. Hence, there is usually high turnover during the summer as employees depart to pursue further schooling in the fall. If you have a target career area, think about the connection between current events and cyclical calendars that may influence an organization's hiring practices. For example, jobs in education mostly hire in the spring and summer and jobs that involve a lot of work outside are typically most active in the spring, summer, and fall.

Finally, remember that the nonprofit sector is a close-knit community and that many positions go unadvertised because they are either filled internally or through a network connection with another organization. This makes getting out and getting involved a vital step toward gaining visibility and finding those unadvertised nonprofit employment opportunities.

common MISTAKES

I'LL JUST FIND EVERYTHING I NEED ONLINE.

Given the level of connectedness that our digital age provides, it is easy to overlook the more traditional (and sometimes more effective) methods of collecting job availability information. You should make a point to read all of the print media (dailies and weeklies) that carry job postings; keep tabs on professional associations that are networks for the type of work you want to do; attend any real-time events (career fairs, business card exchanges) in your area; and look at the local membership of the United Way (these organizations are often some of the better funded ones).

2007 research conducted by the Johns Hopkins Nonprofit Listening Project (*Workforce Recruitment and Retention Soundings, 2007*) shows that four of the six most commonly used recruitment techniques are *not* online. Of the 231 organizations polled for the study, organizations used the following recruitment channels:

- Word of mouth (99 percent)
- Current employee referrals (93 percent)
- Local newspapers (80 percent)
- Postings on others' websites (73 percent)
- Recruitment from recent interns (67 percent)
- Postings on organization's website (64 percent)

Considering the fact that word of mouth, referrals (networking), and local newspapers (print media) topped the list, you may want to spend a fair amount of your job search time *offline*.

Start early

Nonprofit human resources professionals overwhelmingly agree that the earlier you start volunteering, interning, and networking with nonprofits that interest you, the better. For college students, this can mean interning with the same organization for several summers in a row. For emerging professionals working at a "hold it together" (or "B"/"pay the rent") job, this can mean making a commitment to volunteer regularly with an organization. The more exposure you can get to an organization, the more chances you have to get a sense of its culture (see **Chapter Six**) and acclimate yourself to its operational style (see **Chapter Five** for more on internships and volunteering).

Early involvement benefits both the volunteer and the organization. For the volunteer or intern, it allows you to get involved with the organization to see if you are a good fit with the culture and that you share a passion for their mission and activities. For the staff at an organization, they can likewise see how well you fit in and how dedicated you are to the work you do with them. The bottom line is that the more experience you have with a particular organization or cause, the more favorably a nonprofit employer will look upon your resume.

For those without the experience of volunteering or interning with the same organization for a significant period of time, there are two possible approaches to bolstering your nonprofit involvement. The first approach is to look back over your volunteer history and find a common trend in your service. Ask yourself:

- What is the greatest commonality in my volunteerism? Is it a particular cause? A certain structure of organization? A specific demographic served?
- Have I served similar functions within different organizations for a long time?
- Is my service mainly with faith-based initiatives? Advocacy organizations? Direct-service opportunities?

By focusing your networking, cover letter, resume, and interview language to reflect these common trends in your volunteer history, you can better demonstrate to employers your commitment to the cause, as well as the clear trajectory of your social and professional choices (even if they did not seem clear at the time!).

The second option is to explore partner organizations that work with organizations with which you have experience. For example, Daphne Logan from America's Second Harvest points out that her organization works with food banks around the country (often affiliated with religious organizations). Logan says a history of volunteerism and interning with these partners shows the kind of dedication and commitment that employers like America's Second Harvest seek. So, while you may not have direct experience working with an organization that interests you, related experience can be the next best thing.

 Focus your networking, cover letter, resume, and interview language to reflect common trends in your volunteer history."

The challenges of the job market

Nobody said that finding your ideal nonprofit job would be easy. In fact, these days there are plenty of factors that may make it a challenging process. However, people of all ages, backgrounds, and professional aspirations are increasingly willing to seek a job that means more than just a paycheck. With these more holistic requirements in mind for their careers, many people begin their job search in the nonprofit sector. While this invariably increases competition for nonprofit jobs, it also strengthens the sector by attracting the highest caliber employees. As you begin your search for a nonprofit career, know that the process may be daunting in some ways, but the rewards are worthwhile.

> "Nonprofit organizations rarely have the budget or staff to recruit."

Five reasons why finding your ideal job in the nonprofit sector may be a complicated process

1. Heavy competition for coveted jobs

As greater numbers of people seek careers that integrate values, ethics, and a tangible contribution to society, hiring for positions in nonprofit organizations is becoming increasingly competitive. Students, young professionals, and sector switchers are seeking employers that are socially responsible and careers that allow them to make contributions to society. Within this landscape, there are particular organizations and positions that tend to be more attractive than others. People often seek out well-known or larger organizations, as well as positions in public policy, foundations, or international NGOs. When considering a career in the nonprofit sector, be aware that many applicants vie for the same positions at the well-known organizations. Dig deeper. Find lesser known, new, or local peer organizations. Make sure that you are aware of all of your options; some of the best opportunities may take a bit more searching.

2. When nonprofits recruit...

Actually, they usually don't. Nonprofit organizations rarely have the budget or staff to recruit. Because of this, organizations need to employ other strategies for finding qualified, reliable employees. Since nonprofits often have volunteers and/or interns, they already have an ideal pool of ready-made job candidates. When a position opens up, volunteers or interns are frequently the first people considered because it's already apparent whether they will fit well, have a good work ethic, and meet the qualifications of the job. This practice is evident from the findings of a 2003 Idealist.org survey of over 400 nonprofit staffing professionals, which revealed that, when seeking new staff:

- 33 percent of organizations recruit their volunteers.
- 50 percent of organizations recruit their interns.
- 40 percent of organizations recruit through consultants.

3. Nonprofit hiring differs from public and for-profit sector hiring

Nonprofit hiring differs from public and for-profit sector hiring in three key ways: it usually does not follow a regular calendar, nonprofit job postings are often decentralized, and many nonprofit jobs are filled through the organizations' tight-knit networks. The discussion of nonprofit hiring practices earlier in this section elaborates on these three key issues, and it is important to be aware of them because of the impact they can have on your job search. First, know that while some organizations have busier hiring times, it is hard to predict when positions will open up. Compounding this situation, when positions are available, there is often no budget for advertising the opening. Organizations with a hiring budget can utilize online resources like Idealist.org's job posting services. However, without funding (or time), most organizations will simply post openings on their own website or on free, community-based job sites. Additionally, many organizations first look internally and throughout their own nonprofit network for available candidates so these positions are filled before they are ever advertised. The lack of predictable hiring schedules and centralized job posting sites added to the insular nature of many organizations' hiring practices can make knowing when and where to look difficult... unless you get out there and involved!

4. The importance of networking and personal connections

Networking is the main way that nonprofit organizations hire. In a 2003 Idealist.org survey of nonprofit staffing professionals, it was found that, when hiring recent graduates, 66 percent of organizations find out about candidates through networking, while half of the surveyed nonprofits stated that they don't even try to recruit on college campuses. Chapter Four highlighted the importance of personal contacts in finding qualified candidates; this point cannot be overemphasized. To increase your chances of being hired by a nonprofit, get out and meet people! Schedule informational interviews. Ask friends and family if they know anyone who works in the nonprofit sector. Volunteer or intern with an organization. Find out where people who have jobs with your target organizations congregate; attend those networking events and join their professional associations (if you are in school, many of these have student rates). Talk to people in your community. Sending a resume and cover letter may work, but to increase your chances and decrease your search time, networking is key.

5. A candidate needs to be able to hit the ground running

Nonprofit hiring managers want candidates who can show the relevance of their qualifications and skill sets quickly. Many organizations often don't have a lot of time to train a new hire so you need to show that you are the candidate who has the skills, experience, and passion for the job. While passion is undoubtedly important, candidates often focus on this quality while neglecting to demonstrate the experience they have that enables them to do the job. The first opportunity to show relevant experience is through your resume and cover letter. When considering wording, make it clear how your skills fit with the position description. The chapter on resumes, cover letters, and marketing your distinct skills (**Chapter Eight**) gives you guidance on how to do this.

The demand for nonprofit jobs is high, the hiring practices are complex, and it's often about who you know in the sector. Not a great outlook for nonprofit employment. However, the evidence in favor of pursuing a career with a nonprofit easily outweighs the challenges. There are a plethora of reasons people seek nonprofit careers; below are just a few to motivate you for your search.

Five reasons it is worth the effort to pursue a nonprofit career

1. The future is bright

While competition for nonprofit positions is tough, the projected employment outlook is heartening. According to a 2005 article by Lester M. Salamon and S. Wojciech Sokolowski, "nonprofit employment increased by an average of nearly 30 percent in the five jurisdictions for which we currently have time-series data (Maryland, the District of Columbia, North Carolina, Pennsylvania, and Virginia). By comparison, total private employment in these same areas increased by 11 percent, or slightly more than one-third as much."[1] While this limited data points toward an upward trend in nonprofit job creation, demographic shifts coupled with the sector's increasing scope of activities signal an imminent boom in nonprofit hiring. According to The Bridgespan Group, "over the decade from 2007 to 2016, organizations [with annual revenues over $250,000] will need to attract and develop some 640,000 new senior managers."[2] This growing leadership deficit is due to retiring baby boomers and overall sector growth. This means that in the near future there will be more opportunities available, particularly in the areas of management and leadership. Now is a great time to begin your career in the sector!

2. So much potential for change

Working for a nonprofit is a great way of effecting change in local, national, and international communities on a range of issues. According to a 2002 Brookings

Perspectives on nonprofit leadership

In 2008, Idealist.org partnered with the Annie E. Casey Foundation, the Meyer Foundation, and CompassPoint to research nonprofit workforce development. The subsequent report, "Ready to Lead?", offers a comprehensive examination of potential nonprofit leaders' views on their futures as senior managers and executive directors, and of the overall health of the nonprofit sector's "leadership pipeline". The report also offers insight into leadership and leadership development from those working in and outside the sector.

www.meyerfoundation.org/newsroom/meyer_publications/ready_to_lead

---

[1] Salamon, Lester M. and Sokolowski, S. Wojciech. "Nonprofit Organizations: New Insights From QCEW Data" *Monthly Labor Review*, September 2005. Available at www.bls.gov/opub/mlr/2005/09/art3full.pdf

[2] Tierney, Thomas J. "The Nonprofit Sector's Leadership Deficit". The Bridgespan Group, March 2006. Available at www.bridgespangroup.org/kno_articles_leadershipdeficit.html

Institution survey[3], 66 percent of nonprofit workers were "very satisfied" with their opportunity to accomplish something worthwhile, compared to 41 percent of for-profit employees and 47 percent of government employees who were asked the same question. For an opportunity to have a lasting positive effect on society, the nonprofit sector is an obvious choice.

3. There's a mission for everyone

The diversity of the nonprofit sector ensures that if you want to work to protect picas in the Mountain West, advocate for arts education for students in inner city schools, or raise awareness of melting ice caps in the Andes, there is a non-profit organization (or two!) that aligns with your passion. Nonprofit missions run the gamut from conservative to liberal, and focus on concerns affecting the global community as well as issues facing a single neighborhood. With the range of missions and causes, there is an opportunity for everyone to effect change. However, it is important to go beyond a cursory search for an organization that fits with your personal mission. In many cases, there are several organizations that will match your passion, but you'll have to do the research to find them. For example, if you want to teach in an inner city school for a year, Teach for America is a great program, but it's not the only one offering that opportunity. Similarly, Habitat for Humanity is an excellent way to help people afford to own their own home, but there are other organizations that do this kind of work. The best known, most easily researched organizations may be a great fit for you, but be sure to dig a bit deeper to discover all of your options.

4. Nonprofit salaries can hold their own...

"According to a survey by Abbott, Langer, and Associates, the median income of chief executive officers in the nonprofit sector was $88,006 in 2005, but some of the highest paid executives made over $700,000."[4] In industries such as health care and education, where for-profits and nonprofits compete for skilled employees, non-profit salaries are identical to or outpace for-profit pay rates by as much as 30 per-cent.[5] While earning a top salary is not the priority for many people who enter the nonprofit sector, it is important to know that it is still possible to earn a great living while serving in a wide range of roles and working toward a variety of missions.

5. It's about more than the bottom line

As statistics show, many people are realizing that their career choice is about more

Further reading on the nonprofit job market

There are plenty of articles about nonprofit careers, salaries, and employment statistics, as well as analysis of the future of the sector. A few key resources are listed below.

• To find out more about the status of the nonprofit sector in your area, have a look at the *State Nonprofit Employment Bulletins* from the Johns Hopkins Institute for Policy Study, Center for Civil Society Studies, available at:
www.ccss.jhu.edu/index.php?section=content&view=16&sub=104&tri=99#State%20Employment

• For more general information on national and state nonprofits with summaries and comprehensive reports for both, go to the *U.S. and State Profiles* at the National Center for Charitable Statistics (NCCS) website:
http://nccsdataweb.urban.org/PubApps/profileStateList.htm

• Brookings Institute, *Final Topline Report: Health of the Nonprofit, For-profit, and Public Service Sectors.* February 2002.
www.brookings.edu/views/papers/light/NonprofitTopline.PDF

• There are more articles available in this chapter's online resource page:
www.idealist.org/en/career/guide/ch12resources.html

---

[3] Brookings Institute. *Final Topline Report: Health of the Nonprofit, For-profit, and Public Service Sectors.* February 2002. Available at www.brookings.edu/view/papers/light/NonprofitTopline.PDF

[4] Abbott, Langer, and Associates survey data cited by U.S. Department of Labor, Bureau of Labor Statistics. *Occupational Outlook Handbook, 2006-7 Edition.* "Top Executives: Nonprofit Organizations." Available at www.bls.gov/oco/ocos012.htm#earnings

[5] Salamon, Lester M. and Sokolowski, S. Wojciech. "Nonprofit Organizations: New Insights From QCEW Data" *Monthly Labor Review,* September 2005. Available at www.bls.gov/opub/mlr/2005/09/art3full.pdf

than a paycheck; more people than ever are transitioning from other sectors to nonprofit work. These days, people don't expect to be with one organization for their entire career, and there is a growing awareness of the importance of finding positions that provide more than a salary. With this in mind, people are seeking creative solutions that enable them to make meaningful work a part of their everyday lives.

Conclusion

No matter how you look at it, there are a variety of challenges—from disparate job posting resources to a lack of hiring schedules to the insular nature of nonprofit hiring—that make finding a meaningful nonprofit opportunity more difficult. Yet work within the sector is a richly rewarding experience that provides not only a chance to connect passion, purpose, and paycheck but also a wealth of flexible options not available in other sectors. Remember to keep the challenges of mastering the nonprofit hiring process in perspective while also reminding yourself how worthwhile the journey is.

SUMMARY

One key to your success in a nonprofit job search is to fully understand the playing field. It is essential that you know the hiring practices and challenges that you will encounter during your search, as well as reasons why a nonprofit career may be perfect for you. Some factors to keep in mind include:

Nonprofit employers, like their counterparts in the public and for-profit sectors, look first to make sure you have **the necessary skills** to do the job. Next, they look to a key characteristic that is unique to the nonprofit sector: a demonstrated **passion for the work** and the mission of the organization (page 184).

Unlike job openings in other sectors, nonprofit jobs **lack a centralized job posting location**, making the local nonprofit networks and resources in your area all the more important to know. Furthermore, most nonprofits lack the time and resources to recruit to the same degree as government agencies and for-profit companies (page 185).

Nonprofits often have an **unusual (or erratic) hiring cycle**. This makes knowing a particular nonprofit's fiscal calendar and organizational needs all the more important during your search (for example, do a lot of staff leave at the end of summer to return to school?) (page 185).

Starting as early as possible in your job search is key. Nonprofits frequently hire from their intern or volunteer pool, or look for recommendations from colleagues in the sector. **The earlier you get involved** in nonprofit work (through volunteering, interning) the more visible you will be to organizations that interest you (page 186).

Nonprofit positions are **becoming more and more competitive**. Factors like competition for coveted jobs, a lack of recruiting, overworked nonprofit HR staff, a limited nonprofit network, and the need to demonstrate that you can "hit the ground running" if you are hired all make landing the ideal nonprofit job more difficult (pages 187-189).

Even with the unique challenges you must face in order to find a great nonprofit job, there are **a variety of reasons to make the effort**. Projected employment that outpaces other sectors, the chance to create real change, the abundance of organizational missions to suit most interests, salaries and compensation that can hold their own against other sectors, and the ability to do work "beyond the bottom line" all point toward a fulfilling career in the nonprofit sector (pages 189-191).

CHAPTER THIRTEEN

It's not what you think

Dispelling some misconceptions about the nonprofit world

In this chapter you will:

- Read ten common myths about working in nonprofits–and why they may be worth reconsidering.

- Understand why you don't need to be a liberal arts major to be a perfect candidate for the nonprofit sector.

- Consider how to explain your nonprofit work to family (or anyone else) who has reservations about its safety, value, or viability as a career option.

Ten common myths about working for nonprofits

1. "Only rich kids need apply"

No one makes any money in the nonprofit sector.

The nonprofit sector is a multi-billion dollar industry with trillions of dollars in assets, and it employs roughly one in ten people in the United States. The term "nonprofit" relates to the 501(c) tax code in the United States, but elsewhere common terms for nonprofits include nongovernmental organizations (NGOs) and charities. Nonprofits reinvest their surplus revenues back into programs that serve their organizational missions; there are no stockholders receiving annual financial dividends and their employees don't receive bonuses at the end of a good year. However, nonprofit workers still earn salaries, enjoy benefits, and have meaningful careers. You will meet people of all backgrounds working on issues they're passionate about in the nonprofit sector.

2. "Only business rejects apply"

The nonprofit sector is for people who could not make it in the business world.

Nonprofit organizations are full of intelligent people with passion for their work (many with graduate degrees and years of experience). Many people switch between the nonprofit, public (government), and for-profit (private) sectors during their careers. This is especially true in recent times as the traditional lines between the sectors continue to blur. Work in each sector presents its own set of challenges, and there are many talented people in all three sectors. Businesspeople are often surprised to learn how difficult it is to make the transition into the nonprofit sector, which has different, and often rigorous, standards for success.

3. "No upward mobility"

Working for a nonprofit is not really a career path.

Working in the nonprofit sector is sometimes considered "taking a break" from the "real world," with the implication that it's impossible to spend a lifetime doing nonprofit work. In reality, the nonprofit sector provides many people with life-long careers doing exciting and fulfilling work. Nonprofits also tend to offer people more leadership opportunities than other sectors and a greater chance for recent hires to quickly take on upper managerial roles.

4. "Smiles all the time"

Everyone that works in the nonprofit sector is nice.

Most people who work in the nonprofit sector do care about making the world a better place, but so do plenty of people who work in the for-profit and public sectors. Do not be surprised when you encounter the difficult personalities, big egos, and office politics that exist in any professional environment. Perhaps there are a higher percentage of kind-hearted people in the nonprofit sector, but there is no way to measure this, and there are plenty of exceptions.

5. "Collaboration all around"

The nonprofit sector is not competitive.

In a world of limited resources, nonprofit organizations compete with each other intensely for funding, media attention, recognition, and other resources. Competition in the nonprofit sector is similar to competition in other sectors. In some cases, competition among organizations with similar missions may be detrimental to the pursuit of this shared mission; in other situations, competition can be a healthy catalyst prompting nonprofits to adopt more effective practices that make them the most efficient providers of a particular service. In other cases, nonprofit organizations work on alternate solutions to a similar problem, and on certain issues, organizations may have missions that are in direct opposition to one another (abortion, environmental reform, gun control, etc.). While many nonprofits seek to collaborate with other organizations, it's a misconception that all nonprofits "just want to get along."

6. "Wasting time and money"

Nonprofit organizations are inefficient.

Nonprofits do not measure success in terms of bottom lines and profit margins. Instead, success is measured in the steps taken toward achieving the organization's mission—which can be difficult to quantify owing to the complexities of societal problems that nonprofits seek to resolve. Add to this the reality of limited resources and an emphasis on serving clients (often at the cost of organizational maintenance), and it becomes clear why the sector is sometimes perceived as inefficient. There are certainly some inefficient and disorganized nonprofit organizations, just as there are plenty of dysfunctional organizations and agencies in the for-profit and public sectors. In all of these cases, this inefficiency is not a reflection of the sector as a whole. Indeed, there are a multitude of highly efficient and dynamic nonprofit organizations creating innovative solutions to complex problems.

7. "I can't deal with people"

Nonprofits only do direct service work.

When people think of nonprofits, they often picture soup kitchens, mentoring programs, and other organizations that involve staff and volunteers working directly with people who need some form of assistance. However, many nonprofit employees are accountants, computer programmers, salespeople, human resources professionals, managers, fundraisers, and executives. Others are researchers and advocates for certain issues, or are professionals playing vital, behind-the-scenes support roles that enable the more visible direct-service work most commonly associated with the nonprofit sector to happen.

8. "Poor and poorly dressed"

Nonprofits lack resources and are informal.

Many universities, hospitals, and other large institutions with multi-million dollar annual budgets are nonprofit organizations. Cultures within nonprofits vary, but business (or business casual) attire is the norm at many large and small nonprofits.

9. "Only for liberals"

All nonprofits support left-wing causes.

The nonprofit sector itself does not have a political agenda, and many organizations exist to provide services and promote interests that the government and the for-profit sector do not. Organizations within the sector lean left, right, and everywhere in between.

10. "I love volunteering, so why not?"

Working for a nonprofit is just like volunteering.

Nonprofits rely on volunteers to do some of their work, especially in providing direct service. Volunteers, however, are often shielded from the organizational, financial, and other challenges that the actual employees of an organization confront, to say nothing of the burnout issues faced by those who spend a lot of time working in the field. Working at a nonprofit means precisely that—working (albeit often in a role and a field that you're passionate about).

Measuring impacts

Many nonprofits work in fields where a finite measurement of success is extremely challenging, if not impossible. Think of how to best determine the success of a school. Attendance rates? Test scores? The percentage of students who graduate, or who go on to college? Should you consider the percentage of students who rate their education favorably at graduation, or is it better to survey them ten years later? Do you compare a school's academic standing against local, regional, or national ranks, or against all three?

In another example, how can an environmental nonprofit measure its success? Is it by the effect they have on awareness raising, or the influence they bring to bear on policy makers and business leaders? Should they count acres of preserved forest, or species protected, or animals rescued? Does an increase in donations constitute a success, or is effective advocacy on behalf of a single piece of legislation a better metric?

Similar questions can be posed for many of the issues that nonprofits work on every day: poverty reduction, human rights, freedom of expression, community development, civic engagement, health care, and a host of other issues. As these examples demonstrate, there are many benchmarks for success, and since nonprofits often work on complex issues with multiple stakeholders, they have to weigh a variety a factors to judge how effectively they are carrying out their missions.

So, you're not a social sciences or liberal arts major?

The nonprofit sector still needs you!

It is a common misconception that the nonprofit sector is made up solely of social sciences and liberal arts majors. This simply isn't true. While degrees in psychology, sociology, anthropology, political science, art, media studies, history, or English (among others) can prepare you for an exciting nonprofit career, the sector is big enough for everyone. The nonprofit sector addresses an incredibly broad array of issues—everything from poverty to the environment, from housing to the arts, from conflict resolution to literacy—so diverse skill sets and specializations are needed. If you have a passion for creating social change—and you also have a passion for, say, business, biology, or buildings—then you can make an immense impact by working in the nonprofit sector.

The resources below demonstrate some possible career tracks that non-liberal arts majors can pursue in the nonprofit sector. These listings are far from exhaustive. Instead, they are meant to serve as a starting point for further research and to illustrate the wide variety of career opportunities available in the nonprofit sector. You'll also see some sample job postings from the past.

Nonprofit job information websites Here are just a few of the websites where you can search a broad range of nonprofit jobs:

- **Idealist.org**
www.idealist.org

- **Bridgestar**
www.bridgestar.org

- **Chronicle of Philanthropy Careers**
http://philanthropy.com/jobs/

- **Young Nonprofit Professionals Network**
www.ynpn.org

Agriculture

Sustainable agriculture is a pressing issue among farmers, environmentalists, politicians, and consumers. Skilled agriculturalists are needed in the nonprofit sector to research, educate, and guide policy development about agricultural practices. In your job search, consider organizations that are working on agriculture-related issues like clean air and water, urban sprawl, or biodiversity.

Relevant websites

- **National Campaign for Sustainable Agriculture** (http://sustainableagriculture.net) check out their employment section
- **Environmental Jobs and Careers** (www.ejobs.org)
- **Environmental Career Opportunities** (http://ecojobs.com)
- **DEVJOBS**: (www.devjobsmail.com) mailing list for jobs related to agriculture, poverty alleviation, health, population, and natural resource management
- **Organic Volunteers** (www.organicvolunteers.com) volunteer and employment opportunities
- **Orion Grassroots Network** (http://jobs.oriongrassroots.org) job opportunities and additional resources
- **Sustainable Hudson Valley** (www.sustainhv.org)

Sample job postings

- The Center for Science in the Public Interest is hiring a Research Assistant for the Food Safety Project and a Food and Agriculture Policy Director.
- The Watershed Agricultural Council is seeking a Farm to Market Manager to direct the development and implementation of a comprehensive program that will enhance the economic viability of farms in the New York City Watershed Region through farm product promotion, marketing, distribution, and sales systems.

Architecture/Environmental design

Nonprofits need architects, designers, and builders to support sustainable design, an emerging area within the sector. Architects and designers can also have exciting careers in public policy, urban planning, and international development.

Relevant websites

- **Architects Without Borders** (www.awb.iohome.net) look at the local chapter sites, which tend to have job postings on their message boards
- **The Enterprise Foundation** (http://enterprisefoundation.org) sponsors a number of Rose Architectural Fellows each year to work with community development organizations in low-income neighborhoods
- **Community Design Opportunities** (www.designcorps.org) excellent resource for navigating the world of community design, including housing; commercial, industrial, and recreational facilities; health care; child care; and landscaping. The site includes job search advice.
- **Association for Community Design** (www.communitydesign.org) not a job listing site, but has a membership of about 250 community design centers from around the world
- **U.S. Green Building Council** (www.usgbc.org) a coalition of members working to create environmentally responsible, safe, healthy buildings
- **Greener Buildings** (www.greenerbuildings.com) a content-rich site about sustainable design
- **Environmental Works** (www.eworks.org) not a job listing service, but a good source of information about sustainable design

Sample job postings

- Afghans for Civil Society is looking for a professional to oversee the construction of a Skills Training Institute.
- The United Nations Development Program is seeking a Project Advisor to support a $1.3 million straw-bale housing project in Mongolia.
- Conservation Services Group is seeking an Energy Support Specialist to assist in certifying residential construction projects.

"Business"

Nonprofits need employees with business skills including management, finance and accounting, strategic planning, development, public relations and marketing, evaluation and assessment, entrepreneurship, and human resources management. Many organizations in the nonprofit sector are seeking to create a "business" culture emphasizing professionalism, efficiency, and capacity building. A growing trend is for executive directors to be called CEOs, and many nonprofits are hiring CFOs, marketing directors, communications directors, and other traditional "business" roles. There are also many links between business skills and nonprofits' development (fundraising and other revenue creation) functions.

Also note that there is a growing social responsibility movement within the corporate sector. For those who work with for-profit companies, there are ample leadership opportunities related to community investment and engagement, environmental stewardship, and the protection of human rights.

 Many organizations in the nonprofit sector are emphasizing professionalism, efficiency, and capacity building."

Relevant websites

- **DEVJOBS** (www.devjobsmail.com) mailing list for announcing development jobs related to areas including microfinance, poverty alleviation, population, and economic development
- **Business for Social Responsibility** (www.bsr.org) great source of information about socially responsible business practices
- **Sustainable Business** (www.sustainablebusiness.com) be sure to check out the "Green Dream Jobs" section

Sample job postings

- Women for Women International is seeking a Microfinance Consultant to work in collaboration with the Country Director to oversee all aspects of the microfinance program.
- The National Wildlife Foundation is hiring a Senior Financial Analyst.
- New York Cares is seeking a Communications Director to develop campaigns and promotions that inspire and move audiences to action, while achieving concrete marketing objectives.

Engineering

There are many opportunities for engineers to work in the nonprofit sector, both domestically and internationally, on critical issues including clean water, sanitation, renewable energy, transportation, shelter and housing, and capacity building.

Relevant websites

- **Engineers Without Borders** (www.ewb-international.org and www.ewb-usa.org)
- **Environmental Career Opportunities** (http://ecojobs.com) includes a section on engineering careers
- **Global Village** (www.i4at.org) researches promising new technologies that can benefit humanity in environmentally friendly ways
- **Institute for Affordable Transportation (IAT)** (www.drivebuv.org) designs high-quality, low-cost transportation for the working poor in developing countries
- **International Center for Appropriate and Sustainable Technology** (www.icastusa.org)

Sample job postings

- Winrock International is seeking a Program Assistant for their Clean Energy unit to support project implementation, program development activities, and new business activities of the Clean Energy unit. This position also includes serving as backstopper for selected field projects in developing countries.
- Scientists and Engineers for America is looking for an energetic policy research assistant to research and draft concise descriptions of current science policy issues; research elected officials' biographies and voting records on science policy issues and put the information into the science and health policy database; and collect science policy news articles and draft concise summaries of such articles for their website.
- The U.S Green Building Council seeks an Architect or Engineer to participate in the review of applications for project certifications and credit interpretation requests under the LEED Rating Systems; evaluate project documentation; review technical inquiries, and prepare reports and correspondence; and provide comprehensive support to a technical volunteer committee and staff leading the development and implementation of the LEED Rating Systems.

Science/Math

The nonprofit sector has room for professionals in a wide variety of scientific and mathematics fields, including information technology, web development, renewable energy, global warming, agriculture and farming, environmental engineering, and medicine/public health. If you consider the points of intersection between your particular skills and today's most pressing issues, chances are there will be nonprofits in the area that would appreciate your knowledge and abilities.

Relevant websites

- **Bioneers** (www.bioneers.org)
- **Geekcorps** (www.geekcorps.org)
- **Environmental Career Opportunities** (http://ecojobs.com)
- **Association of Science and Technology Centers** (www.astc.org) includes a job bank
- **Public Health Employment Connection** (http://cfusion.sph.emory.edu/PHEC/phec.cfm)
- **Orion Grassroots Network** (http://jobs.oriongrassroots.org) job opportunities and resources
- **PATH** (www.path.org) improves the health of people around the world by advancing technologies, strengthening systems, and encouraging healthy behavior

Sample job postings

- The EthnoMedicine Preservation Project is seeking qualified staff to help preserve the medicinal plant knowledge of indigenous cultures.
- The United Nations Development Programme is hiring a Chief Technical Advisor to the Afghan Legislature.
- The Center for Urban Community Services in New York is seeking a qualified Nutritionist to support residents in a housing facility for tenants with a history of mental illness, homelessness, substance abuse, or HIV/AIDS.

What to tell family and friends about working in a nonprofit

The motivations behind your desire to find a career that matches your values are sometimes lost on parents, partners, relatives, and friends. Other peoples' doubt, confusion, and guilt-giving can add stress to the already hectic process of thinking about what you want to do and trying to locate such a position. Here are just a few possible concerns you may hear:

Concern one: We do not want you working in difficult or dangerous environments.

Your family and friends may think your intentions are noble, and may even support the mission of your organization. However, they may not be comfortable with your role (feeding the homeless, organizing workers in "bad" neighborhoods, or working with crisis victims).

"Can't you have a desk job working for the same cause instead?" they ask.

These concerns are valid: direct-service work is often the most physically and emotionally exhausting work available in the nonprofit sector. These jobs also tend to pay less than administrative positions, and the work typically doesn't have the same prestige as jobs where you spend time promoting or supporting a cause. You may be subject to greater risks, both physically and psychologically, and may be working with a community that is different from your own—in terms of class, race, ethnicity, gender identity, political stability, or other factors.

Direct-service jobs are a great way for newcomers to break into the nonprofit sector, because they provide a quick education on how organizations seek to serve the public's needs. There tend to be more openings for these types of positions (as opposed to administrative support positions), and such experience "in the trenches" is usually seen as fundamental for future supervisory and policy-related roles. This kind of service work also leads you to make a more educated decision about which communities you are most interested in serving, and what work may serve you best in the long term. For example, while working in an after-school program, you may find that you love serving with kids, or that you are passionate about children's issues but have no desire to work directly with children, or that the issue is one that doesn't hold your interest. Such knowledge can lead to a longer career serving the community directly, or it can inform future advocacy on behalf of whichever group(s) you are currently working with.

Jot your thoughts

Note some of the reactions from friends and family to your nonprofit work. Then jot some of your own ideas about how to answer their concerns.

Experience 'in the trenches' is usually seen as fundamental for future supervisory and policy-related roles."

Concern two: You got a college degree so you could make money. How will you make a living working for a "nonprofit"?

The good news is that starting salaries in the nonprofit sector are not significantly different from those in many (but not all) other fields. For an entry-level position in a new field, you would probably be making a similar lower starting salary no matter where you were working. Nonetheless, you will be able to "make a living" in the nonprofit sector—you just may not be able to sustain the same standard of living as some of your relatives or friends who have higher paying jobs.

In the long run, however, this is an issue of your values versus those of your family and friends, and of what sort of work makes you the happiest. Since it is one of the first major career decisions you have made, your family is bound to be nervous. Assure your loved ones that you can pay your bills, even if it means that you must tighten your belt and live modestly at first. Also let them know that your decision to work with a nonprofit is not a waste of your education, and show them how your degree relates to your area of focus and your professional development. Once they see these connections, they should be a bit more understanding of your decision.

Concern three: Take a year "off" to do this stuff, but then we expect you to get a "real job".

This is a classic line, and one you're likely to want to respond to with an equally biting retort. Instead, challenge your friends' and family's preconceived notions and ask them why they don't consider a job at a nonprofit to be a "real" one. Explain to them that the responsibilities of a new job in a nonprofit are extremely challenging, and that your opportunities for advancement in the early stages of your new career may also be much greater than if you were to work in another sector. What aspect of that isn't real? Nonprofit work certainly isn't taking time "off." If anything, due to the greater variety of tasks that your job will probably entail, working at a nonprofit may be a more rapid introduction to the professional world than you would get if you were to take a less dynamic job in a business.

Your family and friends may have a point, however—you may want to change careers one day. Let them know that, for now, you are serious about working in the nonprofit sector. Assure them that one day you may choose to change careers, and that, if you do, you will have some solid work experience under your belt from your time in the nonprofit sector. You will be well suited to make a career transition, if you so choose.

SUMMARY

There are several **misconceptions surrounding nonprofit employment**. Because of the sheer variety of organizations in the sector, there will always be inaccuracies in any sort of sweeping generalization about nonprofits. However, a few misconceptions should be reconsidered when looking into a career in the nonprofit sector.

Several **common myths** come to mind when people talk about the nonprofit sector. These are easily debunked (pages 193-195).

While social science and liberal arts majors are certainly at home in the nonprofit sector, nonprofits also offer plenty of challenging opportunities for people with **backgrounds in such fields as agriculture, architecture, engineering, business, science, and math** (pages 196-200).

Based on the misconceptions discussed in this section, some people still don't consider the nonprofit sector a viable career option. If your **family and friends are having trouble understanding** your desire to work in the sector, there are several ways to address these questions, concerns, or doubts about your decision (pages 201-202).

CHAPTER FOURTEEN

Starting your own nonprofit

Five tips, one warning, and eleven first steps

by **Put Barber**, Senior Researcher, Idealist.org, and Editor of the Nonprofit FAQ

In this chapter you will:

- Read helpful tips to consider when starting a nonprofit.

- Consider some words of warning regarding the difficulty of starting a nonprofit and the amount of research, planning, and work that goes into the process.

- Decide if starting a new nonprofit is really the best route to take and consider alternatives.

- Learn the first steps for launching a new nonprofit organization in the United States.

- Find resources to assist you in starting a nonprofit organization.

The world is in the midst of what has been called an "associational revolution." New nonprofits are being formed for every sort of purpose on every continent at the fastest rate in history. If you are thinking of joining this vast worldwide movement by starting—or helping to start—a nonprofit, this chapter identifies some crucial aspects to consider first, some possible alternatives, and some key steps you'll need to take if you decide to go forward.

Five tips and one warning

Tip one: All nonprofits are local

Even the globe-spanning, well-known organizations that operate in hundreds or thousands of places must learn about, and live with, complicated rules that differ greatly from place to place. Almost certainly, one of the first steps you will take when starting a nonprofit is to register with the local government agency that handles new "nongovernmental organizations" where the organization will be based.

For advice about which government agencies will be involved, consult a nearby organization; see the list at www.idealist.org/if/i/en/faq/166-227/18-67.

Tip two: Local supporters are necessary

No one starts a nonprofit alone and nonprofits don't operate in isolation. All outside funders—foundations, government agencies, corporate contributors, major donors—will want to see evidence that people besides the founder are involved in, and supportive of, the plan for the new organization. Big gifts and grants get a lot of buzz, but even in countries like the United States where organized philanthropy is a major factor in the nonprofit sector, big gifts and grants amount to less than 15 percent of organizational funding. So, one of the very first steps you will need to take when starting a nonprofit is to identify the circles of friends and colleagues who know your work and develop a strategy for earning income, whether it's payment for services by clients or another entrepreneurial approach. Even though you are starting a *non*profit, you need a solid "business plan" at the onset to sustain your work.

There is a lot of information about various approaches to finding financial support in the Nonprofit FAQ at www.idealist.org/if/i/en/faqcat/100-7. For more information on nonprofit "business plans", see www.idealist.org/media/pdf/FAQ/080123NP_Biz_Plan.pdf (PDF).

Tip three: Nonprofits can be–in fact, have to be– "business-like"

If "business-like" means keeping good records, watching revenues and expenditures carefully, and being committed to thoughtful planning about when and how to grow, then every successful nonprofit—alongside its dedication to the community and to the causes being served—is business-like at the heart of its operations. Without financial and service records, it is impossible to provide the community and other stakeholders with reliable information about the scope and value of the organization's work. This means not only being able to demonstrate how your organization's revenues are allocated for maximum impact, but also being prepared to answer to regulators who monitor nonprofits for financial malfeasance.

For an introduction to the many tasks involved, start with Idealist's Nonprofit Management Resources at www.idealist.org/tools/management-resources.html.

Tip four: Often *not* starting a nonprofit at all is the best way to serve

In many communities, a full range of nonprofits is already hard at work. Finding a way to extend and support the work already being done may yield greater benefit more quickly and at lower cost. Helping an existing organization to approach its mission in a new and creative way is often more valuable than starting your own nonprofit. The details will be different, of course, but spending time thinking about alternative paths toward the goal is an essential part of the considerations for starting any new organization.

One possibility that can save you the red tape of founding a nonprofit and let you instead focus your time on running your project is to affiliate with a willing organi-

---

Thinking of starting a nonprofit organization?

You know all about the red tape and paperwork. You've secured sufficient funding to get your organization off the ground. You understand the history, context, trends, and needs in the field your organization will enter. You are, you think, ready.

Even if you have a handle on the logistics of starting a nonprofit, be sure to consider the personal costs of doing this kind of work before you begin. Here are some of the realities for which nonprofit founders should be prepared:

- The risk of burnout–from long hours, low or no pay, and the ultimate responsibility for the organization's success–is very real.

- It may be years before your organization's work is recognized, if it ever is. There are many excellent organizations that haven't received much or any acknowledgment for the good work they do.

- Because the founder of a nonprofit is often the "face" of the organization, you must be comfortable with that kind of visible, public role.

- Especially at the outset, you will need the support of everyone you know. You will need to be comfortable asking friends, relatives, community members, and anyone else in your network for support.

- It is difficult knowing that all paths within your organization end with you. The founder must try to ensure success while being acutely aware of the possibility of failure.

- Founders must recognize when it is time to step away and leave the leadership of the organization to a new generation. With all of the time, energy, and passion that goes into starting and sustaining a nonprofit, separating your identity from that of your organization can be a true challenge.

The decision to start a nonprofit should take into account the organization's short-term commitments as well as its long-term sustainability. The demands on a nonprofit founder are both constant and ever-changing.

zation. And in some places, there are organizations devoted to fostering community service work by providing shared administrative services. You can read more about these alternatives on page 207.

Sometimes the best idea is to find an organization whose work you admire and volunteer to help extend it. Idealist's Volunteer Resource Center can help you explore these possibilities; see www.idealist.org/volunteer.

Tip five: Plan for the long term

If your goal is to do something that can be done quickly, that's all the more reason to avoid creating a new organization (see tip four). Providing a permanent service or tackling a big problem, though, will require an organization that can be sustained for years, even generations. It's essential to have a clear plan for how the work will be carried on once the initial enthusiasms and founding organizers are no longer on the scene (see tips two and three). This long-range plan must include both solutions to governance questions (Who will be on the board? Who will lead the staff?) and management issues (Where will the money come from? How will new services be designed and implemented?). Answering the question, "What would happen if I were hit by a bus?" isn't pleasant, but it's really necessary.

Clear mission statements and good strategic planning are the foundation for long-term success. For advice, see the Nonprofit FAQ discussions at www.idealist.org/if/i/en/faq/66-22/5-5 and www.idealist.org/if/i/en/faq/99-33/11-77.

And a warning

In every part of the world, nonprofits are subject to regulation, scrutiny, and sometimes outright hostility. A great deal is accomplished by people working together to solve problems, meet community needs, and create valued institutions. But rivalries, suspicions, and limited resources have blocked many a good plan. After the initial difficulties have been surmounted, of course, there are further challenges involved in keeping an organization going.

Even under the most favorable conditions, nonprofit leaders are often discouraged by how much of their energy is drawn away from "program work" into the tasks like administration and perpetual fundraising that are necessary for running a nonprofit —any nonprofit—and dealing with external pressures and demands. And despite the essential services that nonprofits bring to the community and the dedication and passion of the people who start them, there are no fail-proof methods guaranteeing the success of nonprofits.

The decision to start a nonprofit organization is not one to take lightly.

Are you new to the sector and thinking about starting your own nonprofit?

This might be a great option for you. However, if you don't have much (or any) work experience in nonprofits, you should consider working for a few years in the sector before starting your own organization. Such experience will allow you to gain a deeper understanding of the community, the work that is already being done, and the people who can help you along the way. Additionally, you can learn some of the best practices to emulate as well as pitfalls to avoid. Given the incredible amount of work and commitment involved in starting your own nonprofit, actual experience in the sector is essential to demonstrate to:

• **Funders** – Experience shows a commitment to the sector and a solid base of knowledge on which to draw. Funders will be less likely to support you if you don't have actual work experience.

• **Future employees** – This goes back to the idea that in order to be taken seriously as a leader, you need to have served in the trenches. Experience in the sector gives you an understanding of what nonprofit employees most need to do to succeed and to sustain meaningful work.

• **Constituents** – It is helpful to have a solid base of understanding right from the beginning so that you can serve your constituents in the most efficient, effective, and innovative ways possible. This knowledge comes from both direct experience and observation.

• **Yourself** – The work that goes into starting a nonprofit is intense regardless of your experience. However, you owe it to yourself to be as prepared as possible in order to mitigate some of the potentially serious personal costs (see sidebar, page 205) involved with running your own nonprofit.

Alternatives to starting a new nonprofit

If any of the considerations above give you pause, there are some very good alternatives to starting a new nonprofit. One obvious option (the subject of most of this book!) is to continue your search for a position with an existing nonprofit organization that offers you the chance to contribute to a cause you care about in a meaningful way. Another, lesser known alternative is to affiliate yourself and your ideas with an existing organization. Ideally your community already has other nonprofits, with complementary missions, with which you could affiliate. This sort of collaborative affiliation can take many different forms depending on your needs.

If you need to be tax-exempt to accept donations, you can approach a nonprofit to act as your fiscal agent. If you have in mind a short-term community project, and simply need a tax-exempt, incorporated organization to accept donations for the project, don't start your own nonprofit! Approach an existing, reputable organization to work with you. You can read more about how fiscal agents in the United States work in the Nonprofit FAQ (see www.idealist.org/if/i/en/faq/205-171/57-95); one way to find out about similar arrangements in other countries is to ask existing NGOs for advice.

Community foundations often allow people in the communities they serve to establish special funds for just this purpose. Let's say you'd like to build a new community garden and you have already won the city's approval, but the catch is that grant money and donations can't be issued directly to you. Your local community foundation may be willing to establish a Community Garden Fund, where grant money and donations can legally be received and held.

If you need to tackle a troubling social problem in an innovative way, rather than taking on the red tape, administrative time, and costs of establishing your own nonprofit, approach an existing organization committed to your shared mission and willing to foster or adopt your project as one of its own. You will need to demonstrate your idea's merit through a plan that shows thoughtful consideration of issues like implementation, sustainability, and staff support. It also requires some tact. But by presenting a sincere and considered approach you can make the value of your ideas apparent and avoid being perceived as an outsider offering unsolicited opinions or unexpected critiques. You may have to contribute the cost of a new phone line, a computer, and some office rent, but you would have more time to focus directly on your mission rather than administrative tasks. You can read more about this type of arrangement, called "fiscal sponsorship", in the Nonprofit FAQ (see www.idealist.org/if/i/en/faq/70-9/21-74).

Giving circles: A modern, philanthropic "sewing circle" or "book club"

A giving circle is a group of donors who pool their charitable dollars and decide as a group which cause to support. Giving circles vary in focus, structure and size. Some giving circles consist of a group of friends with a bank account who meet in each others' homes to discuss and decide on where their funds will go. Other giving circles are much more structured and formal with hundreds of members and governing boards. By combining resources the group is able to make a greater impact toward a common cause. This trend started just a few years ago and has quickly become an established philanthropic force that is estimated to have raised $100 million to support diverse causes.

For example, Shelley Goldseker and her co-founders decided to support women in need. The 52 "founding mothers" established the Baltimore Women's Giving Circle and contributed $1,000 each. Their initial round of grants totaling $52,000 was donated to ten nonprofits organizations that provided legal aid, job readiness, and financial literacy training as well as a women-only Habitat for Humanity project. Their second year, membership grew to 125 members who awarded $100,000.

The obvious benefit of creating or joining an existing giving circle is that an individual can make a big impact with a small donation without going through the lengthy process of becoming a nonprofit organization. Additionally, researching and networking with professionals connected to your cause will help in your career search as you gain information about possible roles, organizations, and volunteering opportunities that might influence your next steps.

- www.givingcircles.org
- www.givingforum.org/s_forum/doc.asp?CID=48&DID=5108

The benefits of affiliating with an existing nonprofit include:

- **Fiscal and administrative support** so you can focus on projects and/or service to clients.
- **Less expense**. By leveraging the work and costs that others have already put in to starting an organization, you can streamline operations and pay a portion of the costs more proportional to your project. A nonprofit willing to work this way with you also benefits, as they can take partial credit for the community benefits your program creates.
- **More support**. By affiliating with an existing nonprofit, people committed to your mission can help foster your project, and you may benefit from its good reputation and visibility, marketing efforts, and fundraising successes. You can also avoid the dangers of burnout and working in isolation.
- **Connections and local knowledge**. Existing nonprofits know the people in their community as well as other organizations engaged in working on similar issues. Even if you know your community well, chances are good that an existing nonprofit will be able to extend your network, and consequently, your ability to be effective and efficient in your work.
- **Time** for your project to grow and become sustainable. After some experience and success, you may choose to create a new nonprofit when the risks are lower.

When is it advisable to start a nonprofit?

So far this section has focused on reasons *not* to start a nonprofit, and on ways to *avoid* starting a new nonprofit. Obviously, the 1.4 million nonprofits registered in the United States and millions more worldwide have a variety of very good reasons to exist.

Communities would simply not be the same without nonprofits. More people would go hungry, be less educated, or feel less connected to their community without nonprofits. Survivors of natural disasters would go unrescued, children would go untutored, and recently released prisoners would go unsupported. Many colleges, hospitals, libraries, and museums would struggle to exist if it weren't for their nonprofit status. Obviously many nonprofit founders have confronted the challenges outlined earlier in order to further their missions, engage their communities in solving complex problems, and create lasting change.

You will know you have a solid case for starting a new nonprofit if:

- You have a clientele or beneficiary with a bona fide need that's not being met by an existing nonprofit or program.
- You have an innovative programming idea or approach to meeting the need.
- You already have (or know how you can secure) the monetary and in-kind donations needed to support the organization for the foreseeable future.

WHEN A FOR-PROFIT MAY SUIT YOUR PLAN BETTER

common MISTAKES

While nonprofits frequently create innovative solutions to community problems, it's going too far to view them as the only game in town. Many people who initially envision starting a nonprofit end up discovering that doing what they want to do through the vehicle of a for-profit is actually simpler and more efficient. This conclusion applies with greater force when the plan involves a lot of transactional revenue (e.g. sales) and does not depend on significant tax-deductible donations or foundation grants. In some cases, a business rooted in a "nonprofit-esque" mission may be the best option for realizing your idea.

While "social entrepreneurs" can be for-profit or nonprofit, searching the internet for "social entrepreneurship" and related terms will turn up some articles and examples that can help you consider the best path to take with your idea.

How to start a new nonprofit

Whatever else a nonprofit organization may be, it is also a legally defined and regulated entity. This means that the process for starting a nonprofit is filled with paperwork and bureaucratic interactions with government agencies. Navigating this process can feel daunting and unfamiliar to people who aren't thinking realistically about the effort involved in starting and sustaining an organization. The following discussion offers a general overview of the process for founding a nonprofit organization in the United States. Be aware that each U.S. state has its own particular requirements, so check with state authorities for the most recent information.

Eleven steps to start a U.S. nonprofit

Assuming you have a group of people who have defined a real need and have some idea of how to approach it; that you know you will have clients to serve or programs to benefit the community; and that you have a well developed plan for securing enough financial and non-cash (like volunteers or in-kind assistance) support—then you begin the process! The first steps to start a nonprofit in the United States are as follows.

Step one: Employer Identification Number (EIN)

The first step is to apply to the IRS for an Employer Identification Number (EIN). You need an EIN whether or not you intend to have other employees. The EIN is needed (later) to apply to the IRS for exempt status and may also be useful, or required, for working with state and local governments. Instructions on applying for an EIN are on the IRS website at www.irs.gov/businesses/small/article/0,,id=97860,00.html.

Step two: Organizing and pre-application planning

Fulfilling the state and federal requirements for starting a new nonprofit will require a lot of planning for the new organization. Some of this planning will be reflected in the documents that you will file with the state to incorporate and with the IRS to secure exempt status and recognition as a public charity (explained below). It is possible to complete all the necessary plans and documents without professional advice, especially with the help of handbooks and guides such as the ones listed in the "Learn More" box on page 215.

Many people working to develop a new organization find it worthwhile to get help from lawyers and accountants who are familiar with the ins and outs of the process. Such advice can cut down on frustrating missteps and delays. If there is going to be a lot of money involved in pursuing the new organization's mission—for employees, buildings, materials, etc.—then the advice of experienced professionals is essential.

Ideas for starting a nonprofit internationally

The process for starting a nonprofit varies considerably by country, owing to different political systems, legal frameworks, and receptiveness to non-governmental activity. To get started, you will need to investigate which government agencies regulate the formation and taxation of organizations (including businesses, faith groups, and NGOs) in the country where you want to work. Some countries do not have a concept akin to U.S. tax-exempt status; instead, organizations that intend to perform "nonprofit" activities may form under a variety of legal structures or informal arrangements—as community groups, voluntary associations, mutual aid societies, and even quasi-governmental agencies and for-profit companies. It may take some time for you to learn the legal landscape that determines how you can create an organization in a particular country, but this knowledge is critical to your eventual success.

Aside from researching the official outlook on nonprofits, conducting informational interviews with the leaders of nonprofits or their local equivalents in the country where you intend to operate will clue you in to the specific steps to take and some of the pitfalls to avoid. As discussed in this chapter, affiliating with an existing nonprofit may be the way to go.

You can search Idealist.org for nonprofits by country at www.idealist.org/if/as/Org/npo and use the information in their profiles to contact them.

Management Support Organizations (MSOs) offer advice, networking, and support to nonprofits. A list of MSOs by country is available at www.idealist.org/tools/support-orgs.html.

Step three: Incorporation at state level (Charter documents)

Registration with a state as a nonprofit corporation (or equivalent) is required before the process of securing IRS tax-exempt recognition can begin. Most states have specific provisions for the formation of nonprofit corporations. Typically, there is a form to file that requires attachments including a list of the people who are forming the corporation ("incorporators"); articles of incorporation and, sometimes, bylaws ("charter documents"); and a fee. In most cases, by this time you will also need to have identified your organization's initial board of directors and to have decided who will serve as officers. The usual and preferred course is to file for incorporation in the state where you live and where initial operations will take place. At this stage, it is not necessary to know the eventual geographic scope of your nonprofit's work, but be aware that a very similar set of filings (for a "foreign corporation") will almost always be required in other states where operations take place. (If you intend to do work in foreign countries, national and local authorities there will require additional registrations, too. See sidebar on page 209).

It is important that the charter documents contain full and accurate descriptions of the organization's purpose or purposes, limitations on the use of revenues and assets to prevent private parties from benefiting from the organization's nonprofit status, and a plan for dissolution that assures that any remaining assets continue to be dedicated solely to charitable purposes. Later, the IRS will examine these charter documents closely for these and other points as it reviews your application for exempt status.

Step four: Internal Revenue Service (Applying for federal tax-exemption)

If you want the organization to be exempt from federal corporate income taxes and for donations to qualify as federal tax deductions when people make them, you apply to the IRS for federal recognition as a tax-exempt organization—often called a "501(c)(3) public charity". You use IRS Form 1023 to apply for recognition as an exempt entity and as a public charity. This form was revised in 2004 and all applicants must use the new version of the form. It is a complicated form, with many attachments related to specific parts of the application.

If your organization plans to be very active politically, it will be ineligible to receive tax-deductible contributions but you will still need to apply to the IRS for tax-exempt status; if successful, your organization will be known technically as a "501(c)(4) social welfare organization." Form 1024 is used to apply for recognition as this type of organization. These "c4s" are also tax-exempt; they operate under much less restrictive rules about lobbying and other forms of advocacy, but donors' contributions to "c4s" are not tax-deductible.

Charter documents
Advice about and examples of charter documents can be found in that section of the Nonprofit FAQ at www.idealist.org/if/i/en/faqcat/5-5.

Incorporation
Contact the Secretary of State or comparable office and ask them for the appropriate application forms and list of necessary attachments.

Addresses for these offices can be found through the IRS website at: www.irs.gov/charities/article/0,,id=129028,00.html.

More local contacts state-by-state can be found in the Nonprofit FAQ at www.idealist.org/if/i/en/faq/210-74/84-86 (A-M) and www.idealist.org/if/i/en/faq/211-108/84-86 (N-Z).

Some listed organizations offer training sessions and manuals covering the specifics of setting up a nonprofit in their state.

For more on the role and recruitment of a board of directors, see: www.idealist.org/if/i/en/faqcat/3-1

There is a lot of information on the IRS website to help with understanding the process and exploring options. The general welcome page is at www.irs.gov/charities/index.html. Some of the more important detailed pages are listed in the sidebar at right.

If everything goes smoothly, it usually takes three to six months for the IRS to process an application. The "Top Ten" reasons the IRS turns down newly submitted 1023s are listed at www.irs.gov/charities/article/0,,id=96361,00.html.

If there is a special circumstance that makes faster review necessary, it can be requested. The IRS toll-free number for exempt organizations—877-829-5500—is probably the best place to inquire about that process.

Step five: "Public Charity" vs. "Private Foundation" (IRS determination)

Organizations that are classified by the IRS as "private foundations" are subject to more stringent limitations on their activities and must pay an excise tax each year based on their investment income. Organizations classified as "public charities" have different rules and don't pay this tax. The law requires the IRS to assume all 501(c)(3) organizations are "private foundations" unless they can prove that they are not. The difference is in the amount of "public support" received; organizations that rely on a few very large gifts are likely to be identified as "private foundations."

A new organization can ask to be treated as a "public charity" for the first five years of its operations while demonstrating that it receives the necessary proportion of public support (the calculations are done as part of Schedule A of the organization's annual Form 990 Information Return filed with the IRS). At the end of five years, the IRS makes a "final determination" about which category applies. This ruling can be reversed, though, if an organization receives funding from too few sources later on, which is why the "public support test" must be completed each year as part of the preparation of Form 990. For more on Form 990, see www.idealist.org/if/i/en/faq/57-95/62-42.

Be aware that many donors, including foundations, require that recipients be recognized by the IRS as public charities before they will consider making a gift or grant.

Step six: Charitable solicitations (Fundraising)

More than 30 states have laws that require some nonprofits and commercial fundraisers to register prior to conducting fundraising appeals and to report on the outcome of their fundraising efforts. If your organization plans to conduct any sort of fundraising that involves broad circulation of an appeal to the general public, you

IRS exempt status
You can find a general Introduction to the IRS application process at www.irs.gov/charities/article/0,,id=96210,00.html

• **Publication 4220**, Applying for 501(c)(3) Tax-Exempt Status (PDF) www.irs.gov/pub/irs-pdf/p4220.pdf

• **Publication 557,** Tax-Exempt Status for Your Organization (PDF) www.irs.gov/pub/irs-pdf/p557.pdf

• **Form 1023**, Application for Recognition of Exemption, 501(c)(3) status (PDF) www.irs.gov/pub/irs-pdf/f1023.pdf

• **Instructions for Form 1023** (PDF) www.irs.gov/pub/irs-pdf/i1023.pdf

• **Form 1024**, Application for Recognition of Exemption, 501(c)(4) status (PDF) www.irs.gov/pub/irs-pdf/k1024.pdf

• **Instructions for Form 1024** (PDF) www.irs.gov/pub/irs-pdf/i1024.pdf

Finally, retired IRS agent Sandy Deja offers a comprehensive resource for preparing Form 1023 at her website www.form1023help.com.

will need to review the laws that apply in every state where you will solicit. The Multi-State Filing Project has a website that describes the charitable solicitations rules in detail and provides a simplified process (the "Unified Registration Statement") for filing the necessary registrations in multiple states. See www.multistatefiling.org. The National Association of State Charities Officials has information about registration and reporting requirements at www.nasconet.org.

Step seven: Other privileges and exemptions

There are special provisions for nonprofits in many state and local tax codes; in federal, state, and local grant programs and government contracts; and in the requirements of foundations and other funders. The only way to learn about these opportunities (and the rules that apply to them) is through local research and developing good relations with other nonprofit organizations.

Many states and some localities have associations of nonprofit organizations and their supporters. The National Council of Nonprofit Associations lists many of these on its website at www.ncna.org. Others are found in the lists of state and local organizations referenced above in step three (Incorporation at the state level).

Step eight: Other state or local requirements

As you work on developing your new organization, be sure to ask state and local officials for any other materials that explain the rules governing hiring employees, employer payroll, and unemployment taxes; registering for licenses and for sales and/or income taxes under state and local law (if any); and any other matters of interest for setting up and managing a nonprofit in your state. These may come from several different offices at both the state and local levels.

Nonprofit organizations are *not* exempt from licensing, employment, safety, consumer protection, and other laws that may require specific permits and registrations before operations begin and for as long as the organization continues to work. Nonprofits are also required to pay many state and local taxes, or to secure specific locally defined exemptions; having federal (IRS) tax-exempt status offers no guarantee that these local taxes can be avoided. Nonprofits must withhold income taxes and pay social security, unemployment, and other taxes related to their employees.

There is no comprehensive resource for locating information on all these subjects. Here too, establishing connections with other nonprofits in your area and attending conferences, orientation sessions, and seminars offered on these subjects by associations and by local and state officials will help you master the requirements. This is another good opportunity to dust off your networking and informational interviewing skills. See if you can arrange to speak with local nonprofit leaders who have already been through these processes and might be willing to offer locally relevant advice.

Establishing connections with other nonprofits in your area will help you master the requirements."

Step nine: Insurance

Nonprofit organizations are protected in some states and by federal laws from some types of judgments concerning organizational liability for accidental injuries incurred by people in the course of the nonprofit's well-run affairs (think of a child being accidentally injured while taking part in a nonprofit after-school program). These protections are usually provided by so-called "Good Samaritan" or "Volunteer Protection" acts. However, this protection is not absolute, and proving that it applies (when it does) can be expensive. In cases where malice or negligence on the part of the nonprofit can be demonstrated, these protections typically no longer apply. Therefore, as a matter of prudence—and also to assure recompense to injured parties in instances of accidental harm—most nonprofits purchase insurance that provides for legal defense and payment of judgments if they are imposed. There are several kinds of insurance that might be useful and policies differ greatly in the protections they offer. Careful study is necessary.

Insurance
Donald A. Griesmann, Esq. has written a comprehensive review of nonprofit insurance for the Nonprofit FAQ; it includes several links to other online resources that will be helpful in sorting out insurance questions. See www.idealist.org/if/i/en/faq/144-221/50-5.

Step ten: U.S. Postal Service (Reduced rates for nonprofit mailings)

Nonprofit organizations can send certain kinds of mail at reduced rates. Recognition by the IRS is not required to mail at these rates (some organizations that qualify with the IRS are not eligible and vice versa). A separate application to the Postal Service is required to obtain a permit to mail at nonprofit rates, and each mailing must fit within the requirements of the program. The rates are only available for "standard mail" (formerly called "bulk mail"), meaning a relatively large number of identical pieces mailed at one time; they have to be sorted by the mailer and then taken to a special location (a "business mail entry" facility) to be mailed. Nonprofits often use specialized "mailing houses" to prepare their mailings. To take advantage of the lower rates, the organization has to have a permit to mail at nonprofit rates even if a mailing house handles production.

There are specialists in the Postal Service regional offices who provide information about the application process. They will also inspect drafts of materials that you want to mail at nonprofit rates and let you know of any potential problems (some of the rules are very specific and can lead to unexpected difficulties). In addition, the Postal Service offers seminars on the rules about standard mail and nonprofit mailing rates. It is worth inquiring about when and where these are offered. The Postal Service webpages discussing nonprofit mailings are at www.usps.com/nonprofits/welcome.htm.

Step eleven: Other considerations as you get going

As you complete all these steps, you'll also need to prepare for the eventuality of actually running your organization on a day-to-day basis. Here are a handful of issues you need to anticipate and plan for:

- **Banking**. In order to receive monetary donations, make purchases, and effect payroll, you'll need an organizational bank account. Mixing your personal finances with those of your organization is inadvisable and could lead to time-consuming—or worse—difficulties with your accountants and the preparation of tax returns.

- **Bricks-and-mortar**. Where will you house your operations? Will you lease an office, seek a donated/shared space, or convert your spare room to an office? There are plenty of examples of the range of ways to do this and there are pros and cons for each; ask around to find out how small, local nonprofits decided where their work would be based. In some communities, there are facilities called "nonprofit incubators" that have been set up to ease the complications of getting started. It's worth exploring whether you can take advantage of something like that.

- **Boards**. As part of the incorporation of your organization, you will already have recruited a board of directors. But even before the official papers arrive, the board should start working to define its role and develop good habits about handling its responsibilities. States have specific rules outlining the conduct and responsibilities of the board of directors, and board members can be held to account for the activities of the organization by various authorities. Thus, building and maintaining a knowledgeable and trustworthy board of directors is critical. You may also find it useful to develop additional advisory boards in order to involve people who can offer expertise on specific topics your organization deals with.

- **Human resources**. Don't plan to go it alone. You will need to locate and support human resources (people!) who can help your organization achieve its mission. This can mean everyone from salaried staff to volunteers, interns, and consultants.

- **Infrastructure**. You will need to acquire office furniture and supplies, telecommunications equipment and connections, and any special tools or materials necessary to run your programs. Subject to state and federal guidelines, your organization's tax-exempt status may be a big help here: in some places your organization may not need to pay retail sales tax on certain purchases (retailers will want proof of your tax-exempt status) and donors who contribute usable equipment (from computers to cars) may be eligible for a deduction equivalent to fair market value. You'll have to research the local rules to take full advantage of these provisions; begin by checking with state and local authorities.

- **Policies**. You will need to develop a range of organizational policies as soon you get going. Creating sensible policies on topics as varied as vacation time, family health insurance benefits, flex time, hiring practices, and volunteer administration cannot be done overnight.

Managing an organization
The following Idealist resource centers offer useful insights and links to more information on many of these nonprofit management issues:

- **Idealist Nonprofit FAQ**
www.idealist.org/npofaq

- **Idealist Tools for Organizations**
www.idealist.org/tools

- **Idealist Nonprofit Human Resources Center**
www.idealist.org/nonprofithr

- **Idealist Volunteer Management Resources Center**
www.idealist.org/vmrc

And finally...

If you do decide to proceed with starting a nonprofit organization, we hope you will find the offerings at Idealist.org helpful—you can list your organization for free, announce events, seek volunteers, describe publications, and recruit interns and staff (U.S. organizations pay a small fee for paid job announcements). Idealist has lots of ways to link up with supporters and draw on networks of colleagues and advisors. You can also use Idealist to identify other organizations working in your community that may be tackling related issues or working toward complementary goals. Idealist's Nonprofit FAQ and its other Resource Centers have discussions of many of the pressing questions you will encounter; they also point to many rich sources of information, advice, and techniques available on the internet. Good luck from all of us at Idealist.org.

Resources for this chapter

One of the most comprehensive resources for any topics related to nonprofits, including starting one, is **The Nonprofit FAQ** (www.idealist.org/npofaq). The Nonprofit FAQ is the work of Put Barber, a contributor to *The Idealist Guide to Nonprofit Careers* (and the author of this chapter).

A widely used reference book is Anthony Mancuso's *How to Form a Nonprofit Corporation* (Berkeley, CA: Nolo Press). The book includes a CD-ROM with outline copies of all the forms and documents needed in the process.

The Nonprofit Handbook: Everything You Need to Know to Start and Run Your Nonprofit Organization by Gary Grobman (Harrisburg, PA: White Hat Communications) offers a comprehensive review of the requirements for starting and operating a nonprofit.

More resources for this chapter online

There are many more resources related to this chapter online at:

www.idealist.org/en/career/guide/ch14resources.html

SUMMARY

If you are **thinking about starting your own nonprofit**, this chapter is essential reading. While no means exhaustive, this chapter offers digestible discussions and links to further resources about many critical considerations for potential nonprofit founders, including:

Five tips (pages 204-206): 1. All nonprofits are local. 2. Local supporters are necessary. 3. Nonprofits can be–in fact, have to be–"business-like." 4. Often *not* starting a nonprofit is the best way to serve. 5. Plan for the long term.

One warning (page 206): The decision to found a nonprofit organization is not one to take lightly.

Alternatives to starting a nonprofit (pages 207-208): Aside from continuing to search for the right job in a nonprofit, there are a variety of ways to affiliate yourself and your ideas with an exisiting nonprofit rather than founding your own. Affiliation offers many advantages, including less bureaucracy and more time to focus on your program work.

Eleven basic first steps (pages 209-215): Navigating your way through the complicated maze of applications and requirements needed to found a nonprofit organization can be daunting. These basic first steps will help you get going in the right direction.

Closing thoughts

Know yourself, the sector, and the points of synergy

In the conclusion you will:

- Review the importance of understanding yourself, the nonprofit sector, and the synergies between the two.

- Recognize the importance of keeping your job search in perspective and staying positive.

Today's nonprofit sector is arguably the most diverse employment sector in our society. Because of this, many of the preconceived notions, generalizations, and myths about nonprofit organizations simply don't hold up sector-wide. From the mission statements that drive nonprofit work to the organizational structures of 2- to 2,000-person nonprofits, there are few universal truths in the sector. To help direct your search for a career in such diverse organizations, Idealist.org created this guide to illustrate the size and scope of the sector, point out commonalities, highlight distinctions, dispel some of the myths, and help you assess where to find your perfect opportunity.

By this point, you've probably realized that working for a nonprofit means serving as a catalyst and connector in a way that transcends any single organization's work. The communal nature of this effort is one of the few sector-wide commonalities: in a simple sense, nonprofit organizations are aligned around the goal of working toward a better world—but how *you* define a better world may differ dramatically from the views of other people and organizations in the sector. The specific missions, strategies, and points of focus for nonprofits vary widely, and finding a group whose efforts mesh with your vision for positive change is crucial as you figure out your role.

Your search should start with a process of **self-discovery**: knowing your skills, experiences, passions, and workplace needs. Next, use this self-knowledge as a framework while you **explore the sector** and your particular areas of interest. Your goal is to **find the points of intersection** between your skills and passions, and the available opportunities.

While the end goal of a successful nonprofit career search is rewarding, the process can be complex, time consuming, and stressful. If you are entering the sector for the first time, you have the added element of transitioning into a new work world where you need to be aware of different vocabulary, positions, and expectations. Searching for a job in any sector can demoralize and frustrate you at a time when you are supposed to be your most proactive and social. It is important to recognize how the psychology of the job search (**Chapter Two**) affects you and your career decisions. Uncertainty about money, self-doubt about your strength as an applicant, and the challenges of your quest to find the right opportunity can coincide with negative interactions with employers either through outright rejection or the quiet "torture" of not knowing whether your resume was received or where they are in the hiring process. It can be difficult to remain optimistic and upbeat. However, being deliberate in your search by taking the time to get to know yourself and understand the sector, and then finding the synergy between the two, is key to ultimately finding the right job.

Know yourself

Any job search begins with knowing what will make you happy to wake up to on a Monday morning. It is an antiquated notion that your only goals should be to get to Friday afternoon and eventually to earn a bigger paycheck. Taking the time to explore your own interests and motivations and then connecting this knowledge to a job search can help you find the meaningful work that you seek. As you look for your first job, a solid sense of self-awareness is essential to find that place where you can both do your best work and have the greatest impact (see **Chapter Three**).

Since you spend so much time with yourself (a bit of an understatement!), it is difficult to step back and get the necessary perspective on your skills and abilities without making time for deliberate self-exploration. This integral element of the job search process allows you to make well-informed choices and, with the right perspective, can also afford you a bit more patience. This patience derives from having a strong sense of what you want and recognizing that it is worth waiting until you find it. You will probably not find the perfect fit immediately, which is why a job search is an ongoing, evolving process. If you are currently not in an ideal position, or if you need to take a less-than-perfect, "hold it together" job to sustain yourself, don't assume that you're "settling." In fact, you are building new skills and experiences that will make you a stronger candidate in your next search. Furthermore, you can continue the search even after you accept a position. And even if you find and accept a great opportunity, keep checking in with yourself regularly to ensure that you are getting what you need from the job to make it more rewarding than just a paycheck. You need to make sure your job is a meaningful, challenging, and sustainable opportunity for you.

The best way to find a tenable and fulfilling position is to be sure that you know your needs and wants. Much of the work that is done in the nonprofit sector is demand-

You are *not* your job search

The most important message you can tell yourself is that you are not your job search. Yes, you are marketing yourself and your skills, but that does not mean that you should take rejection personally. Try to consider the perspective of the employer when you are feeling frustrated. Employers need to make tough hiring decisions and have to weigh the pros and cons of many well-qualified candidates. The "sorry, but we can't offer you a position" response is based on a myriad of factors–skills, experience, and organizational fit, to name a few–and the rejection of a candidate is most often not personal. The reality of the hiring process is that there are always more candidates than available positions.

When you pick yourself up and brush yourself off after a rejection (or two), try to remember that it happened for a number of reasons (most of them not in your control) and there will always be more opportunities, possibly even better ones, in the future.

ing, and the chance of burnout is real. While you'll need to find ways to make whatever job you choose sustainable, knowing your priorities in terms of organizational culture, benefits, responsibilities, and other factors can help you find a job where you can continually do meaningful work.

Know the sector

By beginning with self-knowledge, you can start a targeted job search. Follow this exploration by studying the nonprofit sector to help you see where you best fit into such a diverse employment landscape. This sector analysis involves understanding the lens through which you view the work and recognizing the available opportunities (see **Chapter Three**), and then conducting informational interviews, creating networking opportunities, and taking other deliberate steps to strengthen both your connections to and knowledge of nonprofits (see **Chapters Four** and **Five**).

One of the best ways to get a better understanding of both the sector as a whole and your local nonprofit community in particular is by talking to people who are already involved in this work. As you begin your nonprofit job search (see **Chapter Six**), find ways to strengthen and expand your network (see **Chapter Four**). While networking is vital to any career search, its importance in the nonprofit sector cannot be emphasized enough. When hiring, nonprofit employers seek out referrals from their employees, volunteers, and interns, as well as leads from colleagues and coworkers. Local nonprofits are often connected and the sooner you become a visible, positive part of their community, the sooner you can start taking advantage of your nonprofit network.

While the job search process has certain universals across all employment sectors—knowing your goals, understanding the sector, and connecting with people—there are several unique aspects to a nonprofit job search that you need to keep in mind:

- The unique language of the sector
- An emphasis on collaborating with colleagues and other organizations
- The value of having a passion for the mission

After you've put the incredibly diverse scope of the nonprofit sector into perspective, begin to do some research on nonprofits in your local or target area. Conduct informational interviews (see **Chapter Four**), look for organizations doing work that interests you, and explore issue areas that fit your skills and experiences. Do all of this with the understanding that any information you find is a piece of the puzzle; keep asking, researching, and digging for the myriad other pieces that will give you a more holistic perspective of the nonprofit sector.

"You must study the nonprofit sector to see where you best fit into such a diverse employment landscape."

Find the synergy

With an awareness of what you can contribute and what you need, as well as an understanding of the sector, you can begin to find the points of overlap amid all of the variables in your search. There isn't *one* ideal job for you; there are many ideal ones. But be aware that these opportunities may be elusive, and that you will need to have a strong sense of what you are looking for in order to recognize and pursue them.

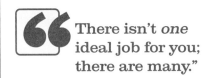

> There isn't *one* ideal job for you; there are many."

As you find and apply for positions, ask yourself if *each position* connects with your priorities. Some questions to ask include:

- Does this position utilize my strongest skill sets?
- Will I be able to strengthen other areas of my knowledge and expertise?
- Can I use my preexisting network to connect and expand the reach of this position?
- What is most exciting for me about this opportunity: the responsibilities of the position, the organization and its mission, the potential for creating change, or the possible career trajectories?
- Does this position look like it will be as challenging as I need/want my work to be? (Finding the range of what challenges you is vital in order to avoid boredom or burnout.)
- Does the size of this organization match what I am looking for?
- Is the compensation package for this position satisfactory? Will I need/be able to negotiate my offer?
- Does this position's work environment (office space, commute time, dress code, etc.) have the attributes that are most important to me?
- Where do I see myself in two to five years if I take this position?

Ultimately, you are the only one who knows all the questions you need to ask to make sure that you have found a great, if not perfect, fit. By asking these questions, you will be well on your way to finding the starting point to a meaningful and fulfilling career, rather than "just another job." This distinction is important because while a career is made up of a series of connected and deliberately chosen jobs, a job does not necessarily lead to a career. You don't need to plot your whole path at the beginning, but deliberately choosing a job with the potential to lead to other exciting professional opportunities can be the first step in creating a career that is as meaningful as the work that you will be doing.

Final thoughts (really!)

Whatever stage your nonprofit career search is in, keep in mind that there is not *one* right way to find meaningful work. Because of this, throughout this book we've offered a variety of exercises, options, opinions, and pieces of advice that fit a range of approaches and steps in a nonprofit job search. However, within these steps, remember the three essentials that you should customize to your unique situation:

- Know yourself and your needs
- Know the sector and the people in it
- Find the synergy between what you want and what opportunities are available

While we'd love to convince you that the nonprofit sector is an amazing place to work (we certainly think so), we know it's not for everyone. If you are unsure, spend some time volunteering, talking with people in the sector, and exploring available opportunities. Even if you decide that you don't want a career in the nonprofit sector, there are other ways to effect change such as getting involved with a company's corporate social responsibility department, engaging in board service or philanthropy, or volunteering regularly.

However, if you are looking for opportunities to do meaningful work every day, with remarkable people in a countless array of issue areas, locations, and organizations, we encourage you to explore the full range of opportunities to participate in and contribute to society through a career in the nonprofit sector. After all, the nonprofit sector continues to address issues of great importance, with innovative flair grounded in necessity. We think there is no better time to take advantage of the incredible potential to make the world a better place—however you choose to define "better." You don't have to be an idealist, you just have to want to make a difference.

SUMMARY

The **steps of the nonprofit job search** resemble the steps you should take any time you are looking for meaningful work, regardless of the sector.

The process of **self-knowledge** involves taking time to consciously reflect on your skill and abilities, wants and needs, and the level of challenge that will keep you invigorated without burning you out (pages 218-219).

Once you understand what you bring to and want out of a job, **explore the nonprofit sector** to see where opportunities in the sector connect with your own interests (page 219).

Finding this synergy is vital to career happiness (page 220).

Recognize that **the job search process can be difficult**, time consuming, and frustrating. Keeping a clear idea of what is important to you as well as a perspective on the reality of the job market (i.e., not taking rejection personally) is vital to your job search peace of mind (sidebar, page 218).

Nonprofitspeak 101

A primer on the nonprofit sector's vocabulary

by **Put Barber**, Senior Researcher, Idealist.org, and Editor of the <u>Nonprofit FAQ</u>

In Appendix One you will:

• Learn to talk the nonprofit talk by brushing up on some of the sector's unique vocabulary.

501(c)(3)

A section of the Internal Revenue Code where the standards for "charitable" status under U.S. tax law are defined. Organizations that qualify are exempt from U.S. corporate income taxes on their program revenues. Gifts to these organizations can usually be deducted from individual income taxes as well.

>>> See **Private Foundation, Public Charity**.

501(h)

A section of the Internal Revenue Code that deals with lobbying by nonprofits.

>>> See **Lobbying**.

Accountability

The responsibility to provide information ("an accounting") to the public. Accountability is also the view that an individual or organization must be "held accountable" and experience consequences for wrongdoings. Standardized reports to funders, government agencies, and the public are sometimes referred to as "accountability mechanisms."

>>> See **Transparency, Form 990**.

Agency

A word that is often used to describe those entities who do community service or nonprofit work.

>>> See **Group, Organization**.

Altruism

An attitude—or, more formally, a philosophy—that focuses attention on the needs of others.

ALTRUISM

There are interesting debates about whether philanthropy and volunteering are primarily altruistic, or whether the personal satisfaction and positive reputation that can follow from such activities are more important motivations.

Annual Report

A voluntary report, usually published yearly by a nonprofit or foundation, that describes its activities, accomplishments, grants, and an overview of its finances. Some funders and regulators require an annual (or other periodic) report that must be filed in a specific format.

Articles of Incorporation

A document filed with a state office providing a legal description of a proposed corporation; often the first legal step in forming a new nonprofit. The minimum contents of articles of incorporation are described in the "corporations statute" but attorneys and other advisors often suggest additional provisions.

Association

A group where the articles of incorporation define membership qualifications and grant members in good standing specific powers (such as electing the board of directors). Nonprofits are often organized as associations, especially those whose members are professionals or enterprises in a certain industry or locality.

Astroturf

A mocking term for advocacy groups with names that sound like grassroots organizations but that owe their existence to other forms of support.
>>> See **Grassroots**.

Board of Directors

The group ultimately responsible for the success of a nonprofit corporation or association. The method by which its members are selected and some guidance about how the Board of Directors will operate can be found in the organization's charter documents (articles of incorporation and by-laws). Above all else, the Board of Directors is responsible for acting, at all times, in the organization's best interest. Commonly accepted elements of the board's responsibilities include: oversight of operations and planning, financial controls, assuring compliance with laws and regulations, assistance with securing adequate funds, and representing the organization's various constituencies.
>>> See **Articles of Incorporation**, **By-laws**.

Business Sector

A way of referring to all the activities of for-profit organizations inclusively—the business sector consists of everything done directly by businesses (companies and corporations) that are organized and operated to provide financial returns to their owners. Also known as the for-profit sector.
>>> See **Sector**.

BUSINESS SECTOR

the GREAT DEBATE

The business sector is often called the for-profit or corporate sector. There is also a blurring of boundaries when it comes to the private sector; this term is often used interchangeably with business and for-profit, but it is broader than those two terms.
>>> See **Private Sector**.

By-laws

A document that contains policies and rules of operation adopted by the Board of Directors; the process for proposing and adopting by-law changes is usually specified in the articles of incorporation.

Charitable Contribution

A gift that supports the work or mission of a charitable organization. Charitable contributions may be money, property, useful items (like clothing or house wares), works of art—in fact anything that will help the recipient do its work directly or indirectly. Charitable contributions may be tax-deductible when individuals and corporations calculate the amount of income tax to be paid.

Charity

An act of generosity, often directed toward assisting a person or a group of people in need or experiencing difficulties. The word "charity" is also used to describe nonprofit organizations, sometimes when referring to nonprofits that provide assistance to people in need and sometimes more generally when referring to community service organizations of all sorts. For the IRS use of the term, see **Public Charity**.

Charter Documents

A term that can be used to describe all the legal and policy documents that an organization has, including the articles of incorporation and the by-laws. These documents can have a wide variety of different names ("constitution," "articles of association," "terms of reference," "policy manual," etc.).

Civic Engagement

Involvement by individuals in activities that guide or contribute to the well-being of the community, such as participation in political campaigns, service on a Board of Directors, soliciting funds for good works, developing or commenting on policy proposals, or volunteering with a service organization or nonprofit.

Civil Society

A term describing the activities and organizations that are not part of government and that are not organized with the goal of producing financial returns for owners. "Civil society" is more general than "the nonprofit sector" because it includes both political organizations and informal groups and temporary associations that do not have any legal standing.

>>> See **Sector**.

Compensation Package

All the elements that contribute to an employee's pay considered together: salary, bonuses, fringe benefits, expense allowances, contributions to pensions and retirement savings, stock options (in for-profit corporations), and any other compensation that the employee and the employer have agreed will be paid.

CIVIL SOCIETY

The word "civil" in this phrase does not imply "polite." Civil society can include organizations that behave improperly or pursue unpleasant or even illegal goals.

COMPENSATION PACKAGE

When considering a job offer (especially a first one), candidates often make the mistake of considering only the salary while ignoring the other benefits. In many nonprofits, the salary may not be that substantial but can be bolstered by factors such as flex time, telecommuting options, and health care provisions.

Community Foundation

A foundation that is supported by gifts from a relatively large number of people in a defined area; community foundations often operate large numbers of *Donor Advised Funds* for which the advice of the donor or members of the donating family are given a voice in the choice of the charitable activities to be supported.

>>> See **Foundation**.

Company

Usually refers to an organization with a goal of producing financial returns for owners.

>>> See **Organization**.

Contract

A binding agreement between government agencies or other funders and nonprofits to provide specific services. In some cases it may be difficult to tell the difference between government grants and contracts.

>>> See **Grant**.

Corporate Giving Program

An organized commitment by a corporation to making charitable contributions or to otherwise support community services and organizations. Some corporate giving programs are run through a corporate foundation that receives financial support from a single corporation or a group of related companies; others are divisions within the corporate structure itself. Corporate giving programs can include charitable contributions and sponsorship support provided from marketing or promotional funds.

Corporate Foundation

A foundation that receives financial support from a single corporation or a group of related companies.

>>> See **Foundation**.

Corporation

An organization that has filed the required charter documents with a state government and has been granted a corporate charter. In general, corporations can engage in any sort of transaction that an individual person may perform and, in addition, may raise money by issuing stock and doing other activities that are only possible for corporations. Broadly, corporations are divided into two groups (though there are many further classifications in each): *for-profit corporations* are formed with the goal of producing financial returns for their owners (usually stockholders); *nonprofit corporations* have many of the same characteristics but focus any excess of revenue beyond expenses on advancing their community services or other mission-related purposes and are not allowed to distribute any profits to owners.

>>> See **Organization**.

COMPANY

Calling a nonprofit organization a "company" can make you seem unaware of the nuances of the sector. While you may hear people use this term, saying "company" when you mean "organization" in an interview setting (especially when transitioning from another sector) could mean the difference between being offered a job and being seen as someone who "just doesn't get nonprofits."

Degrees, Academic

Titles such as "Master of Arts" or "Ph.D." (which stands for Doctor of Philosophy and is the highest academic degree typically awarded by U.S. universities). Various schools and academic subjects, such as Public Policy, Public Administration, Social Work, Nonprofit Management, and Business Administration may have their own names for the degrees that are granted after study. Law schools, for example, may grant a JD or LL.D. to successful students (those initials stand for "juris doctor" and "doctor of laws" and are both based on the use of Latin for academic titles).

Direct Service

A program or activity that works directly with an intended population. The term is used to distinguish such programs from those that seek to change conditions generally through advocacy or public education. This term is also used to distinguish hands-on work with affected populations from background and supporting services in organizations, such as administration, fundraising, and research.

Donor

A person who makes a gift to an organization or program.

Endowment

Income-generating assets held by an organization under special accounting rules that are designed to preserve them, usually indefinitely, while allowing the income they generate to be used to support current operations or expansion. Special care is required by the Board of Directors or other financial officers in the handling of endowments.

Executive Director

The individual responsible for the leadership of a nonprofit organization including managing staff, reporting to the Board of Directors, and overseeing financial, administrative, and program operations. Through these responsibilities, the executive director shapes and implements the mission of the nonprofit. The ED title is a nonprofit-specific term for the CEO or president of an organization.

Fiduciary

As an adjective, "fiduciary" refers to the duty of an officer or the Board of Directors to take proper care of the assets and other financial affairs of an organization; when used as a noun, the word refers to a person with such responsibilities, i.e., "The fiduciaries of the XYZ Foundation have a fiduciary duty to protect the value of its endowment."

Firm

Another word used to describe an organization that may be used for both for-profit and nonprofit groups, although more commonly for the former.

>>> See **Organization**.

EXECUTIVE DIRECTOR

While the Executive Director of a nonprofit often has similar roles and responsibilities to those of a for-profit CEO or president, using these terms interchangeably can suggest a lack of awareness of the distinctions between the sectors. Pay attention to titling conventions at each organization and try to use only the appropriate ones when interviewing or networking with staff there.

Fiscal Sponsorship

An arrangement whereby an established 501(c)(3) organization (the sponsor) agrees to oversee and provide fiscal and sometimes other forms of support for a project or activity that fits within the sponsor's exempt purposes but which has not yet sought recognition as a tax-exempt entity (and may never do so). Contributions made to the sponsor to support the project are usually tax-deductible for the donors. Sponsors typically charge a small administrative fee for serving in this way and must maintain oversight and control to assure that the project remains consistent with the sponsor's exempt purposes and applicable laws and regulations.

For-profit

>>> See **Sector**.

Form 990

The report to the IRS that many nonprofits file annually to document continued eligibility for tax-exempt status and to provide accountability on many topics. Organizations that file a Form 990 with the IRS are also required to make it available to the public on request; completed Form 990s are frequently published online.

>>> See **Accountability**.

Foundation

A specific kind of nonprofit corporation that relies on an endowment or a long-term commitment of continuing support to make grants or operate programs that achieve the charitable purposes of the donor(s). Foundations are subject to different tax and accounting rules from "charities" in the U.S. Internal Revenue Code. There are several different sorts of foundations that are commonly recognized: *Corporate Foundations* are supported by a single corporation or a group of related companies; *Family Foundations* are formed by individuals who involve other members of their families in directing the work; *Operating Foundations* do not make grants, but instead finance programs of their own from endowment income or committed funding; *"Private" Foundations* (the IRS term) depend on the income from endowments to make grants and support research or services. *Community Foundations* are different in that they receive and disperse funds from residents of a given community and offer the donors an opportunity to advise on the uses to be made of their gifts. Community foundations are classified as "public charities" (not "private foundations") by the IRS.

>>> See **501(c)(3)**, **Private Foundation**, **Public Charity**, **Corporate Foundation**.

Founder's Syndrome

This term refers to a condition that occurs when a nonprofit is shaped by a strong founder and gradually loses track of a more general mission. It often begins after the initial growth of an organization and involves a pattern of negative behavior due to the founder's (or founders') resistance to evolution or change in the organization.

COMMON MISTAKES

FISCAL SPONSORSHIP

The term "fiscal agent" is sometimes seen but should not be used. A fiscal sponsor is not an agent for the project; rather, the project is an activity conducted within the sponsor's organization.

Fund

An accounting term used to describe money that is subject to specific controls or restrictions on how it may be used. For example, a foundation may make a grant to an organization that can only be used to buy food for children enrolled in a recreation program. In the financial reports of the recreation program, this amount of money would be described as "restricted" to this specified use. Community Foundations manage large numbers of restricted funds, called donor-advised funds and donor-designated funds, following the wishes of the donors who have made the gifts. "Fund accounting" is a method of bookkeeping (used infrequently today but commonly in the past) that treats the resources of a nonprofit organization as a large number of funds that have been designated for specified purposes.

Fundraising

The practice of soliciting funds (and other support) necessary for the operation of a nonprofit organization or foundation. An event that is held primarily for the purpose of raising money for an organization may be called a "fundraiser." That word is also used to describe an employee or contractor whose principal responsibilities are focused on securing necessary financial support. "Commercial fundraisers" are firms that may have multiple clients on whose behalf they raise money using a wide variety of techniques.

Grant

A form of financial support, usually from a foundation or a government agency. Grants may be "unrestricted"—meaning that the recipient organization can use the proceeds for any legitimate purpose—or, more commonly, designated for a specific purpose or program. *Grantwriting* is the activity of preparing proposals for grants, following the guidelines and requirements of the granting agency or organization. A *grantee* is the recipient of a grant under a specific program. A *challenge grant* requires the grantee to raise additional funds from other sources before the funds will be made available. A *demonstration grant* is intended to illustrate an approach to addressing a problem or need in the hope that further funding to support that approach will be forthcoming from others. *Matching grants* are coordinated among several funders with the goal that by putting together diverse sources of support the full needs of the project will be met.

Grant Application

>>> See **Proposal**.

Grassroots

A word used when describing community-driven projects or activities that involve large numbers of people who do not have an official role or position that gives them specific responsibility for the work. A grassroots organization works with such people.

>>> See **Astroturf**.

FUNDRAISING

Most nonprofit organizations aren't fully funded by fundraising. In 2006, the National Center for Charitable Statistics reported that 71 percent of the nonprofit sector's total revenues were from program service revenues (i.e., YMCA memberships, tickets to the recital); only 23 percent of the sector's total revenues came from contributions, gifts, and grants.

[Source: *NCCS Quick Facts: Public Charity Finances*. http://nccs.urban.org/statistics/quickfacts.cfm]

Group

An organization, agency, or nonprofit corporation can be loosely referred to as a group, i.e., a community group, a grassroots group, or a nonprofit group. Using the word "group" avoids the necessity of determining the legal status.

>>> See **Agency**, **Organization**.

Informational Interview

A conversation between a job seeker and someone who is knowledgeable about the labor market of an area or the requirements of a particular career choice when there is no expectation that the conversation will lead directly to an offer of employment. Informational interviews are often seen as a way of widening one's circle of contacts while simultaneously acquiring better knowledge of employment possibilities.

Infrastructure

Supporting activities or elements, either within a single organization or in the community, that are necessary for the operation of a program or programs. The word is borrowed from civil engineering, where bridges, roads, sewers, disaster preparation work, etc., is called "infrastructure." In nonprofits, it may be used to talk about the human resources, finance, and fundraising departments of a single organization, or the management support organizations, training centers, community loan programs, etc., that are relied upon by large groups of nonprofits in a community.

>>> Compare to **Overhead**.

Intern

A person who is working for a short time in a job that combines assisting in the work of an organization with a specific educational program that builds professional skills or supplements on-campus study. Interns may be paid a nominal amount or serve on a voluntary basis.

IRS

The initials of the Internal Revenue Service, a part of the U.S. Treasury that administers the tax laws. The IRS is responsible for reviewing applications by organizations that may qualify for exemption from corporate income taxes and for assuring that deductions from taxes for charitable contributions are legitimate.

Lobbying

The act of trying to persuade legislators (or other policymakers) to enact legislation that is seen as favorable (or to defeat legislation that isn't). There are restrictions on the amount of lobbying that 501(c)(3) organizations are allowed to do (and even more stringent restrictions on lobbying by Private Foundations). The most straightforward way for a nonprofit to assure that its lobbying is within these limits is to inform the IRS that it will abide by the requirements of section 501(h) of the Internal

INFORMATIONAL INTERVIEW

Informational interviews are valuable for many reasons, but they are *never* an opportunity to ask for a job. This is an unspoken rule that allows people to agree to your request for an informational interview without worrying whether they'll be put on the spot to answer the "Do you have (or know of) any openings?" question. However, these interviews are ideal for gaining information, exposure, and new contacts while sharing a little information about yourself.

INTERN

An internship should never be viewed (by you or the employer) as a form of free/cheap labor or volunteer service. Instead, it should be a structured, professional opportunity for you to gain experience and information about a particular position, organization, or field. Try to ask questions when you are looking for an internship to ensure that the opportunity will be more about helping you develop your skills than about the organization finding someone to answer phones and fetch coffee all day. That said, do be prepared to do what is needed–nonprofit employees often wear many hats!

Revenue Code, which defines lobbying clearly and sets clear financial limits—based on a proportion of total expenditures—for permitted lobbying.

>>> See **501(c)(3), 501(h)**.

Market Sector

A way of referring to all the activities of business organizations inclusively. The market sector consists of all transactions that occur because the participants seek to make a profit from the related business.

>>> See **Sector**.

Mission

The general goals of an organization, the role it seeks to play in the communities it serves.

Mission Drift

A gradual shift in the mission of an organization that may result from external pressures, such as the requirements of funders, or from evolution in the organization's focus or activities. The term tends to have a negative connotation.

Mission Statement

A succinct description of the work of an organization that provides an explanation of what it does for the public and guides the work of staff and volunteers. It should summarize the reason for an organization's existence.

Networking

Creating and using contacts within a community to stay current with developments, find career opportunities, learn new approaches and techniques for addressing issues, establish political alliances, etc. Many conferences and association meetings offer formal networking opportunities. Informal networking can occur at any occasion when people who share common interests or other community ties gather. Sometimes called schmoozing. In some areas, there are organized networking opportunities for people who work in nonprofit organizations or who would like to do so.

NGO

Non-Governmental Organization (or nongovernmental organization). NGO is often used to describe private international aid groups that raise money in some parts of the world to provide services and assistance in others. More generally, the term may be used to distinguish volunteer groups and charities that perform community services that may also be provided by government agencies.

>>> See **Civil Society**.

NETWORKING

COMMON MISTAKES

Networking is essential to both finding and doing work in the nonprofit sector. No matter what position, organization, or field you're looking to work in, networking is key to finding an ideal job because of how important personal recommendations are and the fact that open positions are often filled by word-of-mouth advertising. Similarly, to make a career for yourself and to do really great work, connections become even more important. Networking is definitely not a just-for-businesspeople skill.

Nonprofit

A shorthand term for an organization that does not include making a profit for owners or shareholders among its goals. Nonprofit is often used as a general description for groups that are organized and operate for charitable purposes and that use any surplus of income over expenses ("profit") to expand their services. "Nonprofit" should be spelled without a hyphen in contemporary usage.

>>> See **NPO**.

Nonprofit Sector

A way of referring to all the activities of nonprofit organizations inclusively. The nonprofit sector consists of everything done directly by agencies and organizations that are neither businesses nor governments and that are more or less supported by donations, program service revenues, and volunteers.

>>> See **Sector**.

NPO

Abbreviation for Non-Profit Organization (or nonprofit organization).

>>> See **Nonprofit**.

Organization

Generally, any group of people who share some common purpose or purposes and work together to achieve them (whether as employees, volunteers, or in some other sort of continuing relationship). A "company" is a specific sort of organization, usually operated with the goal of producing profits for its owners or stockholders. There are many terms used to describe organizations that exist to achieve non-financial goals.

>>> See **Nonprofit**. See also **Agency**, **Group**, **Company**.

Overhead (expense)

An accounting term for the expenses of an organization that cannot be linked to any specific service or source of revenue. General management, accounting, personnel administration, and landscaping are examples of activities whose costs might be included in overhead in financial statements.

>>> Compare to **Infrastructure**.

Philanthropy

Organized efforts to apply financial and other resources to community betterment. The term is usually associated with the work of foundations, and occasionally with giving done by a single wealthy individual. Less wealthy individuals and families are often urged to structure their charitable giving by developing a plan for their personal philanthropy.

>>> See **Charitable Contribution**, **Donor**.

NONPROFIT

The term "nonprofit" does not mean that these organizations don't make money. Quite the contrary, in fact. Nonprofits generate a lot of revenue, but they allocate these funds toward programs and operating costs, not toward dividends and other payouts. According to an Urban Institute report from 2006, "the nonprofit sector accounts for 5.2 percent of the gross domestic product (GDP) and 8.3 percent of wages and salaries paid in the United States."

[Source: The Urban Institute, *The Nonprofit Sector in Brief: Facts and Figures from the Nonprofit Almanac 2007.* www.urban.org/ UploadedPDF/311373_nonprofit_sector. pdf]

Philanthropist

An individual, often wealthy, who gives personal attention to making financial and other contributions for community benefit.

>>> See **Charitable Contribution**, **Donor**.

Philanthropoid

An observer or critic of philanthropy, often formerly an employee or executive of a private foundation, who advocates for improvements in the practice of philanthropy and in the laws and regulations that affect foundations and individual donors.

Private Foundation

See **Foundation**. The term "private foundation" is used by the IRS to describe organizations that are exempt from corporate income taxes under section 501(c)(3) and receive most of their support from a single source or a small group of related individuals or companies. Specific, and more restrictive, regulations apply to the operations of private foundations; the IRS uses the "public support test" to identify organizations that can operate under the less restrictive regulations that apply to "public charities."

>>> See **Public Charity**, **501(c)(3)**.

Private Sector

A term used to describe activities and organizations that are not part of any government. Sometimes private sector refers only to for-profit firms and their activities; sometimes it includes nonprofit organizations as well.

>>> See **Civil Society**.

Program Officer

An employee of a foundation whose responsibilities may include reviewing applications, researching possible areas in which the foundation might work, monitoring the performance of grantees, and other program-related assignments.

Proposal

A request for foundation or governmental support in the form of a grant or contract. Often funding agencies provide a format for use in preparing proposals (increasingly online) and specify deadlines by which they must be received in order to be considered.

>>> See **Request for Proposals**, **Grant**.

Public Charity

The IRS term for an organization that is exempt from corporate income taxes under section 501(c)(3) and receives the majority of its support from a large number of small donors or in the form of program service revenue.

>>> See **Private Foundation**, **501(c)(3)**.

Public Sector

A way of referring to the activities of governments inclusively—the public sector consists of everything done directly by agencies and organizations within governmental units and which are more or less supported by taxes.

>>> See **Sector**.

Request for Proposals (RFP)

A public announcement made by a government agency/grantmaking organization or an NPO. An RFP issued by government agencies or grantmaking organizations describes a program and invites organizations to make proposals describing how they would approach meeting the program's goals, including the financial support needed to do so. Many governments, foundations, and associations have set up systems to announce the publication of RFPs and the associated deadlines and other conditions. An RFP issued by a nonprofit is usually for a specific project for which the organization seeks expert assistance to accomplish a task.

Sector

For analytical purposes, economists consider economic activity as occurring in three (and sometimes four) sectors based on the character of the organizations in each: *businesses* are organizations created and operated to make a profit; *governments* are organizations that have the power of lawmaking and can collect taxes to support their work; and *nonprofits* are organizations that call upon volunteers and seek donations to address needs or meet goals that their supporters see as important. Some economists would add a fourth sector: the *family*. In this view, families provide important benefits to their members which should not be ignored in examining the overall working of an economic system.

>>> See **Civil Society**.

Social Entrepreneur

Someone who addresses community needs with creative business practices that can yield financial support for the work or result in significant cost savings through innovative program design.

Tax-Exempt

An organization or activity that is not required to pay a tax. Most frequently used in connection with federal corporate income taxes (many "nonprofits" fit the IRS definition of "tax-exempt entities"). Nonprofits may also be exempt from local or state property taxes on buildings and other assets that they own and from a wide variety of other taxes depending on the rules of the areas where they work. Since many units of government have many different taxes, it is important to remember that being exempt from one form of taxes does not automatically create an exemption from others.

SOCIAL ENTREPRENEUR

Social entrepreneurs often don't create something completely new. Instead, many entrepreneurs identify an issue that they want to address, and before jumping in with their solution, they examine what other work is being done on the issue. This allows them to utilize existing resources, make connections, and find innovative ways to collaborate rather than reinventing the proverbial wheel.

Transparency

Reporting about activities and financial affairs in a way that fosters understanding of the workings of an organization by people and institutions outside it. This is a key element in effective accountability.

>>> See **Accountability**.

Trust

An arrangement under which certain people ("trustees") are designated to care for property on behalf of other people (for example, the children in a family) or in order to support specific activities; trusts may be, but do not have to be, charitable. Most states have laws governing the establishment and operation of trusts; a few, mostly older, nonprofits are organized as trusts, not corporations.

>>> See **Charity**, **Corporation**.

Voluntary Action

Activities that are undertaken without financial compensation in the form of wages or a share in profits, and which are not done as a result of legal requirements or compulsion by a government. *Volunteer Center* is a description of an organization that exists to encourage and facilitate community services performed by volunteers or in volunteer groups and associations.

Volunteer

A person who undertakes a task without expecting or receiving financial compensation. To volunteer is to offer oneself as a candidate for work of that sort. Some volunteers receive living allowances or stipends. Sometimes people who have volunteered to perform a hazardous or onerous task are described as volunteers even when the work itself is compensated; thus the armed services in the United States are sometimes described as a volunteer army.

Watchdog

An agency or organization that scrutinizes the operations of other organizations to increase accountability and provide guidance to the public on their conduct with respect to defined measures of financial performance, governance, and, occasionally, program effectiveness. Some such groups are independent; others are supported by subscribers or by members of an association.

>>> See **Accountability**.

TAX-EXEMPT
Organizations that are granted IRS 501(c)(3) status are exempt from certain federal (and sometimes state and local) taxes. Employees who work for tax-exempt organizations, however, still pay all applicable taxes.

VOLUNTEER
Though you may not have time to volunteer every Saturday planting trees, or three nights a week answering phones, there are a multitude of ways to fit volunteering into your lifestyle, schedule, and skill set. Whether you offer to develop an organization's website from your home office or pick up papers to collate and staple while watching TV at night, most organizations are flexible with their volunteer opportunities–as well as incredibly grateful for whatever you can do! To read more about volunteering and to find opportunities, visit the Idealist.org Volunteer Center (www.idealist.org/volunteer).

SUMMARY

Learning the insider lingo, jargon, and preferred terminology of the nonprofit sector can seem daunting at first. But the vocabulary in this appendix will have you **speaking the language of nonprofits** sooner than you think. And with the right vocabulary, you'll be more confident in your ability to communicate with nonprofit professionals both during your job search and throughout the course of your nonprofit career.